STAR TREK®

PICARD: THE CLASSIC CHRONICLES

TITAN

WWW.TITAN-COMICS.COM

THANK YOU

Titan would like to thank the casts and crews of *Star Trek* and *Star Trek: The Next Generation*, CBS Television, Paramount Pictures, and Marian Cordry and Risa Kessler at CBS Consumer Products for their invaluable assistance in putting this volume together.

Star Trek – Picard: The Classic Chronicles
ISBN: 9781787731875
Published by Titan
A division of Titan Publishing
Group Ltd.,
144 Southwark Street,
London
SE1 0UP

Collecting the best articles and interviews from *Star Trek Magazine*.

A CIP catalogue record for this title is available from the British Library.

First Edition September 2019
10 9 8 7 6 5 4 3 2 1

Printed in China.

Editor Nick Jones
Managing Editor Martin Eden
Art Director Oz Browne
Publishing Director Darryl Tothill
Operations Director Leigh Baulch
Executive Director Vivian Cheung
Publisher Nick Landau

Contributors:

Lou Anders, Abbie Bernstein, Keith R. A. DeCandido, Kevin Dilmore, Chris Dows, Robert Jeschonek, Nick Joy, Andy Lane, Randy and Jean-Marc L'Officier, Emma Matthews, David A. McIntee, Joe Nazzaro, Larry Nemecek, Terri Osborne, Pamela Roller, Marc Shapiro, Paul Simpson, Ian Spelling, Jay Stobie, K. Stoddard Hayes, Dayton Ward.

Please note:

The interviews collected in this volume were originally printed in *Star Trek Magazine*, some of which date back almost 20 years. In order to maintain the originality of the material, we have not modified the interviews unless absolutely necessary.

STAR TREK®

PICARD: THE CLASSIC CHRONICLES

CONTENTS

ENGAGE!

Warping onto screens in *Star Trek: The Next Generation* in 1987, Jean-Luc Picard was a very different kind of *Star Trek* captain: resolute, formidable, and determined, certainly, but also considered, reflective, even somewhat detached. But it was those very qualities that made Picard such an iconic character, helped in no small part by Patrick Stewart's compelling performance.

As Picard returns to our screens, this special collection of articles and interviews taken from the pages of *Star Trek Magazine* is devoted to Picard and his exploits across seven seasons of *The Next Generation* and four big-screen movies.

Patrick

We cannot all be masters, nor all masters cannot be truly follow'd
William Shakespeare, Othello 1:1

The Legacy of Captain Picard

Pamela Roller talks to the man who's perhaps done more than any of *The Next Generation* to shape its direction – and the themes of *Star Trek® Generations*™…

On the *U.S.S. Enterprise* bridge one man *could* be followed. For seven years, Captain Jean-Luc Picard skilfully guided his crew in countless grand adventures through the galaxy of *Star Trek®: The Next Generation*™. The epitome of leadership: strong, forceful and forever dutiful to his purpose, exuding authority and presence, honour and intellect. The same can be said for Patrick Stewart, the actor in the Captain's uniform

As Captain Picard, Stewart repeatedly delivered memorable performances. As a director of five episodes, he added his own experienced perspective and masterful touch. This gifted actor/director has left a tremendous legacy for fans to enjoy through re-runs and now in the debut feature film, *Star Trek Generations*.

Stewart summed up his tour of duty on the *U.S.S. Enterprise* by saying, "I still believe that we've been doing unique television for the past seven years. There has been nothing like it on TV, and the quality of the writing and direction, the production values and all of the performances of the regulars have been outstanding... It's a body of work that I'm thrilled to have been so significantly associated with."

Having achieved some time and distance from the rigor and tumult of the final season, it is now easy for

Stewart to look back at *Star Trek: The Next Generation* with fondness. But, if pressed, he admits that the months leading up to the end of the series were some of the most trying of his career. He exclaims, "I was at times anxious as to whether I would get through that period of work, and I'm not being melodramatic!"

By the end of the series, Stewart was overextended, doing far more than just portraying Picard. He notes that the producers allowed him to do his one-man show, *A Christmas Carol*, in London, during the Christmas season. After the show's run, he immediately returned to production on the series. The producers kept him busy with some complex episodes, as well as one final directorial turn.

Stewart says, "This was followed then, immediately, by the final show, *All Good Things*. In the final two hours, I was in every single scene of the episode and shifting between time periods... I got so tired that things got a little rough and raw for me. I know that there were all kinds of rumours circulating – all of them, for the most part, exaggerated – about my bad behaviour on the set. It was entirely due to the fact that I was trying to do the best job that I could, and, at the same time, there were a lot of people with other needs and demands, and I found it all a bit distracting. But I think it turned out to be a really satisfying episode finally."

Opposite: *Stewart in familar Picard guise....*
Left: *....and in period costume for the opening holodeck sequence of* Star Trek Generations. *"Although we know there is a massive worldwide audience out there for the movie, I didn't want this to be something that would be so elitist that it could only appeal to fans or to those people who had been watching the series for the last seven years."*

Stewart

Top left: *Disguised as a Romulan in* Unification, Part II
Top right: *Wearing period dress in* Time's Arrow, Part II
Below: *Practising his fencing skills*

"And sweets grown common lose their dear delight".
William Shakespeare, Sonnets 102: 15

Although fans never tire of old *Star Trek* episodes, the cinematic debut of *The Next Generation's* crew will delight fans with its newcomer freshness. Stewart believes fans are in for a thrilling dose of big-budget entertainment. Fans will have the opportunity to see the results of a larger budget, greater production quality and, most importantly, more time. Stewart explains, "Instead of being involved in a shooting day which would be putting on film seven to ten pages, we were putting on film two and half pages, which means that everything can be done more slowly, more carefully, many more rehearsals, many more takes. And there would be no moving on until everyone was satisfied that we had done it as well as we could.

"The killer with series television is always speed. You're always having to move on. I can speak as both actor and director on a series that you are constantly looking over your shoulder. You can never really take time to pause and examine something thoroughly. One of the things that makes me feel very good about this film is that a great deal of care was taken at all stages to make it as substantial as possible."

Fans also can expect to see a new and improved "look" with *Generations*. Stewart notes, "What we were able to do was to take the show out of the studio, very significantly, into some spectacular locations and give the show an appropriately epic feeling. *Star Trek* is epic entertainment. It always has been in the way it is

written and the stories that it tells. So that was an exciting factor of the film. Also, in regards to sets, everything was upgraded to film standards, even the sets that we had been looking at and working on for the past seven years. They were, in their own way, given a substantial facelift, which is required when you are looking at a massive screen rather than the conventionally sized television screen."

Given the broad success of the previous six *Star Trek* features, *The Next Generation* cast and crew has quite a reputation to uphold. Everyone involved wants *Generations* to please not only die-hard fans, but also filmgoers who don't know a Betazoid from a Klingon.

This aspect is very important to Stewart, who says, "Although we know there is a massive world-wide audience out there that will see this film, I didn't want this to be something that would be so elitist that it could only appeal to fans or to those people who had been watching the series for the last seven years. I wanted it to be a film that would appeal to someone who had never heard of *Star Trek* - if such a person exists - and that they could sit down and really enjoy it and not feel as if they were being excluded".

Initially, Stewart had concerns about the role Picard would play in the film. He wanted to ensure that a separate storyline for the captain was woven into the main fabric of the film's storyline. Stewart says he is pleased that he and the writers, producers were able to develop "... a very personal, private, intense and emotional story. For me that was the most satisfying and successful part of the preliminary work on the film."

Stewart also found working with Malcolm

Top left: *Armed and dangerous in* Gambit, Part II
Top right: *Looking into the past with Q (John de Lancie) in* Tapestry
Below: *Transformed into the Borg Locutus in* The Best of Both Worlds

McDowell (Picard's new nemesis, Soran) very gratifying. "I was thrilled when I heard that Malcolm McDowell was going to do this film, because I think he's a wonderful actor, but also because Malcolm and I have a history that goes back almost 30 years," says Stewart. "We first worked together with the Royal Shakespeare Company in 1966. This was the first time we have worked together since that year, so it was especially satisfying."

Much has been written about *The Next Generation* crew establishing their own tradition of *Star Trek* features. According to Stewart, when talk began about a *Next Generation* feature film, many people felt that *The Next Generation* crew should immediately stand on its own and relegate Captain Kirk and company to dry dock. Not Stewart: "I strongly felt that this should be seen to be a transitional film, given that Bill Shatner and his colleagues had already made six films. Just to cut them off with the last one and start off with us was going to be missing a really golden opportunity to do something quite intense and dramatic."

Unfortunately, not all of the original *Star Trek* crew members made it aboard *Generations*. Says Stewart, "It saddened me that, ultimately, only three of the original cast members were in it... But, critical to all of this was to have Bill Shatner. Having the two captains share the same screen space is something that I felt people would enjoy."

What happened when the two *Enterprise* captains matched wits and wisdom on the set? Was their alliance an amiable one befitting the Federation's high standard of diplomacy, or did they battle one another like a couple of Cardassian and Bajoran war-

riors? According to Stewart, goodwill ruled over egos. "I didn't know Bill very well. We had met on a couple of occasions... There had been all kinds of legends about what Bill's attitude toward *The Next Generation* was supposed to be – that he was opposed to it and that he was not happy that there was another *Star Trek* series."

Stewart and Shatner attended an industry event In Las Vegas in February 1994, and they flew back to Los Angeles together on Paramount's private jet. This allowed them time to get to know each other.

Top: *Picard acting out a Robin Hood scenario in* Qpid
Bottom: *About to saddle up in a Holodeck-generated scene*

Stewart says, "We talked about a lot of personal things to do with our lives and what had happened to us as a result of the show. I found out what kind of man Bill was."

Their camaraderie extended to the set of *Generations*. "When it came time for us work on this film, we worked very well together," notes Stewart. "We spent a lot of social time together. We had a lot of fun and a lot of laughs. That was the great thing! It was in every sense just a terrific time, and I look forward to the opportunity of working with Bill again. Of course, this is *Star Trek*, so anything can always happen in the future."

"Yield not thy neck to fortune's yoke, but let thy dauntless mind still ride over all mischance"
William Shakespeare, 3 Henry VI 3:3

During filming of *Generations*, the cast and crew left the *Enterprise* bridge to explore new surroundings. This provided some challenges and difficulties that they had never encountered on the soundstage.

"There's a little riding sequence in this film where Bill and I are both on horseback," says Stewart. "As the world knows, Bill isn't just a rider. He's a very considerable, champion-winning horseman. I ride but I am not a horseman. I felt a certain amount of pressure on me that day to at least attempt to get somewhere near Bill's riding skills. I can think of other actors who, given this situation, would have done everything they could to capitalise on the advantages they had. On the contrary, with Bill, I was having some difficulty with this horse, and I remember Bill saying 'just get off. Let me ride him around for a bit.' He rode my horse around for five or 10 minutes and said, 'Okay this what I think you need to do...' And he was absolutely right! I got back on the horse and I followed Bill's instructions, and I had a much more comfortable time."

On the other hand, the comfort of the crew was

compromised for one of the most climactic scenes of *Generations*. The crew was on location in the "alien world" landscape of the Valley of Fire in the Nevada desert, filming on top of a 500-foot tall rock pinnacle. "It was difficult because conditions were extremely grim... for the crew".

Stewart explains, "The temperatures were in the 100s, and there were hot winds and dust. The actual location was quite dangerous. I think everybody was incredibly relieved when we finally pulled out of Nevada. But it is going to look spectacular!"

Not one to rest on the accolades received for his portrayal of Captain Picard, Stewart is distancing himself from *Star Trek* after his seven years with the show. After all, Jean-Luc Picard is but one colour in Stewart's extensive acting palette. He is not a lucky novice who stumbled onto fame. He is a highly respected veteran of the stage and screen, as well as a member of the Royal Shakespeare Company.

The man who portrayed Captain Picard has some surprises in store for fans. Stewart recently completed work on the film, *Jeffrey*, in which he plays a "contemporary middle-aged gay man in New York". Stewart adds, "It's a brilliantly funny script, but the whole story takes with the background nightmare of AIDS... The film is a very life-affirming film, and that's why I was so attracted to it initially. This is the first gay role I have ever played. This is also the funniest role that I have ever played. It's marvellous for me to be playing some comedy".

It's definitely a change from his *Star Trek* role, and he says, "My agent brought this script to me. We had discussed... that the first major project that I should undertake when the *Star Trek* film was completed was something that would take me as far away as possible from Captain Picard, science fiction and ships of any kind."

Does he expect any backlash from fans who see him only as Captain Picard – the man's man and the lady's sex symbol? He answers, "Someone asked me, 'Patrick what do you think fans are going to make of this?' I hope they make a great deal of it... I hope that in same way that they love *Star Trek*, they will love *Jeffrey*, because of many of the similar philosophies the film contains."

> "Lord we know what we are, but know not what we may be."
> William Shakespeare, Hamlet 4:5

Stewart's role in *Jeffrey* is one of his many post-Picard projects. He is finalising plans for a television adaptation of his one-man show, *A Christmas Carol*. He is also working on an hour-long drama he wrote that explores what happened to Pontius Pilate on the day of Christ's crucifixion. He currently stars in the British production of *Let It Be Me*, a feature about ballroom dancing. "Right now it's a matter of finding time to fit all these projects in, and, of course, there are some other stage projects, too. So, life is interesting at the moment."

For Stewart, *Star Trek: The Next Generation* and the soon-to-be-released *Star Trek Generations* are part of his past. Now he moves at warp speed toward the bright horizon of what he hopes will be a prosperous stage and screen career.

For *Star Trek* fans however, Captain Picard will live forever in reruns. And, if *Generations* is a success at the box office – and it certainly looks as though it will be, on both sides of the Atlantic – perhaps Stewart will seize the opportunity to reprise his role as the captain of the *U.S.S. Enterprise* in future big-screen instalments of *The Next Generation*. We live in hope... ∎

Above: *Stranded on an alien world in Darmok*
Left: *The Captain with his trusty crew*

Lost & Found

Star Trek historian Larry Nemecek unearths some rarities from Patrick Stewart's career in the hot seat of the *Enterprise*.

Picard's debuts on the TV and theatrical screen form the basis of this issue's trawl through the archives.

Firstly we travel back to the very beginning: those 20 working days in June 1987 when the bare bones of everything about *Star Trek: The Next Generation* finally took shape during shooting of the series premiere, "Encounter at Farpoint." For Patrick Stewart and audience alike, perhaps the most pivotal and iconic moments of the story came in the waning days of the shoot, on the set for what became dubbed "Q's Courtroom." In these two private off-camera moments, Stewart offers a serious point of gleaned insight with Brent Spiner, in his equally embryonic character of Data... then shares a true laugh with Spiner and Denise Crosby (Tasha Yar) as they and an off-camera Marina Sirtis (Troi) keep their seats in the kangaroo court.

Moving to the other end of the *Enterprise*-D's life, we reach the tale of *Star Trek Generations*, which saw another landmark in the history of Jean-Luc Picard. The captain encounters the towering historical figure of James T. Kirk as Stewart and audiences alike enjoyed the *Enterprise* crew's first big-screen adventure. The shoot began March 28, 1994 on location aboard the *Lady Washington* for Worf's Holodeck promotion, as here we see director David Carson discussing Picard with Stewart, kitted out in his admiralty best.

A few weeks later, somewhere in the Nexus, it appears Kirk and Picard get along famously – or at least actors William Shatner and Stewart do – when visiting TV camera crews show up on location in the Tejon Ranch area.

Once in a while Picard gets a chance to shine
as an action hero in an episode.

NEW AGE CAPTAIN

From his debut in *Star Trek: The Next Generation*'s *Encounter at Farpoint*,
Jean-Luc Picard has proved to be perhaps the perfect Starfleet captain.
K. Stoddard Hayes traces his trajectory.

Jean-Luc Picard is the quintessential civilized man. He is well educated, highly trained and disciplined, thoughtful, tolerant of divergent cultures and values, and possessed of the highest principles and integrity. A man of thought, he always seeks to resolve conflicts with reason and diplomacy rather than force. He has the flawless manners essential to a diplomat, along with considerable tact and poise in the face of bizarre alien customs.

In Starfleet, as in most military services, a commander is considered too valuable to risk in the day-to-day uncertainties of planetary and exploratory missions, so Picard usually remains on the bridge while *Riker* leads the Away Missions. He will usually only visit a planet for a diplomatic mission where security is not an issue.

That's not to say that Picard is never in danger. When the ship is in battle or in jeopardy, the bridge is no safer than any other part of the ship. However, he rarely engages in any kind of direct physical conflict. His battles are usually fought with his mind and the might of his starship. His resources are reason,

cooperation, negotiation and compassion, and, when these fail, shrewd military strategy and the power of a *Galaxy*-class starship.

Once in a while Picard gets a chance to shine as an action hero in an episode. In *Starship Mine*, he finds himself alone in a *U.S.S. Enterprise NCC-1701-D* occupied by ruthless terrorists. He first tricks them into believing he is a harmless ship's barber, then escapes and, using a mixture of guerilla attacks and sabotage, takes them out almost single-handed.

In the *Star Trek* films, however, he has become the quintessential action hero, engaging in lengthy and athletic hand-to-hand conflicts with *Soran*, the *Borg* and *Ru'afo*. In *Star Trek: First Contact*, wearing the action hero's *de rigueur* sweat-stained vest, he even hauls himself up a cable with the *Borg Queen* hanging on his foot. Not bad for a man in his sixties.

Picard's command style is formal, but not harsh. While he sets a high value on military decorum and discipline, he also knows that humour and warmth can go a long way towards making a difficult mission tolerable. Above all, he knows how to value the intelligence and experience of those who work under him. Any of his senior officers can come to him with a problem or even an objection and be sure of a fair hearing. But although he will listen to divergent suggestions and points of view, Picard knows that a ship cannot be a democracy. He always makes clear exactly when his subordinates must stop offering suggestions and start taking orders.

Like any good commander, Picard takes a serious personal interest in the welfare of his crew, not merely as a whole but as individuals. It's natural that he would pay special attention to remarkable officers like *Wesley*, *Data* and *Worf*. He has fostered each in their very different ways: encouraging Data in his aspiration to be more human; inspiring Wesley to mature as a man and an officer; and committing his personal honour and at times his safety to support Worf in the feuds of the *Klingon* High Council.

Of course, Picard's interest in his crew also extends to less important subordinates. This concern has often taken the form of helping people redeem past mistakes. He is the first person to trust *Ro Laren*, giving her the confidence to help her people and to become a reliable officer again. He also requests that *Sito Jaxa*, a disgraced member of Nova Squadron, be assigned to the *Enterprise-D* upon graduation, because he knows that aboard his ship she will be given a chance to prove herself as an officer without prejudice for her past mistakes.

The ship is too large for Picard to be familiar with every crewmember, and so most junior officers take their problems to their immediate subordinates; however, they know that if they ever need to speak to the captain, Picard will listen.

Despite his legendary urbanity, there *are* things that make Picard a bit testy. He often shows impatience with Data's way of giving lengthy, detailed answers to any request for information. And since Picard is ill at ease around children, he feels awkward with the admiration of the ship's youngsters.

Beverly and Jean-Luc rue their misfortune when a rare opportunity to catch a movie is ruined by the constant whispering of the people sitting behind them (*The First Duty*)

Like any good commander, Picard takes a serious personal interest in the welfare of his crew, not merely as a whole but as individuals.

Word Up

As the captain of Starfleet's flagship, *Jean-Luc Picard*'s words carry more weight than most. Here we present some of his more memorable – and in some cases legendary – utterances.

"There are times, sir, when men of good conscience cannot blindly follow orders. You acknowledge [these androids'] sentience, but you ignore their personal liberties and freedom. Order a man to hand his child over to the state? Not while I am his captain."
To *Haftel*, concerning *Data* and his 'child', the android *Lal*, The Offspring

"The claim, 'I was only following orders,' has been used to justify too many tragedies in our history."
To *Data*, Redemption, Part II

"We think we've come so far... the torture of heretics, the burning of witches is all ancient history... then... before you can blink an eye... suddenly it threatens to start all over again."
To *Worf*, The Drumhead

"Some of the darkest chapters in the history of my world involved the forced relocation of a small group of people to satisfy the demands of a large one."
To *Anij*, Star Trek: Insurrection

"Who the hell are we to determine the next course of evolution for these people?!"
To *Admiral Dougherty* on the *Ba'ku*, Insurrection

"How many people does it take, Admiral, before it becomes wrong? A thousand? 50,000? A million? How many people does it take, Admiral?!"
To *Admiral Dougherty* on the proposed forced relocation of the *Ba'ku*, Insurrection

"Beverly, the Prime Directive is not just a set of rules; it is a philosophy and a very correct one. History has proved again and again that whenever mankind interferes with a less developed civilization, no matter how well intentioned that interference may be, the results are invariably disastrous."
To *Dr Crusher*, Symbiosis

"What I didn't put in the report... was that at the very end, he gave me a choice... between a life of comfort... or more torture... all I had to do was say that I could see five lights when in fact there were only four."
"You didn't say it..."
"No... no, but I was going to. I would have told him anything... anything at all. But more than that, I *believed* that I could see five lights."
To *Troi* on his torture at the hands of the Cardassian *Madred*, Chain of Command, Part II

"You say you are true evil? Shall I tell you what true evil is? It is to submit to you. It is when we surrender our freedom, our dignity, instead of defying you."
To *Armus*, Skin of Evil

"Let's make sure history never forgets the name *Enterprise*."
Yesterday's Enterprise

"I know you have your doubts about me... about each other... about the ship. All I can say is that although we have only been together for a short time... I know that you are the finest crew in the fleet... and I would trust each of you with my life. So I'm asking you for a leap of faith – and to trust me."
To the bridge crew, All Good Things...

"Someone once told me that time was a predator that stalked us all our lives. But I rather believe time is a *companion*... who goes with us on the journey, reminds us to cherish every moment... because they'll never come again."
Star Trek Generations

"No. I am *not* dead. Because I refuse to believe that the afterlife is run by you. The universe is not so badly designed."
To *Q*, Tapestry

"Gentlemen, I have the utmost confidence in your ability to perform the impossible."
To *La Forge*, *Wesley* and *Data*, Ménage à Troi

"Can anyone remember when we used to be explorers?"
Just prior to entering another diplomatic engagement, Insurrection

"I would be delighted to offer any advice I can on understanding women. When I have some, I'll let you know."
To *Data*, In Theory

"Five card stud, nothing wild. And the sky's the limit."
At the final poker game, All Good Things...

Perfect 10

The 10 best Picard episodes, in chronological order.

THE BIG GOODBYE: Picard as private eye *Dixon Hill*. Who can resist that hat?
THE BEST OF BOTH WORLDS: Picard's close encounter with the Borg is a fan favourite.
FAMILY: A visit home and a mud wrestling match with his big brother help Picard come to terms with his assimilation.
DARMOK: A monster, a mysterious language and an alien captain with the soul of a bard.
THE INNER LIGHT: In half an hour, Picard lives the entire life of a man long dead.
CHAIN OF COMMAND: Picard's torture by the Cardassians explores the psychology of victim and torturer.
TAPESTRY: Q gives Picard a chance to relive his youth and learn the importance of his mistakes.
STARSHIP MINE: *Star Trek* meets *Die Hard* as Picard defends his deserted ship from terrorists.
ATTACHED: Picard and Crusher uncover their true feelings through a telepathic link.
ALL GOOD THINGS...: Q takes Picard on a magical mystery tour of the past, present and future.

Picard at the mercy of the Borg Queen in *Star Trek: First Contact*

He has an especially hard time when a transporter accident makes him a child again, and in order to fool a gang of *Ferengi* pirates, he has to act like a child and even throw a temper tantrum. (*Rascals*)

No one makes Picard testy faster than Q, who is something of an overgrown child himself – albeit a child with godlike powers and an obsession with a certain starship captain. Q's self-centredness, impulsiveness, irresponsibility and determination to meddle are all direct affronts to Picard's principles of responsibility, reason and respect for all life forms. It's even more annoying that Q seems to like Picard and treats him with a familiarity that the captain finds intolerable.

The isolation that military discipline requires of a ship's commander, combined with his natural reserve, has given Picard a somewhat lonely life. Though he is always available to his officers, and indeed to all members of his crew, Picard himself rarely engages in friendly socialising with anyone. He also keeps his personal problems and feelings very much to himself.

Beverly Crusher and *Guinan*, because of their long friendships with him, and *Deanna Troi*, because of her position as ship's counselor, are the only people to whom Picard opens up, and he only rarely does even with them. However, his experiences in the alternate past, present and future of *All Good Things...* make him realise that he can trust all of his senior officers with his unreserved friendship. He delights them by showing up at their weekly poker game, and as he looks at all their faces, observes quietly, "I should have done this a long time ago."

In the years that he has commanded the *Enterprise-D* (and latterly the *U.S.S. Enterprise NCC-1701-E*), Picard has learned several difficult life lessons. His torture by the *Cardassians* and assimilation by the Borg forced him to see that he could be made to sacrifice his principles under the worst circumstances. This has been a challenge to his perception of himself as a man of integrity and good will. His

Q gives the captain a whistle stop tour of what might have been in *Tapestry*

Picard's command style is formal, but not harsh.

brief romance with *Nella Daren* taught him that if he cared for someone in his crew, his feelings might interfere with his command judgment, a discovery that probably reinforced his natural inclination to solitude. Beverly Crusher's reluctance to explore the romantic feelings she discovered in him while they shared the *Prytt* telepathic link has made him, perhaps, even more cautious about exploring romantic relationships.

Although there's no question these experiences have deepened Picard and matured his wisdom and understanding of himself, he has in essence changed little from the man who first walked out of the turbo lift in the opening scenes of *Encounter at Farpoint*. He was then, as he is now, the quintessential civilized man.

Picard Vs Kirk

In developing a new captain for the 1980s, Picard's creators made him in many ways the antithesis of his predecessor, *Captain Kirk*.

	PICARD	KIRK
Age at beginning of series	58	33
Usual method of conflict resolution	Diplomacy	Fists
Romantic behaviour	Mostly celibate	Ladies' man
Usual post during Away Missions	Bridge	Planet
Hobbies	Archaeology, fencing	Antiques, especially books
Favourite drink	Tea, Earl Grey, hot	Saurian brandy
Most annoying adversary	Q	Harry Mudd
Professional Reputation	Legendary	Legendary

20/20

Star Trek Magazine celebrates

VISION

Star Trek: The Next Generation

STAR TREK
GENERATION

STAR TREK
FIRST CONTACT

STAR TREK
INSURRECTION

STAR TREK

Pictures top right:
The Neutral Zone

ANTI-STAR TREK?

The first season of *Star Trek: The Next Generation* came as a shock to many fans of the original series. Keith R. A. DeCandido recalls those reactions...

n the occasion of *Star Trek*'s 20th anniversary in 1986, Paramount Pictures announced a new *Star Trek* series. It would be released the next year in first-run syndication, something that had previously only been done with game shows.

I was just starting college at the time, and I was thrilled. After all, how many times can you watch the same 79 episodes and four movies? (Well, okay, a lot, but still...) At last, we'd have something new.

It's easy now to forget how controversial *Star Trek: The Next Generation* was when it was first announced. Doing *Star Trek* without Kirk and Spock and McCoy was predicted to be a disaster. (Thank God the Internet as we know it now wasn't around then...)

And then the show itself debuted, and it went out of its way to make itself as different as possible from its predecessor. Yes, many of the trappings were the same, and there were nods to the original – a McCoy cameo, a sequel to a *ST:TOS* episode – but so much else that *ST:TNG* did in its first year was actively trying to be Not The Original Series.

For starters, there was the captain. Small in stature, older, brainy, erudite – Jean-Luc Picard was the polar opposite of James T. Kirk, exemplified in the very first episode when Picard surrendered the ship, something Kirk would never do. (When Kirk gave a surrender order in *Star Trek III: The Search for Spock*, the crew looked on in horror, but Picard's crew doesn't bat an eyelash.) Picard also didn't lead the "away teams," but left it to the first officer.

Picard's approach was more cerebral – the very complaint that was legendarily raised by NBC after seeing the original *Star Trek* pilot *The Cage*. The *Enterprise* crew held meetings to discuss what they would do next in the observation lounge, where Kirk's meetings, when he bothered to have them, were often with fewer people and held in the briefing room. The whole atmosphere of the *Enterprise* was one of warmth and good feeling, down to having civilians and children on board, and the ship's psychiatrist right there on the bridge next to the captain.

Two of the most familiar alien species (Vulcans and Romulans) were nowhere in evidence, though they both got name-checked at different times, and the Romulans showed up at the end of the season. A third, the Klingons, were portrayed as allies, with one on the bridge of the *Enterprise*, in a show that debuted only three years after Kirk's cry of "you Klingon bastard, you killed my son!" On *ST:TOS*, the Prime Directive was usually

PREVIOUSLY ON *STAR TREK*:

James T. Kirk and his crew encountered the PSi 2000 virus in *The Naked Time*.

Captain Picard was in charge of the *U.S.S. Stargazer* at the time of its loss

The Tormed Incident altered relations between Starfleet and the Romulans

The Federation first encountered the neural parasites in *Sins of the Mother...*

The prior lives of the Eugenics Wars survivors discovered by the *Enterprise* NCC-1701-D...

SEASON 1

only mentioned right before
Kirk broke it, though there
were always extenuating circumstances. On *ST:TNG*, the Prime
Directive was mentioned right before
they obeyed it to the letter. *ST:TNG*
portrayed the *Trek* future as a utopia. *ST:TOS'*
notion of a hopeful future had accreted over two
decades into something much more fantastical: not
just a united Earth with no racial prejudice, but a place
that was perfect.

Perhaps the most interesting change was the old
Trek standby, the higher power that tests or manipulates
humanity. The Metrons, Organians, Melkotians, and
Excalbians were all otherworldly and almost ethereal. In
its very first episode, *ST:TNG* gave us Q. He didn't just
manipulate the *Enterprise* from above, he was right
there on the ship — and was obnoxious as hell, making
him a much better foil for the crew.

Some of these changes were a result of the series
being made in the 1980s: meetings, people in touch
with their feelings, an ensemble cast instead of three
stars. But many of the changes made were done
specifically to address criticisms of *ST:TOS*, ones that
were easy to make after seeing the episodes several
billion times. The new show was done differently in part
because we'd seen it all before.

In the end, those differences are what made
ST:TNG a success. If they had aped the original too
closely, viewers might not have responded, especially
since the acting in the first season was rather
lackluster. (Watching the first season now, you
appreciate how much Jonathan Frakes, Marina Sirtis,
Patrick Stewart, and especially Michael Dorn grew as
actors over the years.) But by varying the formula,
by challenging the assumptions of *ST:TOS*, they
made *ST:TNG* into its own thing, one that is still
successful today. ▲

Pictures left: *Star Trek III: The Search for Spock*; *Encounter at
Farpoint*; Majel Barrett as Lwaxana Troi in *Haven*; *Encounter at
Farpoint* Right: Tasha Yar

THE SAGA CONTINUES

The Jellies from *Encounter at Farpoint* reappear in *Orion's Hounds*

The repercussions of Data and Tasha's encounter in *The Naked Now* continue in *Metamorphosis*

The Dixon Hill saga continues in *A Hard Rain*

The parasites from *Conspiracy* reappear in the *ST:DS9* novel series *Mission: Gamma*

20th Century businessman Ralph Offenhouse encounters the Ferengi in *Debtor's Planet*

THE TNG YEARS

Nick Joy continues our history of *Star Trek*...

Following the success of *Star Trek IV: The Voyage Home*, Paramount are concerned the old episodes are running out of steam (How many times can you watch a 20-year-old show?) and that while the movies are good business, they only bring in money every other year. What they want is something that can make them money every week, and so the concept of a new *Star Trek* series (a 'next generation') is mooted. Leonard Nimoy is originally approached to produce the show, but he rejects the offer, not wishing to be drawn into the demands of weekly television. Gene Roddenberry is subsequently lured into the role and immediately assembles a team that includes veterans of the original series – including producer Robert Justman, Eddie Milkis and writers David Gerrold and D.C. Fontana.

The new show features a larger *Enterprise* (designed by Herman Zimmerman) with children and families aboard, thus making it less militaristic. Roddenberry wants *Cagney and Lacey*'s Stephen Macht as Jean-Luc Picard and Bill (*The Rocketeer*) Campbell as Riker before Patrick Stewart and Jonathan Frakes are cast. In a last-minute decision Denise Crosby and Marina Sirtis swap roles, and the show is prepped for a fall debut.

On September 28, 1987 *Star Trek: The Next Generation* launches, with a theme that reprises Jerry Goldsmith's fanfare from *Star Trek: The Motion Picture* and a visit from an aged Admiral McCoy. Written by D.C. Fontana and Gene Roddenberry, *Encounter at Farpoint* establishes the *Enterprise*-D's ongoing mission (no longer limited to five years) as well as the debut of John deLancie's omnipotent god-like-being Q. *The Naked Now* (a virtual remake of *The Naked Time*) fuels the criticism that the show is too beholden to its past, while first Ferengi show *The Last Outpost* showcases a pre-Quark Armin Shimerman as Letek. He'll be wearing those ears for many years to come.

Gene Roddenberry is actively involved with the show as it finds its feet, but soon hands over day-to-day operations to producer Rick Berman. Mrs Roddenberry, Majel Barrett, also has a part to play, as Lwaxana Troi (mother to Deanna), making a striking debut in *Haven*, the last show to air in 1987. The New Year starts with *The Big Goodbye*, the first of the show's many episodes heavily reliant on the much-maligned Holodeck. Other highlights include the introduction of Data's evil twin Lore

(who would later appear in *Brothers* and *Descent*), *Coming of Age* (Wesley attempts to get into Starfleet Academy) and Klingon opus *Heart of Glory*, where Vaughn Armstrong plays the first of his 10 different roles in the *Star Trek* universe. Khan's right-hand man Judson Scott appears in *Symbiosis*, but the biggest shock this year is the unceremonious killing off of Tasha Yar in *Skin of Evil* by a puddle of tarmac. Disillusioned by the way her character was (not) developing, Denise Crosby asks to be written out of the show, thus presenting the writers with their first opportunity to kill off a cast member.

We'll Always Have Paris features Michelle Phillips from The Mamas and the Papas as Picard's love interest, while *Conspiracy* showcases some gruesome special effects of exploding heads. These shots of alien parasites being zapped would later be censored by the BBC, who then forget to take them out of clip show *Shades of Gray*. The first season concludes with *The Neutral Zone*, featuring the return of the Romulans, and a pre-Gul Dukat Marc Alaimo. With respectable (though not huge) ratings, the network announces the show's renewal.

QUOTE-UNQUOTE

"If they do this *Next Generation* nonsense they'll kill it." **James Doohan is unconvinced that *ST:TNG* will be successful.**

"They tried me out with a toupee, but frankly it looked ridiculous." **Patrick Stewart on why 'baldly going' was the best option for Jean-Luc Picard.**

"I can taste the joy of getting something down on film that is entertaining." **William Shatner gets excited about the prospect of directing *Star Trek V*.**

"I wasn't looking to be the star of the show, but I needed more to do than just answering to the captain." **Denise Crosby on why Tasha had to go.**

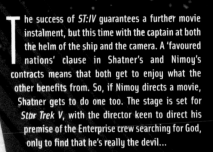

The success of *ST:IV* guarantees a further movie instalment, but this time with the captain at both the helm of the ship and the camera. A 'favoured nations' clause in Shatner's and Nimoy's contracts means that both get to enjoy what the other benefits from. So, if Nimoy directs a movie, Shatner gets to do one too. The stage is set for *Star Trek V*, with the director keen to direct his premise of the Enterprise crew searching for God, only to find that he's really the devil...

SIDE STEPS

(Other *ST:TNG* tales set during this season)

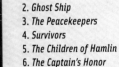

1. *Double Helix 1: Infection*
2. *Ghost Ship*
3. *The Peacekeepers*
4. *Survivors*
5. *The Children of Hamlin*
6. *The Captain's Honor*
7. *Where No One Has Gone Before.*

Picture right: *The Emissary; Elementary, Dear Data; A Matter of Honor*

THEY CALL ME KATHERINE...

One of the biggest changes between the first two seasons of *ST:TNG* (apart from Will Riker's beard appearing) was the appointment of Dr Katherine Pulaski as the new Chief Medical Officer. **Terri Osborne** assesses the effect of the new arrival...

When *Star Trek: The Next Generation* came to television in 1987, the roles of women had undergone a sea change since the late 1960s. Society had adjusted to the idea of women in charge, something that *Star Trek: The Original Series* seemed to shy away from at every step.

In *The Cage*, Majel Barrett's Number One was second in command of the *Enterprise*, but that would change by the time *ST:TOS* went into regular production. After over 20 years of women in the military, Hollywood seemed to have problems with women in the chain of command, to the point that many fans wondered whether there were *any* women captains in Starfleet during Kirk's era. Whenever women were shown as leaders, like Edith Keeler, Natira, or the Dohlman of Elas, they were portrayed more as

victims of their gender than strong representatives of it.

ST:TOS was very much a product of the 1960s, as was its portrayal of the roles of women. The changes women had been seeing for years were only beginning to enter pop-culture prominence in the 1960s, *The Avengers'* Emma Peel being one of the iconic figures. But even Mrs. Peel had her trusty Steed. Women standing alone without need of a man's help wouldn't begin appearing on American television until the 1970s, with super heroines who could be just as rough-and-tumble in *Wonder Woman*, *The Bionic Woman*, and even *Charlie's Angels*. Sitcoms proved to be the more welcoming of mainstream programs at first, with *The Mary Tyler Moore Show*, *Laverne and Shirley* and *One Day At A Time* being torchbearers. At the movies, we watched Princess Leia and Mon Mothma lead a rebellion against an evil galactic Empire.

The 1980s brought the subject into the mainstream for good with the capable female cops *Cagney and Lacey*, the cutthroat businesswomen of *Dynasty* and *Dallas*, and even the genre heroines and villains of *V: The Series*. We left Earth with Sally Ride in 1983, and we all watched Oprah Winfrey take her first steps onto the international stage. Girls in the late 1970s and 1980s were treated to television programs showing they could be anything they wanted to be, just like their brothers.

Society was ready. Could this new *Trek* continue to show us what we could be?

At first, the answer appeared to be no. With *ST:TNG* came Beverly Crusher: the quiet, maternal doctor who barely questioned her captain's orders, followed along, had an excellent bedside manner, and who would've probably been at home in the 23rd Century. When Gates McFadden left after the first season for reasons reported to be everything from the writers not knowing how to deal with the character to McFadden's own displeasure with how Beverly was written, the door was open.

PREVIOUSLY ON *STAR TREK:*

Jean-Luc Picard knew the El-Aurian Guinan for some time before she joined the *Enterprise*-D...

Dr Pulaski wasn't the first *Enterprise* CMO to suffer from an aging virus.

Will Riker had been estranged from his father for some considerable time.

Although it had been kept quiet, Starfleet had encountered the Borg before in the *Star Trek: Enterprise* story *Regeneration*

...and had sent out secret missions to investigate them as revealed in *Star Trek: Voyager's Dark Frontier*

Knowing an opposing ship's prefix codes had got Admiral Kirk out of trouble in *Star Trek II: The Wrath of Khan*

 25

Katherine Pulaski *was* another throwback character, but not to the women of *ST:TOS*. She more resembled a female Leonard H. McCoy than anything else. Could she have been an attempt to get a "Big Three" for the 24th Century? There are stories that Gene Roddenberry himself loosely patterned the character on McCoy. Pulaski and McCoy even share some character traits: transporter phobia, acerbic wit, and similar approaches toward the resident emotionless intellectual. However, Pulaski is neither the old country doctor, nor the long-ago object of the captain's affection. She simply is who she is, with no excuses. That's where she became something more than McCoy with breasts.

A strong, capable, thrice-divorced doctor, who might have reminded viewers of an old favorite character, Pulaski wouldn't take any guff, wouldn't back down from her opinions, and could hold her own in an argument. She was another step on the path women were taking from housewife to head of the household. Pulaski showed us that we'd continue growing capable of holding our own with the men of this, or any other, world.

That would be reflected in Beverly Crusher on her return in Season 3 as well. When Crusher returned, she was a changed woman, more resolute, with the courage of her convictions and the strength to do what she thought needed to be done, even if her life were at risk. It was almost as though the writers learned what Crusher was supposed to be through writing Pulaski.

Katherine — and Beverly, also — from one of those girls in the late 1970s and early 1980s, thank you. ▲

Pictures left: Doctor McCoy and Mr Spock from Star Trek the Original Series; The Icarus Factor; Shades of Gray; Unnatural Selection. Pictures right: The Emissary; Q Who?; Dr Pulaski

THE SAGA CONTINUES

 More revelations about artificial intelligence follow from *The Schizoid Man*...

Lt Selar becomes a key member of the *Excalibur* crew...

 The Iconian gateways discovered in *Contagion* are investigated further by assorted *Trek* crews...

 Kyle Riker's fate is revealed in *A Time To Love*

 Pen Pals' Sarjenka goes on to work with the Starfleet Corps of Engineer team...

THE TNG YEARS

Changes are afoot for the second season of *ST:TNG*. Whoopi Goldberg (soon to win an Oscar for *Ghost*) joins the cast as recurring alien bartender Guinan in the show's new standing set Ten Forward. But gone is Gates McFadden as Dr Crusher is temporarily assigned to Starfleet Medical. She is replaced by *Original Series* guest star Diana Muldaur as Dr Kate Pulaski. The role of supervising producer is filled by Rick Berman following Bob Justman's departure and one of the greatest challenges is getting stories ready for production during the Writer's Guild strike. The season starts late with *The Child*, a rewrite of an abandoned *Star Trek: Phase II* script with Troi filling the Ilia role. Also of note this season is *Elementary, My Dear Data*, which promotes 'cease and desist' threats from Arthur Conan Doyle's estate, *The Outrageous Okona* (with Bill Campbell) and a pre-*Desperate Housewives* Teri Hatcher as the transporter chief, and Klingon exchange drama *A Matter of Honor*, showcasing Brian Thompson's first guest role in the *Trek*verse.

The Dauphin, a weak love story for Wesley, is notable solely for the appearance of a pre-*Twin Peaks* Madchen Amick. Q makes another welcome return in *Q Who?*, which introduces a significant new enemy. Q transports the *Enterprise* crew across the galaxy to meet the Borg, wanting to teach mankind a lesson for becoming complacent – a lesson that would be learned in greater detail in the coming years. Invented by Maurice Hurley, this credible new villainous race would prove to be one of *Star Trek*'s most popular villains.

Samaritan Snare features *Murder One*'s Daniel Benzali in one of his rare forays into sci fi. *The Emissary* is an exciting tale of cryogenically frozen Klingons who don't realise that the war with humans is over, and Suzie Plakson makes her first appearance as Worf's Klingon love interest K'Ehleyr. Cost-cutting season finale clip show *Shades of Gray* is the final downer to a mediocre season, but at least the show has been renewed.

QUOTE-UNQUOTE

"The quality of the first several episodes suffered because of the Writer's Strike... we would have liked to develop and polish them." **Rick Berman on *ST:TNG*'s season two openers.**

"She was a lovely lady. She did have trouble remembering her lines though. We solved it by putting them on cue cards." **Director Paul Lynch recalls new *Enterprise* doctor Diana Muldaur.**

"I've done TV for 11 years and there is no show more difficult that I've ever been involved with than *Star Trek*." **Writer Ira Steven Behr**

"What we really wanted to do, but couldn't because of money, was insects. Insect mentality is great because it's relentless." **Maurice Hurley on creating the Borg.**

DEPARTING
17 March - Merritt Butrick (David Marcus *Star Trek II* and *Star Trek III*)
23 April - Marc Daniels (*ST:TOS* director)

While the script to *Star Trek V: The Final Frontier* is completed by David (*Dreamscape*) Loughery prior to the Writer's Guild strike, many of cast and crew believe that the story is doomed from the outset (How can the crew really meet God?) with DeForest Kelley and Leonard Nimoy particularly unhappy with their roles.

Nicholas Meyer is asked to perform a rewrite, but is too busy with other projects. The movie's shooting is further delayed and Shatner is forced to cut out some of the more complicated effects work. His six rock men are cut down to one, while the demonic cherubs are lost entirely. On June 9, 1989 (October 20 in the UK) William Shatner's motion picture debut finally opens. Eventually making $70m worldwide against a budget of $28m the film can hardly be deemed a failure, but against the success of the preceding movies it's not what Paramount expected. The movie, as released, is a series of compromises, and the culmination of a number of setbacks and disappointments. Having already seen his troop of rockmen reduced to just one, Shatner is told that the footage is unusable and the sequence is deleted (though it appears in the comic book adaptation, is lampooned in *Galaxy Quest* and can be seen in the Special Edition DVD). Was the film's box office failure down to a script that was just too fanciful and underdeveloped? Or was the appetite for *Star Trek* now being sated by a weekly fix of *ST:TNG*?

SIDE STEPS
(Other *ST:TNG* tales set during this season)

1. *Strike Zone*
2. *The Legacy of Eleanor Dain*
3. *Power Hungry*
4. *Many Splendors (S.C.E. 66)*
5. *Metamorphosis*
6. *A Call to Darkness*

27

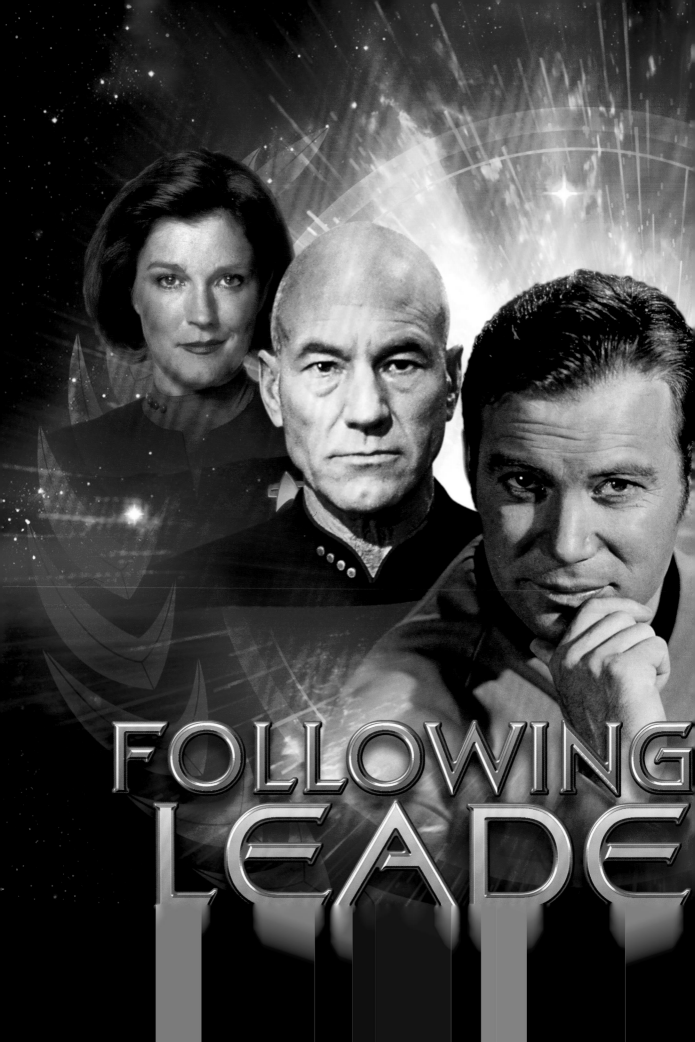

FOLLOWING
LEADE

Throughout *Star Trek*'s four
decades of history, the pinnacle of
leadership in service has been
defined as the captaincy.
Whether leading crews of
a starship or a space station,
the captains of *Star Trek*
exhibit exemplary skills,
unwavering dedication to duty
– and yes, all-too-human
failings. Their individual styles
may vary, but time and again
the captains prove themselves
equally capable and worthy of
occupying that "center seat."
**Kevin Dilmore & Dayton Ward
investigate...**

THE RS

Rank, it's said, has its privileges.
Effective leaders understand that the privileges of command aren't merely bestowed in accordance to the stripes on one's sleeve or the pips on one's collar. They're earned; testaments to an individual's desire to lead, ability to act and willingness to accept all responsibility for consequences of their decisions regardless of outcome.
Yet when asked to name the single highest privilege of rank, a great leader is likely to answer that it's the privilege of serving.
While they are fictional creations, the Star Trek captains frequently are cited by real-world leaders as icons of how to influence, inspire and motivate. Entire books are devoted to lessons in following their example, in everything from success in the business world to fulfillment in finding the perfect spouse.
So, what defines them as great leaders?
Uncounted studies have suggested many qualities of leadership, but over time a handful of these traits have risen to become universally recognized. This is one look at how the captains of Star Trek have exemplified the many critical attributes of a successful leader. This list of examples is by no means exhaustive, and while not every captain might be cited as defining a particular trait, each of them certainly has demonstrated every trait during their adventures in the Star Trek *universe*.

01 INITIATIVE

"Well, a little late, but I'm glad they're seeing it our way."
– Captain James Kirk, *Amok Time* (*Star Trek*)

Leaders don't wait for direction before taking action, perhaps even acting when others fail to see such a need. They may face situations where they're unable – or perhaps unwilling – to stand by until someone else gives the orders, or can't afford to hold out until they're presented with the ideal set of circumstances in order to proceed.

Sometimes it's as simple as being the first to volunteer for an assignment, such as when Jonathan Archer insists in *Broken Bow* that he and the newly-constructed NX-01 *Enterprise* return a Klingon – the first encountered by humans – to his home world deep in unexplored space. It's also demonstrated by a willingness to take on personal risk, as James Kirk does when he attempts to steal a Romulan cloaking device in *The Enterprise Incident*. Benjamin Sisko, after accidentally time-traveling with Dr. Bashir to 21st Century Earth in *Past Tense*, takes on the persona of Gabriel Bell when the man is accidentally killed before he can bring about the peaceful end to the violent "Bell Riots," thereby preserving Bell's contributions to Earth history.

In *Star Trek*, the captains often are portrayed as being "on their own," either at the edges of explored space or simply out of communications range, and forced to act without benefit of higher authority or any form of support system other than their own talents as well as those of their crews in order to accomplish their mission. Kirk faces that very dilemma when he chose to pursue a renegade Romulan vessel into prohibited space in *Balance of Terror*, or when Jean-Luc Picard orders the *Enterprise* back to Earth to participate in defending against a Borg invasion in *Star Trek: First Contact*.

How leaders react in such instances often determines the success or failure not just of the mission at hand, but also their own ability to inspire others to follow them – now and in the future.

02 JUDGMENT & DECISIVENESS

"A hundred decisions a day, hundreds of lives staked on you making every one of them right."
– Commodore Stone,
Court Martial (*Star Trek*)

Effective leaders weigh information available to them before making timely and accurate decisions, communicating intentions to subordinates in a clear and confident manner. What if you don't have all of the facts, or you suspect that some or all of the information you've gathered is questionable or faulty? Sometimes, you have to make a decision anyway.

Each of the *Star Trek* captains personifies the decisive leader who employs experience, sound judgment and instinct in order to determine the best choice for a given situation. There are numerous examples of each captain listening to the advice of their trusted colleagues before implementing a bold course of action. On many occasions, they've even dispensed with any sort of counsel and instead issued orders seemingly off the cuff or from the gut, trusting their crews, their own intuition and even a bit of luck to see them through whatever crisis they faced.

Naturally, some of those decisions proved unpopular or controversial, fraught with excessive risk or simply incomprehensible to the casual bystander at the time action was initiated: Archer giving information to the Andorians about the covert military facility hidden beneath the Vulcan monastery on P'Jem in *The Andorian Incident*; Kirk calling for the destruction of the planet Eminiar VII in *A Taste of Armageddon* or deactivating the Landru computer in *The Return of the Archons*; Kathryn Janeway's choosing to destroy the Caretaker array, saving the Ocampa and yet stranding her own vessel and crew in the Delta Quadrant (*Caretaker*), or her later decision to reverse the transporter malfunction responsible for fusing Tuvok and Neelix into a single being (*Tuvix*).

Despite the outcomes of such choices or the moral and ethical dilemmas plaguing the decision-making process, effective leaders put aside doubt or hesitation and take critical action when required.

Pictures: top left inset: *Amok Time*; bottom left: *The Enterprise Incident*; *Past Tense*; top center inset: *Court Martial*; bottom center: *The Andorian Incident*; *Tuvix*; top right inset: *The First Duty*; bottom right: *In the Pale Moonlight*; *Pegasus*

03 INTEGRITY

> "The first duty of every Starfleet officer is to the truth... whether it's scientific truth or historical truth or personal truth. It is the guiding principle on which Starfleet is based."
> – Captain Jean-Luc Picard, *The First Duty* (*Star Trek: The Next Generation*)

The 19th Century American evangelist Dwight L. Moody wrote, "Character is what you are in the dark," and in the utter darkness of deep space, the *Star Trek* captains proved themselves as shining examples of integrity. Without the scrutiny of higher authority, encounters with unknown alien cultures might offer an ineffective leader opportunities to follow paths of lesser resistance or even temptations to act in dishonest or wicked ways. Yet in such situations, these captains continually demonstrated uprightness of character and sound adherence to their moral principles.

A benchmark of integrity in *Star Trek* is a captain's willingness to follow Starfleet's Prime Directive, the General Order prohibiting interference with the development or internal affairs of an alien species. While each captain found occasion to push its bounds or even violate it (arguably one of the most egregious being Sisko's duplicitous actions to involve the Romulans in the Dominion War in *In the Pale Moonlight*), they all continually cited the Prime Directive as the overall rule and guide to their actions in their commands.

Time and again, Picard proved his high standards of integrity. In *The Pegasus*, he stands clear on his support for the Treaty of Algernon and his willingness to prosecute those involved in its violation during the *Pegasus* "experiment." In the wake of a deadly accident within an elite flight team in *The First Duty*, Picard's adherence to truthfulness proves inspirational to Wesley Crusher. The captain's honor also rises to conquer his desires to infect the Borg with a genocidal virus in *I, Borg*, when signs of humanity within a single drone force him to re-evaluate his convictions.

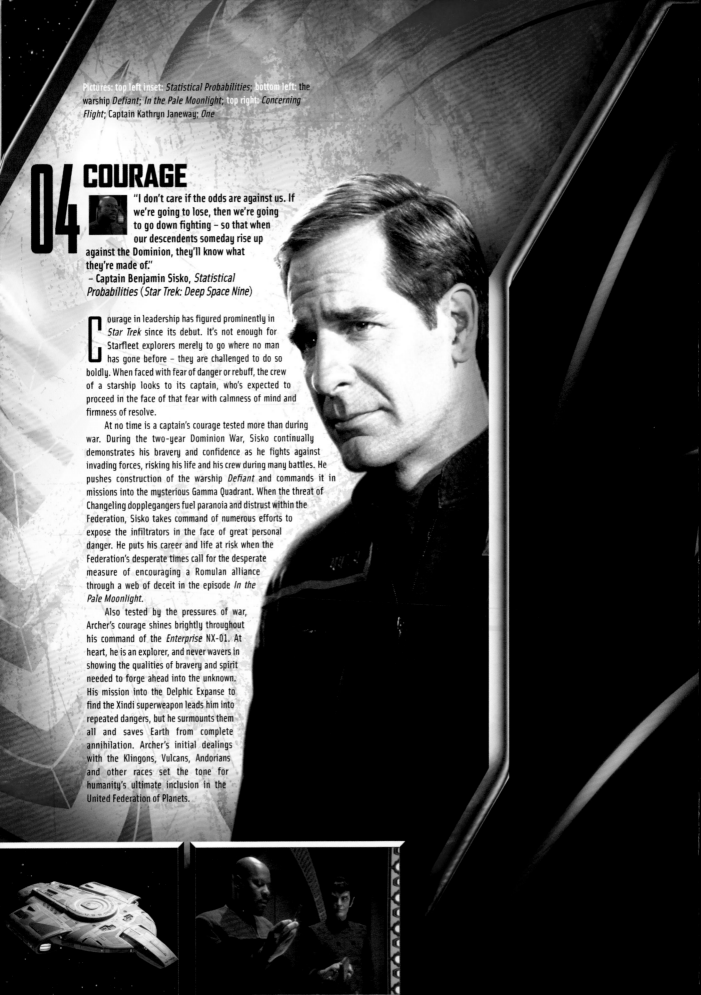

04 COURAGE

"I don't care if the odds are against us. If we're going to lose, then we're going to go down fighting – so that when our descendents someday rise up against the Dominion, they'll know what they're made of."
– Captain Benjamin Sisko, *Statistical Probabilities* (*Star Trek: Deep Space Nine*)

Courage in leadership has figured prominently in *Star Trek* since its debut. It's not enough for Starfleet explorers merely to go where no man has gone before – they are challenged to do so boldly. When faced with fear of danger or rebuff, the crew of a starship looks to its captain, who's expected to proceed in the face of that fear with calmness of mind and firmness of resolve.

At no time is a captain's courage tested more than during war. During the two-year Dominion War, Sisko continually demonstrates his bravery and confidence as he fights against invading forces, risking his life and his crew during many battles. He pushes construction of the warship *Defiant* and commands it in missions into the mysterious Gamma Quadrant. When the threat of Changeling dopplegangers fuel paranoia and distrust within the Federation, Sisko takes command of numerous efforts to expose the infiltrators in the face of great personal danger. He puts his career and life at risk when the Federation's desperate times call for the desperate measure of encouraging a Romulan alliance through a web of deceit in the episode *In the Pale Moonlight*.

Also tested by the pressures of war, Archer's courage shines brightly throughout his command of the *Enterprise* NX-01. At heart, he is an explorer, and never wavers in showing the qualities of bravery and spirit needed to forge ahead into the unknown. His mission into the Delphic Expanse to find the Xindi superweapon leads him into repeated dangers, but he surmounts them all and saves Earth from complete annihilation. Archer's initial dealings with the Klingons, Vulcans, Andorians and other races set the tone for humanity's ultimate inclusion in the United Federation of Planets.

05 BEARING & TACT

"If you respect our customs and we see that respect, we will be friends ...."
– Lutan to Captain Jean-Luc Picard, *Code of Honor*
(*ST:TNG*)

With the possibility of encountering new life and new civilizations a constant, *Star Trek*'s captains ultimately served as diplomats of deep space, responsible for making the best impressions on behalf of the United Federation of Planets. Of equal importance was the need to deal with others – whether known quantities or disturbingly alien entities – without creating offense.

Picard seems to revel in such opportunities. In *Manhunt*, he rises to his diplomatic best despite initial anxieties while entertaining a shipload of ambassadors and dignitaries from a myriad of cultures. In *Darmok*, Picard's uncompromising efforts to understand and relate to Captain Dathon's metaphoric language lead to a break-through in establishing relations where previous efforts had failed. Years later, the typically modest captain shows no outward shame when outfitted with a less-than-flattering Evoran headdress in *Star Trek: Insurrection*.

As Starfleet's sole representatives in the Delta Quadrant, Janeway impresses upon her entire crew the importance of maintaining a level of bearing and tact that was in keeping with Federation expectations. Her embodiment of Starfleet ideals as well as her carriage as an officer and leader in *Caretaker* favorably impress members of two species – the Ocampa and the Talaxians – to the point that they join her crew to explore the quadrant alongside them. With each encounter of a new race, the Kazon, Vidiians, Krenim and Hirogen notable among them, Janeway keeps her dignity and that of her people through her decisions to maintain her conduct and bearing in line with Starfleet ideals.

Pictures: top left inset: *Deadlock*; *Counterpoint*; main image left: *The Killing Game*; *Death Wish*; bottom right: *Darmok*; *Caretaker*

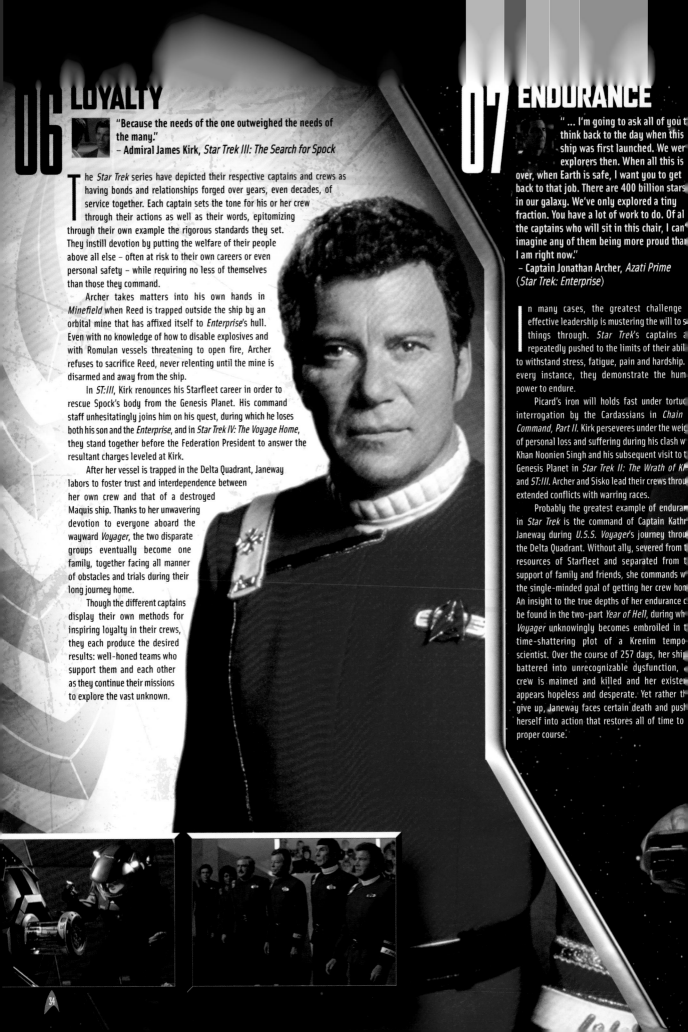

06 LOYALTY

"Because the needs of the one outweighed the needs of the many."
– Admiral James Kirk, *Star Trek III: The Search for Spock*

The *Star Trek* series have depicted their respective captains and crews as having bonds and relationships forged over years, even decades, of service together. Each captain sets the tone for his or her crew through their actions as well as their words, epitomizing through their own example the rigorous standards they set. They instill devotion by putting the welfare of their people above all else – often at risk to their own careers or even personal safety – while requiring no less of themselves than those they command.

Archer takes matters into his own hands in *Minefield* when Reed is trapped outside the ship by an orbital mine that has affixed itself to *Enterprise*'s hull. Even with no knowledge of how to disable explosives and with Romulan vessels threatening to open fire, Archer refuses to sacrifice Reed, never relenting until the mine is disarmed and away from the ship.

In *ST:III*, Kirk renounces his Starfleet career in order to rescue Spock's body from the Genesis Planet. His command staff unhesitatingly joins him on his quest, during which he loses both his son and the *Enterprise*, and in *Star Trek IV: The Voyage Home*, they stand together before the Federation President to answer the resultant charges leveled at Kirk.

After her vessel is trapped in the Delta Quadrant, Janeway labors to foster trust and interdependence between her own crew and that of a destroyed Maquis ship. Thanks to her unwavering devotion to everyone aboard the wayward *Voyager*, the two disparate groups eventually become one family, together facing all manner of obstacles and trials during their long journey home.

Though the different captains display their own methods for inspiring loyalty in their crews, they each produce the desired results: well-honed teams who support them and each other as they continue their missions to explore the vast unknown.

07 ENDURANCE

" ... I'm going to ask all of you to think back to the day when this ship was first launched. We were explorers then. When all this is over, when Earth is safe, I want you to get back to that job. There are 400 billion stars in our galaxy. We've only explored a tiny fraction. You have a lot of work to do. Of all the captains who will sit in this chair, I can't imagine any of them being more proud than I am right now."
– Captain Jonathan Archer, *Azati Prime*
(*Star Trek: Enterprise*)

In many cases, the greatest challenge of effective leadership is mustering the will to see things through. *Star Trek*'s captains are repeatedly pushed to the limits of their ability to withstand stress, fatigue, pain and hardship. In every instance, they demonstrate the human power to endure.

Picard's iron will holds fast under torturous interrogation by the Cardassians in *Chain of Command, Part II*. Kirk perseveres under the weight of personal loss and suffering during his clash with Khan Noonien Singh and his subsequent visit to the Genesis Planet in *Star Trek II: The Wrath of Khan* and *ST:III*. Archer and Sisko lead their crews through extended conflicts with warring races.

Probably the greatest example of endurance in *Star Trek* is the command of Captain Kathryn Janeway during *U.S.S. Voyager*'s journey through the Delta Quadrant. Without ally, severed from the resources of Starfleet and separated from the support of family and friends, she commands with the single-minded goal of getting her crew home. An insight to the true depths of her endurance can be found in the two-part *Year of Hell*, during which *Voyager* unknowingly becomes embroiled in the time-shattering plot of a Krenim temporal scientist. Over the course of 257 days, her ship is battered into unrecognizable dysfunction, her crew is maimed and killed and her existence appears hopeless and desperate. Yet rather than give up, Janeway faces certain death and pushes herself into action that restores all of time to its proper course.

08 JUSTICE

"In a part of space where there are few rules, it's more important than ever that we hold fast to our own."
– Captain Kathryn Janeway, *Alliances* (*Star Trek: Voyager*)

As any experienced leader will tell you, justice involves far more than reading and heeding a rule or law from a book or a piece of parchment. Sometimes it means seeing past the mere words and realizing a deeper or perhaps untested interpretation in order to serve a greater good. There may be occasions when leaders find themselves standing in direct contradiction to such directives in order to foster true fairness and equality. *Star Trek* captains have faced such trials numerous times; forced to take controversial or perhaps even illegal action as they seek justice, either for themselves, a friend or shipmate, members of an alien species or even an entire race.

Kirk finds himself bending the letter of the Prime Directive in *A Private Little War* in order to uphold its spirit, by ensuring that the Hill People of the planet Neural received the same weapons as those being furnished by the Klingon Empire to rival villagers. Taking this action maintains a delicate balance of power between the contending groups, offering not swift defeat for either side but instead the hope that both parties might eventually see the futility of the escalating conflict and seek peace.

Picard often stands in opposition to rules and regulations when it comes to the welfare of his crew. In *The Measure of A Man*, the *Enterprise* captain defies Starfleet decree when he calls for a board of inquiry to determine once and for all Data's status as an individual with the same inalienable civil rights as any other sentient member of the Federation. On several occasions, Picard comes to the support of Worf when the demands of his heritage cause conflict, as when the Klingon seeks revenge against his lover's murderer in *Reunion*, or when his cultural and personal beliefs drive him to refuse offering a blood transfusion for a Romulan in *The Enemy*.

It's a dilemma Picard acknowledges in that same episode, when he tells Worf, "Sometimes the moral obligations of command are less than clear. I weigh the good of the many against the needs of the individual, and try to balance them as realistically as possible. God knows I don't always succeed." Leaders can only be effective so long as they strive for that balance – even if they don't always find it. ▲

Pictures: top left inset: *Star Trek III: The Search for Spock*; bottom left: *Minefield*; *Star Trek IV: The Voyage Home*; top center inset: *Azati Prime*; bottom center: *Chain of Command, Part II*; *ST:III*; top right inset: *Alliances*; bottom right: *A Private Little War*; *The Enemy*

Pictures top right:
Yesterday's Enterprise

BROADENING THE CANVAS

Chris Dows examines how the scope of the *Star Trek* universe was suddenly expanded in the pivotal third season episode *Yesterday's Enterprise*...

When an episode starts off with Lieutenant Worf declaring prune juice a warrior's drink, you know you're in for a good time. As it turns out, this is only one of several memorable incidents in arguably the best single *Star Trek: The Next Generation* episode ever made – an episode that, on first viewing, I vividly remember thinking was one of the finest pieces of television I'd ever seen. But the real impact of *Yesterday's Enterprise* comes after the credits have rolled and everything is back to normal in the *Star Trek* universe, a universe that is suddenly and dramatically expanded in one powerfully written and beautifully acted installment.

Coming just over halfway through Season 3 of *ST:TNG*, *Yesterday's Enterprise* benefits from a substantial amount of continuity, and while the events of the first five movies were also known by the episode's first transmission in 1990, their timeframe only went up to the 2290s. Sure, our knowledge of Klingon culture and history had been greatly enhanced with episodes such as *Heart of Glory* and *A Matter of Honor*, but the events of *Star Trek VI: The Undiscovered Country* and the whole Khitomer business were twinkles in the mind's eye of Leonard Nimoy. So the time was ripe to bridge some of the 70 year gap in *Star Trek*'s history left between the movies and the 43625.2 Stardate at that time.

Yesterday's Enterprise is delightfully rich in continuity development, making it one of those episodes that presents *Star Trek* in its very best and brightest light. Disregarding Tasha Yar's alternate reality and the link formed by Guinan between the 'proper' and 'war' timelines (a nice touch introducing aspects of the El-Aurians later developed in *Time's Arrow* and *Star Trek Generations*), we have the introduction of the *Ambassador*-class Starship *U.S.S. Enterprise* NCC-1701-C, the logical extension of ship design on the *Constitution*-class and *Excelsior*-class vessels. Add to that a female Captain in the shape of Rachel Garrett and the lineage of the Starship *Enterprise*, while not entirely complete, became considerably more comprehensive.

While that certainly pleased fans, there is more Starfleet information implied in the episode than actually shown. The chilling, often subtle suggestions of an organization now entirely dedicated to war permeates throughout, from Captain Jean-Luc Picard's 'Combat Log' entry to Tasha's proud boast that the *U.S.S. Enterprise* NCC-1701-D is a battleship capable of carrying 6000 soldiers. All of this goes to form an unnerving mirror reflection of how easy it would be for Starfleet to veer from missions of peace to an entirely military purpose, a function made all the more alarming by the admission that 40 billion Federation citizens had died during the 20 year war – a war they were losing.

While this view of an alternative future is intriguing, from a continuity perspective it is conjectural. The 2344 battle at Narendra III is, however, pivotal. The temporal rift caused by the intense exchange of fire between the *Enterprise*-C

PREVIOUSLY ON *STAR TREK*:

The *Enterprise*-A suffered similar systems failures to its successor in *Star Trek V: The Final Frontier*...

The *Enterprise* NX-01 crew had problems with the Duras family in the 22nd Century...

Picard and Phillipa Louvois' went head to head at his court martial over the loss of the *Stargazer*...

Enterprise Captains have problems on *Shore Leave* planets...

Rachel Garrett was a highly regarded Captain of the *U.S.S. Enterprise*-C...

Sarek's history between *Star Trek VI: The Undiscovered Country* and *Sarek*

Lal is not the first android unable to cope with emotional distress: Rayna Kapec sufferered similarly in *Requiem for Methuselah*...

and the four Romulan Warbirds pulled Garrett's ship out of the fight before the doomed Klingon outpost on the planet below realized their distress signal had been heard, and the sacrifice of the Federation ship did not take place. One is to assume that relations with the Klingon Empire broke down irrevocably during the following couple of years, with the war having lasted two decades at the time of the *Enterprise*-C's appearance in this altered timeline.

The key aspect to these events – and to the additional depth of understanding regarding the Klingons – is brought up by Lieutenant Commander Data during the stormy briefing in which Captain Picard informs the Senior Officers of his plan to send the *Enterprise*-C back to its certain destruction. The almost belligerent Executive Officer Riker cannot see the point of sending 125 crew to a meaningless death, but Data says it is not necessarily meaningless because the Klingons regard honor above all else. If the crew died trying to defend the outpost, it would be considered a meaningful act by the Klingon Empire. Their deaths could prevent a war because of the status the Klingons would attach to an *attempt* at doing the honorable thing even if it did not succeed.

With the *Enterprise*-C returned (along with Tasha, generating the whole 'Is Sela *really* her daughter?' debate in *Redemption Part I* and *II*), 'normality' is resumed. Lieutenant Worf is back on the *Enterprise*-D's Bridge, the lights are bright and the bandoliers gone. But as an audience seeing *Yesterday's Enterprise* for the first time, the changes lasted far longer than the episode's duration on air. We were given things to think about, a richness of detail to ponder that showed the *Star Trek* Universe was getting bigger – and better – all the time. ▲

Pictures top left: *Yesterday's Enterprise*
Pictures center right: Tony Todd as Kurn in *Sins of the Father*; James Cromwell in *The Hunted*

THE SAGA CONTINUES

 The Ferengi from *The Price* were eventually found by the crew of the *Starship Voyager*...

 Narendra III and the destruction of the *Enterprise*-C are detailed...

The battle of Wolf 359 from a different perspective in *Star Trek: Deep Space Nine's Emissary*

 Commander Shelby's career continues on board the *U.S.S. Excalibur*

THE TNG YEARS

Returning on September 25, 1989 *ST:TNG*'s third season witnesses two significant changes. Replacing the restrictive one-piece spandex suits, new two-piece cotton uniforms are sported by the crew, forever to be tugged down in the 'Picard Manoeuvre' when rising from a chair. But of far greater importance is the return of Beverly Crusher after her one-year Starfleet sabbatical. Gates McFadden is coaxed back while Diana Muldaur goes off to *L.A. Law*.

Saul Rubinek plays a sinister pre-eBay collector in *The Most Toys*, while Kathryn Leigh Scott (*Dark Shadows*) and Ray Wise (*Twin Peaks*) fill the guest spots in *Who Watches the Watchers?* Geordi's virtual girlfriend Leah Brahms debuts in *Booby Trap*, while *The Enemy* sees Andreas (*Babylon 5*) Katsulas in his first episode as Romulan Tomalak.

The Hunted features the first *Star Trek* appearance of James Cromwell, who will later be immortalised as warp engine creator Zefram Cochrane in movie *First Contact* and *Enterprise*'s *Broken Bow*. *The High Ground*'s tale of terrorists strikes a chord with the BBC,

who ban it because of a reference to a victory by the IRA. *Deja Q* reveals a vulnerable Q, stripped of his powers by *L.A .Law*'s Corbin Bernsen, while Bernsen's screen wife Jennifer Hetrick plays Picard's occasional love interest Vash in *Captain's Holiday*.

Fan favorite *Yesterday's Enterprise* allows Denise Crosby to return to the show as an alternative Tasha Yar, while *Candyman* Tony Todd debuts as Worf's brother Kurn in *Sins of the Father*. Other guest stars in this starry selection of shows include a pre-Rom Max Grodenchik (*Captain's Holiday*), a pre-*Buffy* Harry Groener (*Tin Man*), former *A-Team* member Dwight Schultz as recurring character Barclay, and the return of Spock's father in *Sarek*. Add to this some naked Trois and the first ever (and arguably the best) *Star Trek* season cliffhanger, the Borg-packed *The Best of Both Worlds*, and you have the best season so far.

When asked why the BBC are not get showing *ST:TNG*, controller Jonathan Powell confirms that he has seen it (in reality, just part of the pilot) and that it was "terrible". He further adds that "sci-fi is not popular" and that it might "pop up on BBC2." Of far greater concern is Gene Roddenberry's deteriorating health. He suffers a stroke and never fully recovers, becoming confined to a wheelchair.

SIDE STEPS
(Other *TNG* tales set during this season)

1. Double Helix: Vectors
2. A Rock and A Hard Place
3. Gulliver's Fugitives
4. Doomsday World
5. Exiles
6. Q in Law
7. Fortune's Light
8. Eyes of the Beholders
9. Boogeymen
10. Federation
11. Contamination

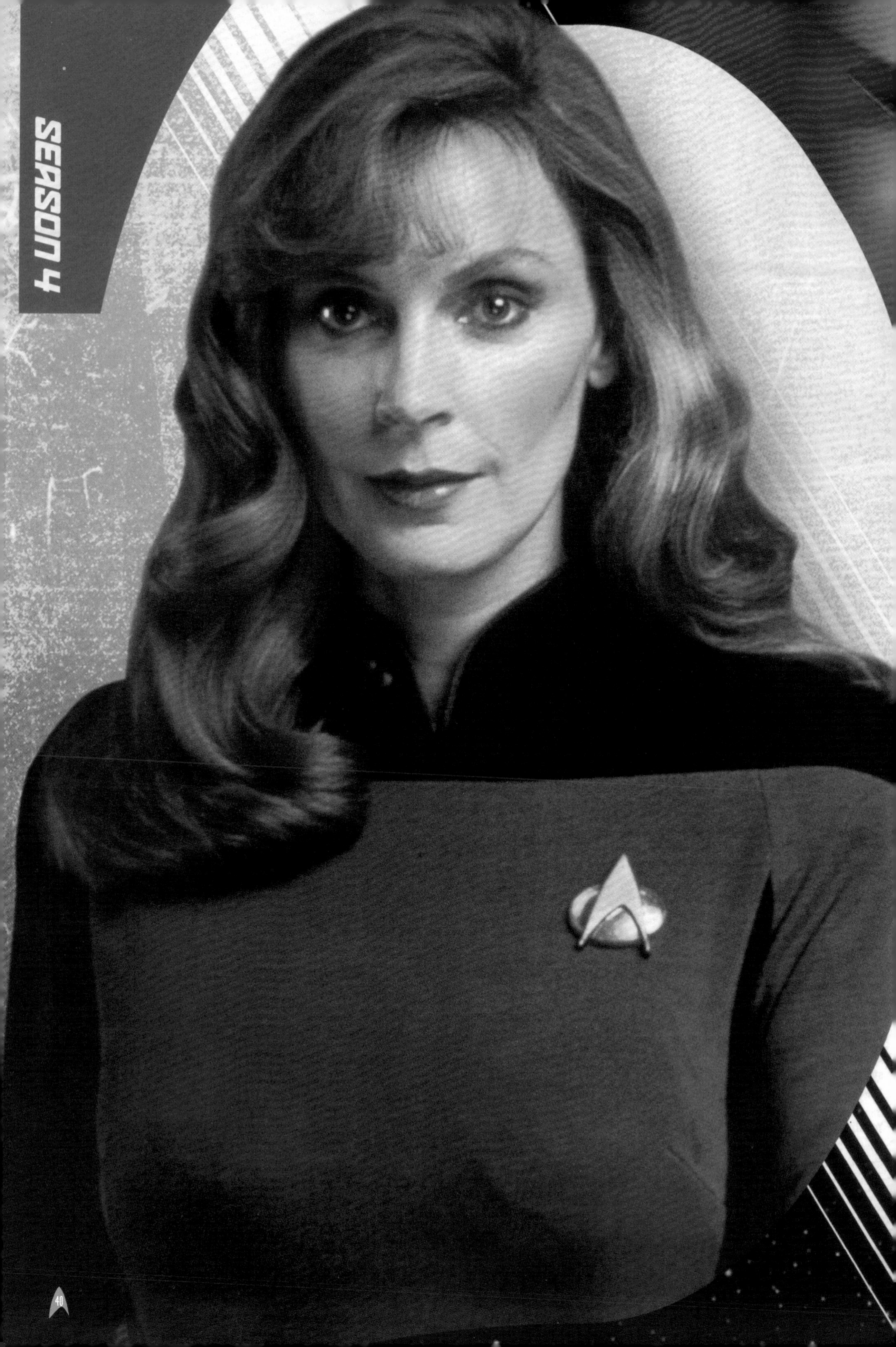

A BOY NAMED (MARY) SUE

Was Wesley Crusher really an embodiment of Gene Roddenberry's hopes for the future of the human race? Or simply a 'Mary Sue' figure, fulfilling his creator's fantasies? David A. McIntee investigates...

The fourth season of *Star Trek: The Next Generation* was one of changing focus. Story-arcs, later to come to the fore in *Star Trek: Deep Space Nine*, began to appear more overtly in *ST:TNG*. The development of the Romulans, and the machinations of Klingon politics, brought *Star Trek* out of the standalone format of episodes that could be swapped round in transmission order.

A familial theme also emerged, with many episodes focusing on the crew's relationships with friends and family. This domestic element would last throughout the series, reaching a prominence in season seven. Domesticity was a theme missing from *Star Trek: The Original Series* – limited to Spock's father appearing once – and was almost as rare, Riker's father excepted, in earlier *ST:TNG* seasons.

Of course there had long been family issues on the *Enterprise*-D: the Crusher family. This, too, changed in season four with the departure of Wesley as a regular character in *Final Mission*.

Wesley had been quite an unpopular character among fans. Wesley's defenders sometimes suggest that the reason fans dislike him is that he reminds them of themselves, but there are more practical dramatic reasons for his unpopularity. Firstly, he was the latest in a long line of smarter-than-the-adults kids-who-save-the-day in US science fiction. The second explanation has to do with the lack of payoff to the setting-up of Wesley's character. As Ron Moore put it, if Wesley was so special and unique, then why was he going through a boring Academy process? Certainly not to show us realistic teenage life, because he was still the Will Robinson type savior on several occasions, even though the ship was crewed by Starfleet's finest.

Eugene Wesley Roddenberry himself claimed in interviews to never have understood why the audience so disliked Wesley Crusher, as "who wouldn't like to have grown up on a starship?" Note the creator's middle name: Wesley Crusher was unashamedly created in his image. Fandom often decries creators putting avatars of themselves into their stories, tagging them with the label of Mary Sue.

The requirements for the Mary Sue label are simple: a super-character who gets off with a regular, is superior in every way, and is usually written by a female. Mary Sue fiction is particularly associated with *Star Trek*, because the original fanfic that gave the genre its name back in the 1970s was a *Star Trek* story. *ST:TNG* was the first US SF series to open up to the possibility of fans who had grown up with the original series contributing to the new one. That meant it was also the first to be open to the arrival of Mary Sue stories. *In Theory*

PREVIOUSLY ON *STAR TREK*:

Using the deflector as a weapon had worked against the Xindi...

The Soong family have plagued previous *Enterprise* crews...

Captain Kirk and his crew encountered the Devil in *The Magicks of Megas-Tu*

certainly seems to fit the pattern: a young lieutenant fancies Data and must prove herself worthy. The truth is rather different: the story is about Data's nature and potential failings, and it was written by two men.

Once the precedent had been set, even if only in a perceptual rather than actual sense, there could be no stopping the arrival of Mary Sue stories at the show's production office. If we want an example of a *ST:TNG* episode that fulfils all the requirements, then *In Theory* isn't nearly as good an example as *Lessons*, in season six.

What about Wesley, then? Is he a true Mary Sue, superior to the regulars? Saving the ship makes it seem that way, but Ron Moore has a point. The term usually refers to a character put into an existing series by an author who is a fan, and who wants to show their suitability to be put on a pedestal as high as those of the heroes in the series. Wesley is an avatar for the show's own creator, is a regular, and is as often the cause of a problem as its solution.

The concept of an author putting his or her self into a story in the form of a character is far from new – it was an important element of the New Mythology of the German Romantics in the 18th Century. However, the authors of original works had always put themselves into their stories in order to explore their feelings and experiences, or to work through matters that held great importance for them in their lives and philosophies.

In this respect, Wesley is a creation in the true romantic ("romance" being the archaic word for a work of imaginative fiction) sense. Which means he is a part of the longest story-arc in the world: the story of storytelling. All of which fits nicely with the arc-oriented direction that *Star Trek* began to take in *ST:TNG*'s fourth season. ▲

THE SAGA CONTINUES

 Leah Brahms and Geordi La Forge have to work together to combat *The Genesis Wave*...

 Troi's dreams are violated again in *Star Trek Nemesis*

 Odo tries the same trick to hide from Mrs Troi as Picard did in *Half a Life* – with the same lack of success...

Pictures left: *Remember Me*; *In Theory*; *The Final Mission*; *The Final Mission* Pictures center right: Bebe Neuwirth in *First Contact*; Bob Gunton in *The Wounded*; David Ogden Stiers in *Half a Life*

THE TNG YEARS

By being renewed for a fourth season *ST:TNG* eclipses the original series, with *Legacy* marking the critical 80th show. Cast members get a chance to direct, with Stewart helming *In Theory* and Frakes *Reunion*. Wesley leaves the show in *Final Mission* (alongside *Space: 1999*'s Nick Tate), while the production staff is bolstered by the addition of Jeri Taylor as supervising producer, who would later co-create *Star Trek: Voyager*. After the dramatic resolution to *The Best of Both Worlds*, *Family* offers a low-key character piece with Jeremy Kemp and Samantha Eggar, while *Brothers* gives Brent Spiner the chance to play not only Data's brother, but his creator too. *Reunion* brings the return of the regular cast of supporting Klingons and the tragic death of K'Ehleyr, and Worf's woes are compounded when his son Alexander arrives.

Notable guest stars making their mark this season are *The Shawshank Redemption*'s Bob Gunton as a renegade captain in *The Wounded*, former Hollywood starlet Jean Simmons (*The Drumhead*), *M*A*S*H*'s David Ogden Stiers as Lwaxana Troi's love interest in *Half a Life* and *Frasier*'s Bebe Neuwirth in *First Contact* (not to be confused with the movie). Of note is the debut of the Cardassians, with leader Gul Macet played by Mark Alaimo prior to his seven-year stint on *Star Trek: Deep Space Nine* as Gul Dukat.

Another race to be popularised in *ST:DS9* are the Trill, who debut in *The Host*, though less freckled than Dax would prove to be. *Devil's Due* is a fun reworking of an abandoned *Phase II* script, Barclay makes a return visit in *The Nth Degree*, while Q and Vash join the crew on the Holodeck for the Robin Hood romp *Q-Pid*. Michelle Forbes (later to return as Ensign Ro) appears in *Half a Life*, John Fleck (later to return as Silik, *Enterprise*'s lead villain) is a Romulan in *The Mind's Eye*, while the 100th episode is also the season cliffhanger, *Redemption*. But is that really Tasha Yar in the shadows?

QUOTE-UNQUOTE

"When we finished the first half we had no idea what the second half would be." **Rick Berman admits that** *The Best of Both Worlds* **was a real challenge for the writers.**

"I am Locutus of Borg... have you considered buying a Cadillac?" **An on-set Patrick Stewart, in full Borg regalia, provides a memorable out-take.**

"Patrick was upset with the way Picard was being treated, and he had every right to be." **Michael Piller on why Picard's character needed to change.**

"He's a very sensitive man and did a great job. He was also lucky that he got a Data show as his first." **Jonathan Frakes praises Patrick Stewart on his directorial debut,** *In Theory*.

LeVar Burton gets his star on the Hollywood Walk of Fame, while William Shatner wins Razzie Awards for Worst Director and Actor in *Star Trek V*. DeForest Kelley gets away lightly with just a nomination as Worst Supporting Actor. Elsewhere, Gates McFadden becomes the first actress to play Jack Ryan's wife in *The Hunt for Red October* and *ST:TNG* finally debuts in the UK, three years late.

While *Star Trek V: The Final Frontier* didn't set cash registers alight, Paramount still see potential in the movie franchise, particularly with the 25th anniversary looming in 1991. Harve Bennett immediately reacts with his long-gestating premise of a Starfleet Academy movie, following a young Kirk and Spock in their cadet days. Fan fears of a '*Police Academy*' style film, backed up by the condemnation of original cast members (already upset at their ousting by *ST:TNG*, and now seeing the final nail in the coffin), lead to the project being shelved, and Bennett's departure from the series. Instead, Leonard Nimoy is asked to help out on the movie. Together with Lawrence Konner and Mark Rosenthal (*Superman IV*) he develops a storyline that reflects the end of the Cold War. The studio love the idea, Nicholas Meyer signs on to co-write and direct, and the first draft of *Star Trek VI* is ready before Christmas 1990.

SIDE STEPS
(Other *ST:TNG* tales set during this season)

1. *Reunion*
2. *Spartacus*
3. *Perchance to Dream*
4. *Dark Mirror*
5. *Vendetta*
6. *Chains of Command*
7. *The Forgotten War*
8. *Imbalance*

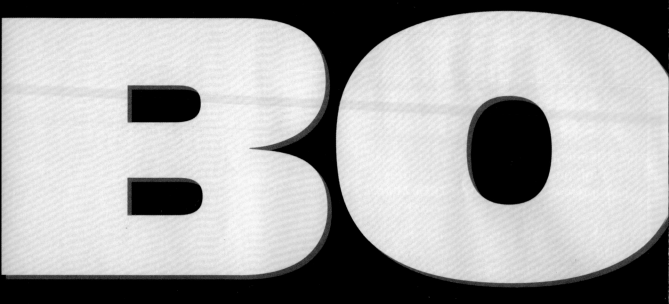

BO

When the *Borg* first appeared on *Star Trek: The Next Generation* they were originally intended to be insects, but building and operating the costumes was deemed too expensive. A careful rethink turned them into cybernetic organisms ('cyborgs') and that's how they appeared on screen. Who knows how successful they would have been with compound eyes and six limbs, but with their distinctive artificial design – a cross between a leather-clad biker, a Michelangelo muscle man and an expensive matt black stereo unit – they've captured the imagination of *Star Trek* fans world-wide. Now they've reached the big screen in *Star Trek: First Contact* but, before we all get blown away by the scale of the film, let's remind ourselves how much they've changed over the years.

RG

This page: *Captain Picard is assimilated into the Borg Collective in* **The Best of Both Worlds**
Opposite bottom: *The cybernetic beings as we first knew them in* **Descent...**
Opposite top: *... and today, even more menacing in* **Star Trek: First Contact**

he first we see of the Borg is one of their spaceships in *Q Who*, a featureless cube with no specific bridge, engineering section or living quarters. There is something about it that says, 'We don't care about design, we don't care about form, we just want this ship to do what it does best – move fast and fight hard.' According to the *U.S.S. Enterprise*'s sensors, the Borg inside don't register as life forms in their own right – they are a collective consciousness: each body being a mindless cell linked to the rest by continuous subspace messages. 'They don't have a single leader,' *Deanna Troi* realises. "It's the collective minds of all of them."

The Borg travel in straight lines, examining the technology of the races they encounter along the way and, if it offers them something they haven't already got, taking it by force. There's no rancour there, no aggression – they are strong, other races are weak and that's the beginning and the end of it. They almost wiped out *Guinan's* entire race, the *El Aurians*, at more or less the same time that *Captain James T. Kirk* first took command of the *U.S.S. Enterprise NCC-1701*.

That was a long way from Earth – somewhere in the Delta Quadrant – but 100 years later, a Borg ship passed by the Federation. The crew of the *U.S.S. Enterprise NCC-1701-D* see the result in the season one episode *The Neutral Zone*. There's very little left of the Borg's target, Science Station Delta Zero Five – it looks as if it has been scooped from the ground by a giant hand. The station is on the edge of the *Romulan Zone*, and at first it seemed the Federation's oldest enemies were to blame for the attack, but later events show how lucky they were.

In 2365, a second Borg ship is encountered over 7,000 light years away from the Federation in *Q Who*. We don't know what direction it was going in, but as a result of the information it downloaded from the *U.S.S. Enterprise*'s databanks, it changed its direction and headed straight for the Alpha Quadrant. And that's bad news for everyone. "You're just raw material to them," Guinan warns *Captain Picard*, and who knows better than her what the Borg can do?

In their first appearance the Borg are regarded as a definite race in their own right. They aren't interested in kidnapping other races and turning them into new Borg – all of that came later. All they want is technology. "The Borg are the ultimate user," Q tells Picard. "They're not interested in political conquest, wealth or power as you know it. They're simply interested in your ship – its technology. They've identified it as something they can consume." No mention there of assimilating the crew of the *U.S.S. Enterprise* – it's the starship itself they are interested in. They are the ultimate in high-tech shoplifters. As Guinan says, "They swarmed through our system, and when they left there was little or nothing left of my people."

From the little we have learnt of the Borg we know some, at least, are a race quite separate to the collection of assorted cybernetic hybrids kidnapped from different planets we have also seen, because of the presence of a Borg nursery in their ship. During their explorations, the Away Team who beam over to the Borg ship discover a cache of

baby Borg – cute little 'rugrats' with appealing mechanical contrivances fitted to their heads, their bodies and their limbs. The clear impression is that the Borg are born (or, perhaps, cloned) just like any other mammalian life form, and their artificial add-ons are added on shortly after birth. The babies look just like Human babies – there are no funny foreheads, no odd noses – and, if you remove their appurtenances, the adult versions could be mistaken for any pale, anorexic people you might bump into in the street – fashion models, for instance, or students.

Between 2366 and 2367, the Borg entered Federation space heading for planet Earth. (While this attack was anticipated by the Federation based on reports of the *U.S.S. Enterprise* encounter, it came months sooner than Federation strategists predicted, and defenses were not fully prepared.) During this second appearance, in *The Best of Both Worlds, Parts I and II*, their *raison d'etre* had shifted. Now they wanted people as well as machinery. "I thought they weren't interested in Human life forms – only our technology," *Lt. Commander Shelby* says, referring back to the behaviour of the Borg in *Q Who*. "Their priorities seem to have changed," Picard replies. The Borg Collective later tell Picard about their new-found mission in life. "We wish to improve ourselves... We will add your biological and technological distinctiveness to our own. Your culture will adapt to service ours."

The Borg start with Jean-Luc Picard himself, of course – kidnapping him, infiltrating his body with cybernetic material and altering his DNA in the same way they do with the little baby Borg. Even his heart is stopped and his blood drained away – his healthy pink skin tone rapidly altering to an ashen white as he lies, strapped to their operating table, a single tear trickling from his remaining Human eye. Their aim is to create the first Borg from another race – someone who can explain to the rest of Humanity what they want. "We only wish to raise quality of life for all species," Picard explains to Riker after his transformation into the entity known as *Locutus of Borg*.

THE BORG FACTS

STRUCTURE

The Borg Collective appears to operate on a group-mind principle, with many individuals linked through a type of subspace communications network. Neither the decision-making process, nor any central source of command, is known. The exact method of distribution of tasks is unknown. Command structure is known to be divided into three major subcommands – Communication, Navigation and Defence – which cover the range of necessary actions. A high degree of redundancy has been observed in the Borg command structure, eliminating dependency on any individual, so that even if significant percentages of the Collective are damaged or destroyed, it will not effect overall performance. The individual units of the Borg are cybernetically enhanced biological life forms, and are technologically differentiated for various functions. The Borg appear to have acquired their numbers and their vast technological capabilities largely through assimilation of other species and cultures. ■

TECHNOLOGY

Little is known of Borg technology other than what has been observed in confrontation, since virtually all encounters have been hostile.

They possess the ability to travel through vast distances at speeds appreciably faster than our practical warp limits. Of their vessels, we have usually confronted the cube-shaped vessel, believed to be their archetypal design. The renegade Borg group encountered in 2370 utilised a very different design, asymmetrical and highly unusual, and not possessing the typical outward attributes of Borg technology. It is not known whether or not this vessel was of Borg origin.

Their weaponry is highly advanced and very powerful.

Their defensive capabilities adapt quickly to all forms of weaponry we have used, including to weapons whose operating parameters are changed constantly, e.g. automatic phaser re-tuning has had some limited effect, but they have been able to adapt their defences against it before cumulative damage becomes significant.

The personal technology resident in each Borg unit seems similarly advanced, allowing them, for instance, to function as both fighting units and computer terminals virtually simultaneously. ■

CULTURE

Virtually nothing is known of Borg culture in the usual sense. All Borg are apparently interconnected with all other Borg, and the concept of individuality is apparently destructive to this organisation.

Their only known pursuit or intention seems to be the assimilation of other cultures and technologies, and the perfection and export of their form of organisation. ■

BORG BUSTER!

David Bassom talks to actress Elizabeth Dennehy about her battle with the Borg in the classic _Star Trek: The Next Generation_ two-parter, _The Best Of Both Worlds_.

F ew of _Star Trek: The Next Generation_'s guest stars made more of an impression than Elizabeth Dennehy. As ambitious Starfleet Tactical Specialist Lieutenant Commander Shelby in _The Best Of Both Worlds_, Dennehy challenges Commander Riker's position aboard the _U.S.S. Enterprise_, serves as his first officer following Captain Picard's abduction by the Borg, and ultimately plays a key role in saving the Human race from the insidious bio-organic conquerors.

For Dennehy, the initial appeal of making the show was obvious. "I loved the script and I really liked the character," she recalls. "I had never seen a _Star Trek_ show or movie, but I thought the storyline of _The Best Of Both Worlds_ was terrific and Shelby was wonderful. She was a very well-written character and she was very unpredictable. The nice thing was that I could see her point of view but I could also see how she could be so annoying!

"People have very strong feelings about my character," she continues. "Some people hated her, and some people really loved her. I'd go to _Star Trek_ conventions and people would debate about whether I was a bitch or just trying to do my job. Usually, women would defend me and men would defend Riker, which was interesting! But one way or another, she made an impact."

Shelby certainly experiences more than her fair share of the action in _The Best Of Both Worlds_. Besides beaming aboard the Borg ship to sabotage its warp engines, she commands the _U.S.S. Enterprise_'s Saucer

Above: _Lt. Commander Shelby does battle with more than just the Borg in_ The Best of Both Worlds
Right: _Captain Picard as Locutus Borg in_ The Best of Both Worlds

"You will become one with the Borg." His first attempts at improving the 'quality of life' meet with fierce resistance from a massed Federation armada at Wolf 359, destroying 39 starships and costing 11,000 lives.

Fortunately, Picard isn't a Borg for long enough to become one fully – "Their brains grown dependent on the biochips," he explains in a later story – and he is rescued and restored to Humanity. The scars run deep, however, and he doesn't like to be reminded of what he became – or what he did while assimilated.

By the time the Borg reappear in _I, Borg_, they seem to have made a Collective decision to assimilate the biological material of other races as well as their technology. "We assimilate species," says the Borg designated Third of Five (later to become better known as _Hugh_). "Then we know everything about them." Driving the point home later, he tells Picard, "The Borg assimilate civilisations, not individuals."

Hugh is sent back to the Borg ship from whence he came with a little gift, courtesy of the crew of the _U.S.S. Enterprise_. In a clever twist, they've assimilated _him_ into the Human race by treating him as an individual, looking after him and by becoming friends with the being. The results, for Hugh and his fellow shipmates, are fairly drastic. When the crew next come across a group of Borg, in the two-part story _Descent_, it's a group from the same ship Hugh came from, and they're different. _Very_ different.

"They were fast, aggressive... almost vicious," Riker complains – and, unlike the Borg of old, they seem to have feel-

Section during a desperate attempt to retrieve Captain Picard/Locutus. Ironically, however, the biggest challenge Elizabeth Dennehy faced whilst filming the episode came when her character was required to beat Commander Riker at poker!

"I haven't a clue about playing poker and I had to try to look like I knew what I was doing," she laughs. "If you're doing space stuff, you can do anything and people might believe you. But if you're faking it with poker, people can tell! So that was hard."

Although she spent most of her time on the show fighting the Borg, Dennehy speaks highly of her foes. "The Borg are cool! I felt really sorry for the actors who played them; they were all bound up in their rubber suits and were completely encased – they couldn't even go for a pee! But they do look very impressive with their fake arms and machinery; it's certainly not difficult to be scared of them! The set for the Borg ship was really incredible too, because it was almost like walking on an actual ship.

"The amount of effort and resources that go into [Star Trek] are very impressive," she adds. "It's great that Paramount Pictures care about the fans so much to produce a quality show time and time again. It's a tribute to the fans really."

The first instalment of The Best Of Both Worlds was shot as Star Trek: The Next Generation's cliff-hanging third season finale, while the concluding part was filmed several months later as the fourth season première. During the hiatus, viewers were left wondering if Captain Picard had truly been lost to the Borg and was destined to die. According to Dennehy, the show's cast and crew were equally intrigued about the outcome.

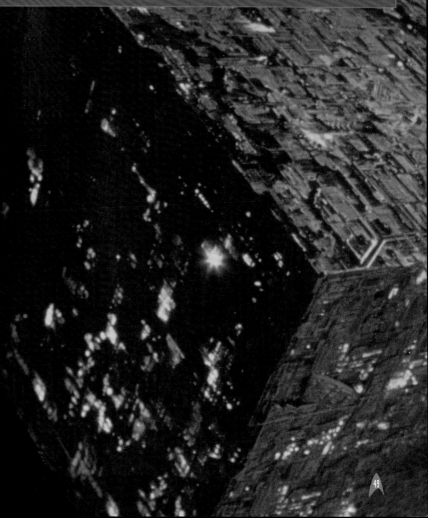

"When we shot the first one, the second part hadn't been written," she reveals. "As a result, over the summer, nobody knew what was going to happen: nobody knew if Picard would be rescued, if Shelby was going to replace Riker, or even if Shelby was going to be exposed as a Borg spy! Nobody knew.

"When I was getting ready to do the second one, I was talking to someone in the wardrobe department and I asked them what was going to happen. But they wouldn't tell me in case the phone was tapped! It was a cliff-hanger and they were trying everything to keep the ending a secret. So we didn't know what was going to happen until we showed up on the set."

Since serving aboard the U.S.S. Enterprise, Dennehy has been kept busy by a multitude of projects, including Prophecy II: Ash Town, The Eighth Day, The Game, Clear And Present Danger, The Waterdance, Quantum Leap and The Lazarus Man. While she admits to being disappointed that Lieutenant Commander Shelby does not appear in the big-screen Borg-fest Star Trek: First Contact, Elizabeth Dennehy still hopes that she will reprise the role one day, possibly in an episode of Star Trek: Deep Space Nine or even Star Trek: Voyager.

"I had a great time doing Star Trek: The Next Generation," she states. "It's amazing but I still get [fan] mail and I still get recognised for playing Shelby. I think that's incredible, because there's not a lot of work you can do that has such a strong recognition factor; the only other thing I can think of is a soap opera. It's very touching and pretty amazing to still be remembered for that role. So I would love to get another crack at it again!"■

was centred around acquiring cultures and technology," Picard responds, clearly stunned by the change and, perhaps, temporarily forgetting that the creatures had no interest in culture until they met him. This new set of Borg had a different set of aims again. "We do not assimilate inferior biological organisms," one of them says, "we destroy them."

These Borg proved to be a renegade band 'infected' by the sense of individuality that Hugh gained while previously in the care/custody of the U.S.S. Enterprise crew. Their command structure had been destroyed, and they wandered aimlessly until they found leadership in Data's 'brother' Lore, who promised to guide them to a new era of leadership among life forms. (The Borg appear to venerate both Data and Lore as more perfect than themselves, being fully artificial life forms.) Data shoots Lore with an energy weapon, effectively killing him, and the Borg group continue together, cut off from the collective, their current whereabouts and activities unknown. "We can't go back to the Borg Collective," Hugh says at the end of the story, indicating that there is still an unchanged Borg Collective to go back to. Well of course there is. They're the ones in Star Trek: First Contact.

Relentless. Unstoppable. Unforgiving.

"You can't outrun them," Q gleefully tells Picard in Q Who? "You can't destroy them. If you damage them, the essence of what they are remains. They are relentless."■

HAT TRICKS

She's the hostess with the mostest. Advice, that is, not to mention an enormous capacity for listening to problems and some nifty hats to boot. She's also something of an enigma, wrapped up in a paradox, sealed in a conundrum. She's *Guinan*, the *El-Aurian* proprietor of Ten-Forward on the *U.S.S. Enterprise NCC-1701-D*, and K. Stoddard Hayes is determined to get to the bottom of her.

Guinan Profile

Guinan has a sixth sense that seems almost clairvoyant. Everyone who knows her well has learned to respect this sixth sense, and they use her as a barometer for trouble.

Guinan has a sixth sense that seems almost clairvoyant. Everyone who knows her well has learned to respect this sixth sense, and they use her as a barometer for trouble. In *Q Who*, *Geordi La Forge* sees Guinan staring out the windows of Ten-Forward with a troubled look on her face. He interrupts his conversation and asks her if everything is all right.

"I don't know," she answers uncertainly.

That's all it takes to put the usually calm Geordi into a mild panic. "I think I'll go check on Engineering," he says and hurries from the room.

Guinan's most extraordinary ability is a perception of time that transcends the linear. When she sees the *U.S.S. Enterprise NCC-1701-C* emerge from a temporal rift, Guinan looks around at a room suddenly full of armed officers talking about war, and she knows that something has gone very wrong. It's not just a perception that there might be an alternate timeline to the one in which the war is proceeding.

She knows that the war timeline is the wrong one, that there should be children and families aboard, that the *Enterprise-D* should be a peaceful vessel, not a warship.

"Who's to say that this history is any less proper than the other?" *Captain Picard* demands.

"I suppose I am," she answers, with a certainty that comes not from stubbornness, but from knowing with senses she can't even describe.

No one but Guinan could have convinced Picard that the war timeline is wrong and must be corrected, even if this requires the loss of the *Enterprise-C*. She can persuade him to do things no one else could even get him to consider, because he trusts her advice absolutely, even when it goes completely against his own judgement. This trust was established through a relationship Picard describes as "far beyond friendship", and which began many years before Guinan joins the *Enterprise-D* as hostess and bartender. We

Guinan meets *Data* for the first time. No, sorry, *his* first time... no, no, that's not right... Oh I give up! (*Time's Arrow*)

The wise woman of *Star Trek* wears rich colours, stunning sculptural hats and an enigmatic smile. And she listens. As a member of a race that defines itself as "listeners" – the El-Aurians – Guinan seems to know everyone on the *U.S.S. Enterprise NCC-1701-D*, and she can see right into the soul of each and every one of them.

She listens to *Wesley Crusher* pour out his heart about his first romance, and assures him that he's right, he'll never feel the same about anyone ever again, because each time you fall in love it's different. She introduces a sceptical *Worf* to what will become his favourite non-alcoholic drink, prune juice, and suggests that he try dating some of his human crewmates. And she is surely the only person who can get away with calling him a coward, when he rejects her advice.

Young at heart: Keiko, Guinan and Ro in *Rascals*

don't know anything about these earlier experiences that have created so much trust between them; we can only see the results.

Because of the temporal adventure of *Time's Arrow*, the first time Picard met Guinan was not the first time she had met him. He only discovers this when he travels to late 19th Century San Francisco and realises that Guinan first met him when she was visiting Earth – disguised as a woman of letters – to "listen" to humans. It seems Guinan's interest in humans has lasted not years, but centuries.

When Picard leaves Guinan in the past, she tells him the hardest part for her will be waiting nearly 500 years to meet him again. When she does meet him again in his own time, she does not mention that incident, for fear of altering the timeline. We can guess, though, that she would take pains to pursue the acquaintance, because of her memory of meeting him so long ago.

Tasha Yar and Guinan begin to realise something's wrong in *Yesterday's Enterprise*

Little is known about Guinan's life, not even her age. Her father was born in the late 17th Century, and she travels to Earth in the late 19th Century, so she is probably between 500 and 600 years old. She has had several children. Known dates in her chronology are as follows:

circa 1890

Guinan visits Earth for a while to study humans. She passes as human, and becomes a celebrated literary figure, counting among her friends the great American writer Samuel Clemens.

1893

Guinan meets Picard and several of his officers when they time travel to old San Francisco to stop an alien incursion.

circa 2185

Guinan has unknown but hostile dealings with Q, ending about this time. Q knows her under a different name.

2265

The Borg destroy the El-Aurian system, reducing Guinan's people to bands of refugees scattered across the galaxy. Guinan is not on her home world at the time of the attack.

2293

Guinan and other El-Aurian refugees are rescued by the *U.S.S. Enterprise NCC-1701-B* when their ship comes into contact with the Nexus.

circa 2327 – *circa* 2363

Sometime in this period (presumably after Picard's graduation from the Academy and before he takes command of the *Enterprise-D*) Guinan meets Picard again and they become close friends.

2365

Guinan joins the *Enterprise-D* at Picard's invitation, to become hostess of the new Ten-Forward crew lounge.

2371

Guinan's whereabouts after the destruction of the *Enterprise-D* are not known. ■

When Q is stripped of his powers, Guinan stabs him with a fork to find out if he really is flesh and blood, and as he howls with pain, observes, "Seems pretty human to me."

We know almost nothing of Guinan's long relationship with Q, except that they met over 200 years ago, and only hostility lies between them. Each one regards the other as a major troublemaker. Knowing Q and knowing Guinan, we can speculate that perhaps Guinan prevented Q from tormenting some hapless species in the past.

Whatever Q did, it was enough for Guinan, this most compassionate of souls, to have no compassion whatsoever for the omnipotent meddler. When Q is stripped of his powers, Guinan stabs him with a fork to find out if he really is flesh and blood, and as he howls with pain, observes, "Seems pretty human to me." After an alien energy beam leaves him stricken on the floor and screaming for help, she remarks with ironic satisfaction, "How the mighty have fallen."

Guinan and her people also have a long history with the *Borg*, who destroyed their home world, and she reacts to any Borg much as she does to Q. The *Enterprise-D*'s rescue of the young Borg, *Hugh*, is one of the very few times Guinan shows anger and hostility. She is adamantly against rescuing Hugh, because of what will happen "when that kid's big brothers come looking for him." When Picard is wondering about the ethics of using Hugh as a weapon against his own people, Guinan tricks him into letting her win their fencing match, by making him think she has hurt herself.

"You felt sorry for me, and look what it got you," she says.

Yet she is a listener, and when Geordi challenges her to meet Hugh and see what he's really like, her innate honesty prompts her to take up the challenge. She knows she must see and judge for herself. And that one brief meeting is enough to convince her that Geordi is right: Hugh is no longer Borg.

Although Guinan is excellent at giving advice, she can also be frustratingly reticent at the times when one would like her to say the most. When Q drops the *Enterprise-D* in Borg space, Guinan gives Picard very little information about either Q or the Borg, although it's clear she knows much more than she is telling.

A moment of dialogue gives a hint as to why she may be holding back. As Q tries to persuade Picard to accept him as a crewman, Guinan and Q suddenly start talking over Picard's head about whether or not the humans are ready to meet the challenges of the galaxy. They sound like two parents discussing a child. When Q argues that the humans don't have a clue what awaits them, Guinan replies, "They will learn and adapt. That is their greatest advantage." Perhaps she is obeying her own 'non-interference directive' by allowing her human friends to solve their own problems and learn from their mistakes.

Guinan lives very much in the present, as we see when she and several crewmates are transformed into children by a transporter accident. While Picard, *Keiko* and especially *Ro* treat the change as a misfortune, Guinan welcomes her second childhood as an opportunity. She turns to the gloomy Ro with a grin and says, "You make a pretty cute kid."

To Ro's exasperated complaint that they should be *doing* something, she replies, "You're right. Let's go play... I haven't been young for a long time, and I intend to enjoy every minute of it." She skips through the corridors, bounces on the bed, and even persuades Ro to play with her. Even when her adult body has been restored, she prolongs the delight of childlike play by settling down to do some colouring with Ro.

"That's the wonderful thing about crayons. They can take you more places than a starship," she says.

Guinan is both enigmatic and transparent, a contradiction often found in deeply spiritual people. She can speak with the wisdom and understanding that come only from depths of experience and knowledge. Yet her own life seems simple and serene, focused on the present, and on helping those around her to help themselves. She wants nothing for herself but to be able to listen. ■

Guinan tries to convince Picard that the timeline must be altered in *Yesterday's Enterprise*

RENDEZVOUS ON RISA

Guest star Jennifer Hetrick proved a match for both the stalwart *Captain Jean-Luc Picard* and the omnipotent *Q* as the brash archaeologist *Vash*, as Joe Nazzaro discovers...

Jennifer Hetrick didn't think *Star Trek: The Next Generation* would ever catch on with television viewers. "I hadn't watched it, and when they were just beginning to create the series I had an opportunity to audition for it, and I said no. I said, 'It's a spin-off of *Star Trek*? It'll never work!' Those were famous last words!"

Hetrick's involvement with *Star Trek: The Next Generation* started when she auditioned for a guest-starring role in the third season episode *Captain's Holiday*. The episode saw *Captain Picard* getting involved with a mischievous archaeologist named Vash (Hetrick) while vacationing on the planet *Risa*.

Hetrick admits that she really didn't know much about the *Star Trek* phenomenon before working on the series. "I actually thought that Jonathan Frakes was the captain!" the actress laughs. "I really didn't know what I was getting into, but I looked at the script and loved it. I actually laughed aloud and it takes a lot for me to do that, reading a script. I was impressed and really loved the story and wanted to do it."

According to Hetrick, it didn't take long to establish an on-camera relationship with Patrick Stewart. "I think we hit it off well right off the bat. Patrick was very open and available; he wouldn't just show up and then run off to his trailer." Not long after finishing *Captain's Holiday*, Hetrick and Stewart also became involved off-screen. Luckily, they managed to keep their relationship fairly low-key, avoiding the usual media pitfalls that affect most Hollywood couples.

Viewer response to Vash in *Captain's Holiday* must have been extremely positive, because Hetrick was invited back the following season, in *Q-Pid*, in which Picard's reunion with the brash archaeologist is interrupted by the arrival of Q, who transforms the *U.S.S. Enterprise* crew into characters from the Robin Hood legend. "It wasn't really unexpected," says Hetrick of her return in *Q-Pid*, "but it was a great opportunity, because I didn't really know the other cast members at that point, and it was fun to finally work with them."

Q-Pid was one of the more unusual episodes of *Star Trek: The Next Generation*'s fourth season. For Hetrick, the juxtaposition of Robin Hood with *Star Trek* presented an interesting challenge. "I had chosen for Vash to be quite uncomfortable in those clothes. At one point, I trip over the long dress. The head-dress was very awkward, and I'm sure she wasn't used to that kind of attire."

Ironically, the actress continued her on-screen partnership with John De Lancie after *Q-Pid*, not on *Star Trek: The Next Generation* but an episode of the western series *The Young Riders*. "Actually, it happened after that episode. We joked about it because at the end of *Q-Pid* he says, 'I can take you anywhere,' and where we ended up was the wild west in the mid-19th Century!

"John is extremely focused," says Hetrick of her co-star, "but not to the exclusion of having fun. He's able to do both. He's not reclusive, he doesn't hide away."

Hetrick re-teamed with De Lancie for *Q-Less*, one of the first-season episodes of *Star Trek: Deep Space Nine*. "There were two difficult aspects to that episode," she explains. "The first was the scene with John when we're arguing in my quarters. We have this fight while I'm busy unpacking, and he keeps throwing my packed bag back onto my shoulder, and I have to unpack again. It was a seven-page scene, and there were so many details with the bag. Then there were the entrances of the doctor and Armin Shimerman, and all this stuff. We were trying to play it like farce.

"There was also the scene where Q keeps zapping me into the different phases of deterioration," she continues. "That was a total of 10 hours in make-up for just a few seconds of camera time, but I love doing that stuff. It's fun, and it's a departure from always having to look so damn glamorous out here. I didn't find it unsettling at all."

Although Vash has yet to make another appearance in the *Star Trek* Universe, Jennifer Hetrick has managed to stay in touch with its fans. She's attended a number of recent conventions, and still receives a fair bit of mail. "I was already used to getting fan mail because of *L.A. Law*," she says, "but the mail from *Star Trek* started happening a few months after the first episode aired and just continued on since then.

"They've also come out with *Star Trek* trading cards which I'm on, and I even have an action figure. That's pretty wild!" ∎

Photo courtesy of Jennifer Hetrick

Pictures top right:
Sarek; Encounter at Farpoint; Unification

THE RETURN OF THE WORTHY

Spock, McCoy, Scotty – even Jim Kirk – would eventually appear in the 24th Century alongside their successors on board the *Enterprise*-D. But were they the people we remembered? **Dayton Ward** and **Kevin Dilmore** examine the evidence...

While the creators of *Star Trek: The Next Generation* worked to establish a unique identity for the show, once in a while they dipped into the well of characters and events from the original *Star Trek* – and those efforts met with mixed reactions from fans of both series.

ST:TNG's inaugural episode, *Encounter at Farpoint*, took a moment to note a symbolic passing of the *Star Trek* baton between the shows with an appearance by a withered yet still irascible Dr. Leonard McCoy. An admiral at age 137, the original series' spacefaring country doctor was a welcome face aboard the *Enterprise*-D while behaving more cantankerously than ever. Fans loved the quiet, even touching scene in which McCoy tells Data that this new ship bears the right name, and advises the android to "treat her like a lady, and she'll always bring you home."

It wouldn't be until the third season that another familiar face from the 23rd Century paid a visit to the *Enterprise*. In an episode bearing his name, Spock's

father Sarek was shown continuing his efforts as Vulcan's ambassador to the Federation after more than 100 years. Unlike McCoy's earlier appearance, seeing Sarek here was not cause for celebration. Advancing age had finally begun to take its toll, with the Vulcan shown suffering the early effects of a degenerative neurological disease. This turn of events tangibly affected how the character behaved, with his emotions taking a stronger grip on him at inopportune – even public – moments.

Fan reaction to *Sarek* was vocal, with a good share of criticism leveled at the decision to inflict the Vulcan equivalent of Alzheimer's disease upon one of the original series' most beloved characters. That disapproval would rise sharply when Sarek died two seasons later, during the two-part episode *Unification*.

In many fans' eyes, *Unification* itself seemed to contradict its noble intentions as *ST:TNG*'s 1991 salute to the 25th anniversary of the original *Star Trek*. The stage appeared set to honor and embrace this milestone, complete with Leonard Nimoy guest-starring as the nearly 140-year old Ambassador Spock on a mission to bring Romulans and Vulcans together in peace.

Presented as a tribute episode (as well as offering a few teasing hints about events of the feature film *Star Trek VI: The Undiscovered Country* starring the original series cast poised for release just a few weeks later), *Unification* initially seemed not to resonate with fans of either series. At the heart of many complaints was Spock's portrayal as a man obsessed, apparently willing to turn his back on Federation and Starfleet ideals and risk an interstellar incident as he pursued his goals. Fans also took exception to how easily the normally-shrewd Spock seemed to be duped by deception on the part of his Romulan counterparts.

Captain Montgomery Scott was the next character to come to the 24th Century in *Relics*, which showed how the resourceful engineer escaped certain death after a transport crash by beaming himself into a transporter pattern buffer – for 75 years – before being rescued by officers of the *Enterprise*-D. The episode featured numerous nods to the original series – including a loving

PREVIOUSLY ON *STAR TREK*:

The reasoning behind Spock's presence on Romulus is explained...

The computer records of the *U.S.S. Enterprise* were corrupted by Ben Finney in *Court Martial*...

Captain Picard isn't the first person to deal with a difficult passenger in *Perfect Mate*; James T. Kirk had to cope with the Dohlman of Elas...

tribute to the original *Enterprise* (as Scotty himself said, with "No bloody A, B, C or D.") by including a scene set on a holodeck recreation of that famed starship's bridge. That moment, shared between Scotty and Captain Picard, has grown into one many fans cite as a favorite among *ST:TNG*'s entire run.

Despite all of this, initial fan reaction to *Relics* was also mixed. Many took issue with the despondent "funk" in which the legendary engineer wallowed as he faced his new life in the future, and reaction to Scotty's early treatment at the hands of the *Enterprise* crew — specifically Geordi La Forge — unsettled many viewers. However, by the end of the episode, the Scotty known and loved by longtime fans was back in true form, crafting yet another miracle and helping LaForge to rescue the *Enterprise* from being trapped inside a mammoth Dyson Sphere.

Conspicuously absent from the *Enterprise*-D's seven years of adventures were any clues as to the fate of *Star Trek*'s original leading man, James T. Kirk, (apart from one comment by a still-disoriented Scotty when he first was rescued) with many fans hoping to see the legendary captain pay his own visit to the 24th Century. That wish would come to pass — as would Kirk himself — when Captain Picard and his crew leapt to the big screen in 1994's *Star Trek Generations*. Relatively few complaints were heard about Kirk's portrayal, with many believing his presence easily overshadowed Picard's more reserved demeanor during their time together onscreen. Still, fan furor over Kirk's death continues to this day, with numerous grassroots campaigns aimed at seeing the character returned to at least something resembling his former glory.

And what of the other original series characters? There were no mentions of Sulu, Chekov, or Uhura during *ST:TNG*'s television run, though Chekov does appear — along with Sulu's daughter, Demora — in the opening scenes of *Star Trek Generations*. What of these beloved characters? So far as the 24th Century is concerned, they have fates as yet untold... ▲

*Pictures top left: *Unification*; *Star Trek: Generations*, *Relics*; *Relics* pictures center right: *Cause and Effect*; *The Game* picture bottom right: *Ensign Ro**

THE SAGA CONTINUES

Koral's story continues in *ST:DS9*'s *Sword of Kahless*...

Robin Lefler's epic journey continues on board the *U.S.S. Excalibur*...

Sela returns to plague the *Enterprise* crew...

Spock's efforts towards Unification continue

Neral's rise to Praetor is recounted in *ST:DS9*'s *Inter Arma Enim Silent Leges*

After Miles O'Brien was possessed in *Power Play*, it was his wife's turn in *ST:DS9*'s *The Assignment*...

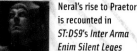

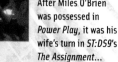

Captain Bateson becomes the first captain of what would be renamed the *U.S.S. Enterprise*-E...

THE TNG YEARS

Brannon Braga joins as story editor for season five (and later co-creates *Enterprise*). He helps formulate the resolution to the *Redemption* cliffhanger – it's actually Tasha's half-Romulan daughter Sela. *Darmok* is an *Enemy Mine*-type adventure welcoming *Star Trek II: The Wrath of Khan*'s Paul Winfield back to the franchise, and *Ensign Ro* introduces not only the eponymous recurring character (as played by Michelle Forbes) but the Bajoran race, to be pivotal players on sister show *Deep Space Nine*. *Disaster* is an Irwin Allen-style disaster movie, while *The Game* allows Wesley to return with a pre-mainstream Ashley Judd as Robin Lefler. Biggest casting coup of the year (and tying in with the release of *Star Trek VI: The Undiscovered Country*) is Leonard Nimoy's return as Spock in the *Unification* two-parter. *Part II* is the highest rated show since the pilot and provides the final bridge between the shows.

Patrick Stewart directs his second episode, *Hero Worship*, about a traumatised boy linking with Data, while *Violations* is a rape story and *Ethics* tackles euthanasia following Worf's paralysis. The Frakes-directed *Cause & Effect* starring *Frasier*'s Kelsey Grammer is a classic time anomaly tale, *The First Duty* investigates Wesley's rogue cadet friends (including a pre-*Voyager* Robert Duncan McNeill), Mrs Troi returns in *The Cost of Living*, and in *The Perfect Mate* Patrick Stewart appears alongside his future *X-Men* co-star Famke Janssen and *Buck Rogers*' Tim O'Connor.

The Inner Light (Picard lives his life in an alternative world) proves to be one of the best-ever shows, *I, Borg* tackles prejudice (Hugh would return), and the season concludes with the *Time's Arrow* cliffhanger. The show is still featuring some great action adventures amongst its social allegories, with each member of the cast regularly getting episodes to develop their characters. ▲

QUOTE-UNQUOTE

"There's less experimentation now. I think there's less stretching of the envelope than we did in the first few years." **Brent Spiner on *ST:TNG* getting too comfortable.**

"Spock becomes an emissary against prejudice and discovers, during the course of the story, his own prejudices." **Leonard Nimoy on Spock's journey in *ST:VI*.**

"It was very difficult. There were scenes at the end that were very, very emotional. It was particularly intense for me because it was the first time I'd worked with my son on camera." **Patrick Stewart on filming *The Inner Light*.**

DEPARTING

October 24 - Gene Roddenberry (*Star Trek* creator)

On February 13 the sixth *Star Trek* movie is officially approved, with the stipulation that it's in cinemas before Christmas (still within the 25th anniversary year). The budget has been dropped from $46m to $30m, resulting in the loss of some set-pieces and the necessity to redress and use *ST:TNG* sets during the show's hiatus. Filmed from April, Christopher Plummer's villainous Klingon Chang is cut from the same cloth as Khan, Kim Cattrall's Vulcan Valeris is a great variation on Saavik, and David Warner (previously in *Star Trek V*) plays Chancellor Gorkon. Michael Dorn play's Worf's grandfather, and *ST:DS9*'s Rene Auberjonois has his scene edited out of the cinema release, though it is reinstated for the DVD. With Sulu finally taking command of the *U.S.S. Excelsior*, and a story that allows all of the regulars to shine, this is a fitting final adventure for the whole crew, with a worldwide take of $94m.

At the 25th Anniversary Convention at the Shrine Auditorium the *ST:TOS* cast gather with a wheelchair-bound Gene Roddenberry. It will be their last public appearance together; Roddenberry dies in October 1991. While he gets to see a pre-release cut of *ST:VI*, he misses DeForest Kelley getting his Star on the Hollywood Walk of Fame on December 18.

SIDE STEPS
(Other *ST:TNG* tales set during this season)

1. *The Badlands* Book One
2. *Imzadi*
3. *The Last Stand*
4. *War Drums*
5. *Nightshade*
6. *Sins of Commission*
7. *The Devil's Heart*
8. *The Romulan Prize*
9. *Grounded*

1

2

3

4

5

6

7

8

9

Schisms; Realm of Fear; Chain of Command; Chain of Command

DARKENING THE UNIVERSE

Captain Picard's encounter with Gul Madred in *Chain of Command* marked a turning point in the *Star Trek* universe, as **Andy Lane** explains...

I n Gene Roddenberry's universe, every human is perfect and, as a result, humanity itself is perfect enough that it can challenge its own gods for supremacy – a typically 1960s Southern Californian attitude, but one strangely at odds with Roddenberry's military background. There are plenty of examples, however, both in *Star Trek: The Original Series* and in the first few movies, of times when Roddenberry vetoed ideas that he felt went against his policy – Harlan Ellison's original script for *City on the Edge of Forever*, for instance, was heavily rewritten to remove the idea of drug-dealing on board the *Enterprise* on the basis that the crew, *Roddenberry's* crew, just wouldn't *do* that – while a fan could lose count of the number of deities who get their come-uppance in various ways.

It's noticeable, by the way, that Roddenberry almost never allowed an evil human character in the original series: they could be mad, they could be mistaken, but they were almost never actively evil. Even after Roddenberry's death, his influence persisted, testament to both his willpower, his tenacity and perhaps the fact that his beliefs supported the entire series like the foundations of a pack of cards, and the new show-runners were worried that pulling some of them out would send the entire edifice crashing down around their ears.

It was only by season six of *Star Trek: The Next Generation* that one can see the gradual deconstruction of Roddenberry's ideals and beliefs. *Star Trek: Deep Space Nine* was being prepped for launch at the same time, and despite what members of the production team may now say, it *was* a darker version of *Star Trek*: one in which nobody wanted to be where they were and they all rubbed each other up the wrong way. Back on *ST:TNG* a more subtle version of the same process was going on. First we had the return of Reginald Barclay in the second episode of the season, *Realm of Fear*. Barclay was the most flawed but sane and functional human character we'd seen in Starfleet up to that point: paranoid, cowardly, neurotic, obsessive, but still a hero, rather than a villain. Later, the episode *Schisms* gives us graphic and horrific medical experiments, including the surgical severing and reattachment of Riker's arm.

The dark heart of the season, however, is the two-part story *Chain of Command*, in which: a new captain is assigned to the *Enterprise* and proceeds to put everyone's nose out of joint; Riker is relieved of command; and, most

PREVIOUSLY ON *STAR TREK*:

Captain Montgomery Scott last stood on an *Enterprise* bridge in *Star Trek Generations*...

Mackenzie Calhoun encountered Edward Jellico while at Starfleet Academy...

The Preservers were believed to be responsible for the spread of human-type species across the galaxy...

A duplicate Captain Kirk had already plagued the *Enterprise*...

...as had a duplicate Spock!

tellingly, Picard is tortured for precious tactical information by the Cardassians. Actually, the telling thing is not that Picard is tortured – plenty of characters, from Kirk onwards, have had pain inflicted on them in the course of their duty. No, the telling thing is that Picard actually breaks under torture. Physically and mentally abused by his captor, Gul Madred (chillingly played by British actor David Warner), Picard can clearly see that there are four lights suspended in the darkness above the Cardassian's head, but Madred tells Picard that there are only three lights, and if Picard admits that he can only see three lights then he will be released. The problem is, of course, that by saying that there are only three lights, Picard will have taken the first step towards collaborating with his captors, and his false admission will be exploited in true Orwellian fashion. Picard is rescued, of course, but back on the *Enterprise* he is forced to admit that, for a moment, just before the rescue occurs, he actually did see three lights. The deprivation, the abuse, the desire to stop the pain – they all got to him. The Cardassians won – they just never got the chance to use their victory. It's a moment that would be unthinkable in any previous season of *ST:TNG* or in *ST:TOS*: the main character admitting that he gave in to torture.

It's not as if season six of *ST:TNG* marked a massive sea-change in the style of the show – there were still plenty of fluffy episodes (*Rascals, Tapestry*), episodes based around puzzles (*Aquiel, Man of the People*) and episodes in which it's not entirely clear why we are watching (*Frame of Mind, Lessons*), but Reginald Barclay would be back, as dysfunctional as ever, and there would be suicides and dark doings on the *Enterprise* in the next season. In all, season six of *ST:TNG* marked a sea-change in the way *Star Trek* would be portrayed, and *Chain of Command* is, arguably, the point at which the tide turned. ▲

Pictures left: *Chain of Command*
pictures center right: Tim Russ in *Starship Mine*;
Stephen Hawking in *Descent*
picture bottom right: Reginald Barclay

THE SAGA CONTINUES

 Scotty attempts to go back in time to save Jim Kirk's life...

 Admiral Jellico helps to decide the fate of Federation President Min Zife...

Gowron's story continues in *ST:DS9*'s *House of Quark*...

Tom Riker reappears in *ST:DS9*'s *Defiant*

THE TNG YEARS

S T:TNG is renewed for a sixth (and rumoured final) year, concluding the *Time's Arrow* yarn, Barclay returns for the third time in *Realm of Fear* (there are creatures in the transporter stream), *Man of the People* features an ageing manhunting Troi (shades of ST:TOS' *The Deadly Years*), and Q returns in *True Q*. The show experiments with high concept shows, including a western (*A Fistful of Datas*) and the crew turned into 12-year-olds (*Rascals*). *Schisms* sees the crew being operated on (cut apart and stitched back) at night by hooded aliens, and Data recites his classic poem 'An Ode to Spot' (his cat).

Season highlights include the return of a 147-year-old Scotty (*Relics*), with a beautifully visualised original *Enterprise* bridge set, and Cardassian two-parter *Chain of Command* with Ronny Cox (*Robocop*) as the no-nonsense temporary captain, Jellico, and David Warner (back in the franchise, after appearances in *Star Trek V* and *VI*) as torturer Gul Madred.

Again, the cast get opportunities to explore their back stories and the histories that have been built up over the preceding five years. *Ship in a Bottle* features the return of Moriarty, while *Face of the Enemy* has a surgically altered Troi posing as a Romulan alongside Carolyn (*Survivors*) Seymour. In *Tapestry*, Picard recalls being fitted with an artificial heart following a run-in with a Nausicaan, while the *Birthright* two-parter visits DS9 and meets Dr Bashir. *Part II* features Richard Herd, who would later play Tom Paris' father in *Star Trek: Voyager*. *The Chase* (directed by Frakes) features Linda (*The Avengers*) Thorson as the first female Cardassian while *Starship Mine* has a pre-ST:VOY Tim Russ as a ship saboteur. Guest cameos this year are former astronaut Dr Mae Jemison in *Second Chances*, while Professor Stephen Hawking plays himself in the show's second Borg season cliffhanger, *Descent*. Data appears to have gone rogue and joined up with his brother Lore...

QUOTE-UNQUOTE

"We didn't intend to do a cliffhanger this year, but once DS9 was announced, there were rumours that *The Next Generation* was being cancelled." **Michael Piller on why *Time's Arrow* had to be split over two episodes.**

"*Time's Arrow* is a particularly fun episode. I have no plans over the hiatus, so I'm going to spend that time in anticipation about what happens to Data." **Brent Spiner on solving the mystery of Data's disembodied head.**

DEPARTING

15 December – William Theiss
(*TOS* Costume Designer)

W illiam Shatner and Leonard Nimoy take to the road for their '25 Year Mission Tour', Nichelle Nichols gets her Star on the Walk of Fame and Smithsonian's National Air & Space Museum in Washington host *Star Trek: The Exhibition*. And if we are to believe what we heard in *Space Seed*, this is the year that Khan Noonien Singh rises to power in the Middle East and Asia...

New year. New show. January 2 1993 sees *Star Trek: Deep Space Nine* launch with *Emissary*. The pilot features Patrick Stewart in the dual roles of Locutus and Picard, locking horns with new commander Sisko. For the first time ever, two new *Star Trek* shows are in production at the same time, with ST:DS9 being the first to have no input from original creator Gene Roddenberry. Instead of exploring the galaxy, the crew are on a static space station, inviting the action to come to them. Created by Michael Piller and Rick Berman, it offers a darker vision of the future.

Miles O'Brien and wife Keiko cross over from ST:TNG, while other links to the past are Q and Vash (*Q-Less*) and Lwaxana Troi (*The Forsaken*). New villain Gul Dukat is in the show from the pilot, as is enigmatic Cardassian Garak. Season finale *In the Hands of the Prophets* introduces Oscar-winner Louise Fletcher as villainess Winn, as well as Kira's recurring love interest Bareil.

SIDE STEPS
(Other ST:TNG tales set during this season)

1 2 3 4 5 6

7 8 9 10 11

1. The Best and the Brightest
2. Here there be Dragons
3. A Fury Scorned
4. Debtors' Planet
5. Guises of the Mind
6. The Death of Princes
7. Double Helix: Red Sector
8. To Storm Heaven
9. The Romulan Stratagem
10. Foreign Foes
11. Requiem

Who would have
thought that
an immortal,
omnipotent and
totally erratic
being could
grow and learn
in a very
human way?

TRUE

Without Q's steering influence, Captain Picard and the crew of the
U.S.S Enterprise NCC-1701-D would have followed a markedly different
path, and he's even made a nuisance of himself on *Deep Space Nine* and
the *U.S.S. Voyager.* K. Stoddard Hayes chronicles Q and the *Q Continuum.*

Q squares up to Picard for the first
time in *Encounter at Farpoint*

Only in *Star Trek*: Q meets Isaac Newton

Blimey, Data looks a bit weird. Oh no, my mistake:
it's Q in *Hide and Q*

Every epic ought to have a trickster
character to break the rules, cause all
kinds of mischief and open the door
to any kind of unpredictable story.
Star Trek's trickster *par excellence* is Q.
His godlike powers combine with a
love of mischief and a childlike irresponsibility to make him "next of kin to
chaos" (*Picard, Deja Q*). And like the true
trickster of mythology, Q can be sometimes the adversary and sometimes,
though rarely, a kind of hero.

Q would be an important character in the *Star Trek* mythology if he
had done no more than introduce us
to the *Borg*. But Q's significance goes
far beyond the events of *Q Who*
Between his capricious nature and
his almost limitless powers, the
writers have the freedom to create
almost any kind of story for Q,
from a fantastic trip to Sherwood
Forest, to a chance to undo the
mistakes of one's youth, to a
hearing on the individual's right
to commit suicide. Seeing John
de Lancie's name at the opening
of an episode is almost a guaran-
tee of an entertaining ride, full
of unexpected twists and razor
sharp repartee.

Nothing indicates Q's importance to the *Star Trek: The Next
Generation* storyline more than the
central role he plays in both the
pilot and final episodes of the series.
In fact, Q spends so much time pestering the *Enterprise*-D, and Picard in
particular, that it's hard to imagine
what he did for fun in all the millennia
of his existence before he met his
"*capitaine*". From that first *Encounter at
Farpoint*, when he tests humanity, and
specifically Picard, to find out if we are as
civilized as we claim, Q goes on to seven more

Q taunts the future Picard in *All Good Things…*

adventures with the *Enterprise*-D, plus three other
Starfleet encounters.

In all these adventures, just when we think we
have Q figured out, he changes. Who would have
thought that an immortal, omnipotent and totally
erratic being could grow and learn in a very human
way? Q begins as a petulant child-being, ready to
manipulate any corporeal creature with his tests and
games. Sure, he claims to represent the Continuum
in testing humans, but it's a good bet he thought of
these little torments all by himself. The Continuum
expresses its displeasure with his activities quite
forcefully, first by whisking him off the *Enterprise*-D
when he seems likely to break his bargain with
Picard (*Hide and Q*), and finally by stripping him of
his powers and making him a mortal (*Deja Q*).

Mortality is the making of Q. It's ironic that he
learns more in a few hours of being mortal and finite
than he learned in countless millennia as a Q. He is
humiliated by his experiences as a human and

When Q encounters the *U.S.S. Voyager* in *Death Wish,* he immediately takes a shine to *Janeway.*

Mortality is the making of Q. It's ironic that he learns more in a few hours of being mortal and finite than he learned in countless millennia as a Q.

shamed by the compassion and altruism of *Data* and his crewmates, who risk their own lives to protect him from his well-merited enemies. Their nobility inspires him to the first selfless act of his infinite, self-centred life: he leaves the ship to prevent the *Calamarain* from destroying it in their quest to capture him.

Of course, he'd rather die than admit that he cares about the *Enterprise*-D and her crew, so he pretends he has left the ship just to end his miserable mortal life. Yet clearly, he has changed. Each time he returns to the *Enterprise*-D after this, his actions are purposeful, and even at times altruistic. It may amuse him to drop the *Enterprise*-D crew into a facsimile of Sherwood Forest in *QPid*, but his motive is real; he is trying to pay a debt and help Picard patch up his relationship with *Vash*. And he genuinely does help Picard appreciate the mistakes of his youth in *Tapestry*, by letting the captain relive one of those mistakes and see what happens to his life.

Finally, he shepherds Picard through the remarkable test of *All Good Things*.... When Q first tests Picard at *Farpoint*, he is furious that Picard passes the test, and departs in a huff. This time, Q appears not as tormentor and judge, but as guide, giving Picard hints of what he should be looking for and how to solve the puzzle. At the last, he tells Picard the Continuum was testing him to see if he was capable of thinking outside the normal space-time continuum. And far from being miffed at Picard's success, Q is genuinely pleased.

Mr and Mrs Q in *The Q and the Grey*. Don't they make a lovely couple?

TO BE CONTINUUM

So what's it like in the Q Continuum?

If we believe Quinn, it's as dull as a desert gas stop. If we believe Q, it's a battlefield of the American Civil War. But of course, both of these images are only representations created by the Q to put their world in terms that their human associates can comprehend. The Continuum itself seems so limitless that humans would not be able to perceive its reality.

With the flash of a hand, the Q can throw a starship halfway across the galaxy, or take it back to the moment of the Big Bang, or reduce it to subatomic size. The Q can take the officers of the *Enterprise*-D on an adventure that seems to last for hours, and return them to the moment that they left, without so much as a ripple in the space-time continuum. If they can do all these things to us, surely the restrictions of time and space and corporeal existence have no hold on the Q. They can literally do whatever they can think. For them, to wish is to have, and to think is to be.

There is no birth or death in the Continuum. Quinn is the first Q ever to die, and the child conceived by Q and the female Q is the first child ever born in the Continuum. It seems likely that the Q in their natural state simply exist, with none of the life transitions we are accustomed to. It's easy for us mortals to grasp the notion of immortality, of never dying, but what are we to make of never being born? How

did the Q come into existence in the beginning? Did they evolve to their energy state from mortal tissue and then once they reached that form, did they simply continue in it? And if they don't reproduce, why do they have male and female genders? All these questions, like countless others, remain unexplained.

However, the Q do have a couple of experiences in common with humanity: conflict and boredom. When Quinn introduces Janeway to his desert version of the Continuum, he tells her, "Everyone has heard everything, seen everything. They haven't had to speak to each other in 10 millennia. There's nothing left to say." (*Death Wish*)

Apparently, omnipotence and immortality engender nothing but boredom, because there is no challenge. Quinn tells Janeway that Q's mischief-making was the result of boredom, and that it had a salutary effect on the Continuum. "We paid the price by forcing you to stop. But for a moment there, you really had our attention... You gave us something to talk about."

The Q finally solve their boredom problem by creating their own conflict. One faction, led by Q himself, wants change, while the mainstream wants to preserve the stagnant status quo. In fighting each other, the Q find that their interest in life is rekindled enough that they try something new: giving birth. What will happen to the Continuum now? Q knows? ■

Q never seems to fit on *Deep Space Nine*. Perhaps *Sisko* is too blunt, too direct to have any patience with the kind of mind games Q plays. When Q whisks him into an old fashioned bout of "fisticuffs" and dares him to "take a poke at me", Sisko decks him.

"You hit me!" whines Q, aggrieved and astonished. "Picard never hit me!"

"I'm not Picard," Sisko retorts. (*Q-Less*)

When Q encounters *Voyager* in *Death Wish*, he immediately takes a shine to *Janeway*. We can tell by the sweet talk he sends her way: "Did anyone ever tell you you're angry when you're beautiful?" And, "You would have me put [*Quinn's*] future into your delicate little hands? Oh, so touchably soft!"

Like Picard, Janeway leads with her intellect, trying to think her way through problems, which makes

her a perfect straight man for Q's antics. And when Janeway proposes an asylum hearing to resolve the claims of the rival Qs, Q's heart is won. The idea of a legal hearing appeals instantly to his natural love of games, rules and structured competition. Which isn't to say that he won't bend those rules to gain advantage; he even tries to bribe Janeway with the offer to return *Voyager* to Earth, if she will rule in his favour.

The hearing reveals some home truths about both Q and the Continuum. Quinn explains that all of Q's misbehaviour in the past was the result of pure boredom in the stagnation of the Continuum.

"I miss the irrepressible Q, the one who made me think," he says.

No one is more startled than Q to hear that he was Quinn's inspiration for change, and that his own

Q Continuum

surrender to obedience actually preserved the status quo that he had once rebelled against.

"He was right when he said the Continuum scared me back into line," he says. "This was a man who was truly irrepressible. I only hope I make a worthy student." He abandons his obedience to the Continuum, and helps Quinn to end his life. When Janeway observes that the Continuum won't be very happy with him, he smiles. "I certainly hope not!" (*Death Wish*)

And with the civil war that follows, Q brings his mischievous and irresponsible nature to the leadership of a new movement to end his people's stagnation, and finally, in *The Q and the Grey*, becomes that most responsible of beings: a father. With Q, anything is possible! ■

In *Tapestry*, Q takes Picard on a tour of what might have been

THE Q EPISODES

STAR TREK: THE NEXT GENERATION
Encounter at Farpoint
Hide and Q
Q Who
Deja Q
QPid
True Q
Tapestry
All Good Things...

STAR TREK: DEEP SPACE NINE
Q-Less

STAR TREK: VOYAGER
Death Wish
The Q and the Grey

Q spends so much time pestering the *U.S.S. Enterprise NCC-1701-D*, and Picard in particular, that it's hard to imagine what he did for fun in all the millennia of his existence before he met his *"capitaine"*.

MIND YOUR PS AND QS

Though Q is known for his fast quips, he is just as likely to provoke a sizzling retort from an adversary. A few choice comments on our favourite Q.

Q: "What must I do to convince you people [that I'm mortal]?"
Worf: "Die!"
Deja Q

Q2: "You know, you're incorrigible, Q. You're a lost cause. I can't go to a single solar system without having to apologise for you, and I'm tired of it."
Deja Q

Q: "I'm immortal again! Omnipotent again!"
Riker (deadly monotone): "Swell!"
Deja Q

Picard: "He's devious and amoral and unreliable and irresponsible, and definitely not to be trusted!"
QPid

Picard: "I refuse to believe that the afterlife is run by you. The universe is not so badly designed!"
Tapestry

O'Brien: "Why don't you do something constructive for a change? Like torment *Cardassians*!"
Q-Less

Janeway: "If you think this puerile attempt at seduction is going to work, you're even more self-deluded than I thought."
The Q and the Grey

Q: "I know you're asking yourself, 'Why would a brilliant, handsome, dashingly omnipotent being like Q want to mate with a scraggy little bipedal specimen like me?'"
Janeway: "Let me guess. No one else will have you?"
The Q and the Grey

Q: "I just thought you could give me some advice, man to man [on how to seduce Janeway]."
Tom Paris: "My advice would be to give up before you embarrass yourself more than you already have."
The Q and the Grey

Neelix: "Do you want to know what Captain Janeway likes about me? I am respectful, loyal, and most of all, sincere. And those are qualities which someone like you could never hope to possess."
The Q and the Grey ●

Pictures top right:
Ensign Ro; Lower Decks; Deja Q; Realm of Fear; Lower Decks; Lower Decks; Lower Decks

HERE COME THE LOWER DECKERS

As *Lower Decks* focuses on the secondary characters on board the *U.S.S. Enterprise*, **Robert Jeschonek** sings the praises of those whose lives intersected regularly with the command crew...

C ould *Star Trek: The Next Generation* do without Guinan? Reg Barclay? Ro Laren? Of course it could. The Big Guns – Picard, Riker, Data, Geordi, Troi, Crusher, and Worf – carry the show. So what, if anything, do the bit players from the *Enterprise*-D's lower decks add to *ST:TNG*?

Illumination of the Big Guns, for one thing. The Lower Deckers shine a light on surprising facets of the Big Guns. Guinan, for example, brings out a soulful warmth in Picard. Miles and Keiko O'Brien help Data explore human concepts of romance and marriage. Reg Barclay pushes all the Big Guns' buttons with his Adrian Monk-style hyperphobic oddness.

But that's not all the Lower Deckers accomplish. They also make great cast filler, giving the show the ensemble flavor so fashionable in late 1980s/early 1990s television. In the era of *Hill Street Blues*, *St. Elsewhere*, *L.A. Law*, and *thirtysomething*, ensemble dramas were pure gold.

But *ST:TNG* is no *Hill Street Blues*. Picard still gets the lion's share of the attention, especially after the success of *The Best of Both Worlds*. The rest of the Big Guns dominate the remaining limelight, leaving the supporting crew to settle for scraps.

That's all the more reason to applaud the Lower Deckers. They do a lot with a little. They're virtually nonexistent in season one, and they fade out again in seasons six and seven. Still, in their limited appearances, they play a vital role in setting the course for the future of the *Trek* franchise.

They do it by adding diversity to a whitebread starship. In the beginning, the *Enterprise*-D isn't much of a melting pot. The crew reflects a colonial model of race relations, with whites in the majority (Riker, Beverly, Data, Tasha, and Wesley), and white alpha male Picard (French by name but with an accent straight out of the British Empire) leading "assimilated" lesser powers (Betazoids, Vulcans, a Klingon, etc.) in an illusion of egalitarian power-sharing.

The Lower Deckers change this by adding diversity to the crew. In their heyday in seasons two to five, the supporting players make the *Enterprise*-D a more multicultural place. In doing so, they blaze a trail for future series. The *Enterprise*-D gains a black bartender (Guinan), a Bajoran navigator (Ro Laren), a Japanese botanist (Keiko O'Brien) and a Japanese nurse (Alyssa Ogawa), among others.

The next series, *Star Trek: Deep Space Nine*, features a black man commanding a diverse crew of aliens (Trill, Bajoran, Founder, Klingon, Ferengi), with only one white male cast regular: ironically, one of the original Lower Deckers, Miles O'Brien. *Star Trek: Voyager* continues the trend wih a white woman

leading a Latin American Indian, a black Vulcan, a half-Klingon woman, a Chinese male, a holographic doctor, and a Borg female. Again, the main crew includes a solitary white male – Tom Paris.

In *ST: DS9* and *ST:VOY*, the world of *Star Trek* looks more like a believable far-future community of peoples. The humble Lower Deckers help make this vision possible. Their reward? Some get a chance to shine. Guinan saves the timeline in *Yesterday's Enterprise*. Miles O'Brien prevents war with the Cardassians in *The Wounded*. Ro Laren attends her own funeral in *The Next Phase*. Reg Barclay whips up warped holodeck versions of the Big Guns in *Hollow Pursuits*.

Then the Lower Deckers vanish as if struck by a cloaking device. Guinan, Ro, and the O'Briens disappear in season six (though Ro and Miles each bow once more in season seven). By the final year, *ST:TNG* turns its focus on the Big Guns and beams the Lower Deckers into space.

It hardly seems fair that the supporting crew members are discarded so easily. They accomplished so much: revealing new facets of the core crew, giving the show an ensemble flavor, boosting a trend in diversity.

However, as the supporting crew fades, an episode comes along that serves as a tribute to their experience. *Lower Decks* in season seven tells the story of four junior officers (including Nurse Ogawa), one of whom dies on a secret mission. *Lower Decks* makes the ultimate statement about the supporting crew: their lives go on in parallel with those of the command crew – sometimes intersecting, sometimes even affecting the lives of their superior officers. They live, and sometimes die, as bit players in the shadow of larger events. Ultimately, like most of us, they are important only to each other.

This time, the supporting cast's role is clear: they represent the common man. They represent us. ▲

Pictures top left: *Lower Decks*; *The Wounded*; *The Next Phase*; *Hollow Pursuits* pictures center right: Robin Curtis in *Gambit*; Kirsten Dunst in *Dark Page*; Terry O'Quinn in *The Pegasus*; Eric Pierpoint in *Liaisons* picture bottom right: Guinan

THE SAGA CONTINUES

Abandoning her pursuit of Picard, Mrs Troi turns her attentions to Odo...

Riker's decisions in *The Pegasus* are influenced by his revisiting of the first *Enterprise* in *ST:ENT*'s *These are the Voyages*..

After the experiences of the *Enterprise* in *Genesis*, Tom Paris would suffer a similar evolution on *ST:VOY*'s *Threshold*...

The Maquis continue to battle on *Deep Space Nine*...

Wesley Crusher's preparation as a Traveler is described..

Ro Laren eventually ends up on board *Deep Space Nine*...

...while Q turns his attentions to Kathryn Janeway...

THE TNG YEARS

ST:TNG's final season starts with *Descent, Part II*, and the return of Hugh Borg. *Liaisons* guest stars *Alien Nation*'s Eric Pierpoint (to return in *Star Trek: Enterprise* as Harris), while *Gambit* marks Robin Curtis' return to the *Trek* world. Lwaxana Troi makes her final *ST:TNG* visit in *Dark Page*, featuring a young pre-*Spider-Man* Kirsten Dunst.

The *Pegasus*, directed by LeVar Burton, stars Terry O'Quinn (*Lost*'s Locke) as Riker's former captain, and provides the framework for the final *Star Trek* TV episode to date, *ST:ENT*'s *These are the Voyages*. *Sub Rosa* (directed by Frakes) give Crusher one final romantic fling, this time with Duncan Regehr, who would later be Bajoran resistance leader Shakaar. Gates McFadden also gets a chance to direct in 'creature feature' *Genesis*, while her screen son Wesley reaches his final destiny

with *Journey's End*. Ferengi tale *Bloodlines* gives Patrick Stewart the last chance to direct on the show, and the whole seven-year run is rounded off on May 23 1994 with two-hour finale *All Good Things...* Featuring the return of Q, Tasha Yar and Miles O'Brien, the episode takes the series full circle and wins a Hugo Award for Best Dramatic Presentation. ▶

QUOTE – UNQUOTE

"I always knew what her career would be about, and what she'd aspire to; Uhura would be an Admiral and head of all communications on Earth and everywhere else in the universe!"
Nichelle Nichols on Uhura's likely future.

While *Star Trek: Deep Space Nine* continues to prosper in its second season (about which more in the *ST:DS9* Special issue coming soon) Leonard Nimoy appears as a yellow-skinned caricature of himself in *The Simpsons*' *Marge vs the Monorail*, James Doohan is Scotty (no relation, honest!) in *National Lampoon's Loaded Weapon 1* and Patrick Stewart gets to don his Q-Pid Robin Hood tights again as King Richard in *Robin Hood – Men in Tights*. Brent Spiner croons on his album *Ol' Yellow Eyes is Back*, supported by backing singers The Sunspots (Frakes, Dorn, Stewart & Burton) and Shatner releases his first biography, *Star Trek Memories* (with Chris Kreski).

SIDE STEPS
(Other *ST:TNG* tales set during this season)

1. *Engines of Destiny*
2. *Blaze of Glory*
3. *Star Trek: Klingon*
4. *Possession*
5. *Embrace the Wolf*
6. *Dyson Sphere*
7. *Infiltrator*
8. *Into the Nebula*
9. *Q Squared*
10. *Balance of Power*
11. *Dragon's Honor*
12. *Rogue Saucer*

HEIR APPARENT

Ian Spelling talks to former *Star Trek* executive producer Rick Berman, a primal force in the shaping of the modern series, about his integral role in the making of *Star Trek: The Next Generation*...

STAR TREK *Magazine*: How did *Star Trek* creator Gene Rodenberry and the other series producers think of you as someone to help develop *Star Trek: The Next Generation*?

RICK BERMAN: Well, after being a writer and producer in New York, I came to Los Angeles in 1984. After a short stint at Warner Bros., I got an executive job at Paramount and, although I often read people talking about the fact that I was a suit and an executive, I had been everything from a sound man to a film editor to a writer and producer of films and documentary television my whole life.

This job I got at Paramount was my first taste of 'executive-ing', and after quite a short period of time where I was the executive director and then later vice president of current programming at Paramount, where I was dealing with both hour shows and half-hour shows from a kind of studio oversight position, I learnt that one of the new shows that was being developed was a new *Star Trek* series with Gene Roddenberry.

Because Roddenberry was known as being kind of curmudgeonly and somewhat difficult to deal with from the studio's point of view, they asked me to be in charge of the series from the studio point of view, because I was the least tenured vice president at Paramount at the time. I went to the first meeting, the very, very first meeting I had with Gene and his attorney, Leonard Maizlish, and some of my bosses at the studio. The meeting ended and I got a call from Leonard the same day,

saying, "Can we have lunch?" I went and had lunch with him the same day. And he said, "Gene really likes you, and he was wondering if you'd be interested in leaving your job as a Paramount executive and coming and producing the show with him."

Now, I had been an executive for about a year and I was not really enjoying it, and the thought of getting back into production was something that I was really hungry for.

STAR TREK *Magazine*: When did you realise just how big an undertaking you'd signed on for?

BERMAN: Well, at first, it was kind of risky. I had a contract and a job and a pregnant wife, and this show was going to be a syndicated sci-fi sequel, and none of those three things had been very successful on television. Sci-fi certainly wasn't around at the time. There were very few sequels that worked. And it wasn't going to be on a network. These were all very risky things. But the thought of getting back into production was strong enough for me that I wanted to do it. Gene had had people like [producer] Bob Justman and [former *Happy Days* producer] Eddie Milkis involved with the series, and a couple of other people, and we started it up. I had no idea it was going to be successful, mostly for the three reasons I just mentioned.

Probably the best thing for *TNG* was that the studio treated it like a network show, even though it was a syndicated show. They put the kind of

WHO'S WHO

GENE RODDENBERRY The original creator of *Star Trek* was the brains behind the resurrection of the saga in *Star Trek: The Next Generation*. His contribution to modern televison is legendary to this day: on 4 September 1986, his fans presented him with a star on the Hollywood Walk of Fame, the first writer/producer to be honoured in such a manner. Sadly, he died in 1991 – but his guidelines for *Star Trek* storytelling remain in place to this day. Web Link: www.roddenberry.com

LEONARD MAIZLISH Attorney to Gene Rodenberry, Leonard Maizlish had strong views on the shaping of *Star Trek: The Next Generation*. Despite the changes in public attitudes between the 1960s and the 1980s, writer David Gerrold has accused Maizlish of being one of the prime opponents in his attempts to feature gay characters. One of his scripts for the show, *Blood and Fire*, which featured a gay male couple and infectious alien creatures called bloodworms that were an allegory for AIDS, was apparently dropped partly due to Maizlish's resistance to the idea.

BOB JUSTMAN Robert Justman's career spans many years, and includes vital contributions to over 35 motion pictures and 500 television episodes, pilots, and movies – including *Star Trek: The Original Series*, detailed in the book *Inside Star Trek*, written with Herb Solow – and *Star Trek: The Next Generation*. " I liked Gene very much," he said during an online interview for startrek.com in 1996. "I think he liked me too. He let me pull a number of practical jokes on him, and he took them graciously, so I liked him even more because of that!"

MAURICE HURLEY Hurley, whose writing credits on *ST:TNG* include *Datalore*, *The Child* and *Q Who?* was producer on the show and became co-executive producer for its second season. As writer of *Q Who?* he is, of course, the creator of the Borg – *ST:TNG*'s enduring arch-nemeses.
Hurley left *ST:TNG* at the end of its second season, apparently following difficulties with Gene Roddenberry, to be replace by Michael Piller. His recent writing credits include episodes of *24* and *La Femme Nikita*.

PETER LAURITSON Head of the television post-production department at Paramount Pictures, Lauritson first got involved with *Star Trek* in 1981 with *Star Trek II: The Wrath of Khan*. He continued to be heavily involved in the franchise, and worked as supervising producer in charge of all post-production on *Star Trek: Enterprise* – a role that involves sound, music, visual effects and editorial.

money into it that was more befitting a network series than a syndicated series. Most of the syndicated television at the time was being done in Canada, with budgets that were a third of what network television budgets were. And it wasn't until a half a dozen episodes into the show airing that we realised people liked it. There were a lot of people who were angry at the thought that we were putting a middle-aged English guy into Captain Kirk's shoes and that we were doing another show with a ship called *Enterprise* and that it was in a different century. We had no idea how it was going to work, but Gene had a very, very clear vision and everybody stuck to it. Gene was running the ship and certainly within six months we knew we had a hit on our hands, and it just kept getting better.

STAR TREK Magazine: What were you feeling when the time came to take over from Roddenberry? Did you feel beholden to stick with what he'd developed?

BERMAN: There wasn't a day where they suddenly said, 'You take over.' It didn't happen like that. Gene was very, very involved in the first season. In the second season, when I was sort of running the show with Maurice Hurley under Gene, Gene decided he wanted to step back a little bit. He put a lot of faith in Hurley and myself. He still gave notes, he still watched the shows – but he just started stepping back. Then, in the third season, when Michael Piller joined me, Gene stepped back

a little further. Eventually, he became ill and his illness caused him to step back even more and get less and less involved. He and I spoke every day and he had trust in the way I was doing things, and in the way that Michael was doing things, and he was comfortable with that. But the more ill he got, the less involved he got. So, by the time the studio came and asked me to develop a second series, *Deep Space Nine*, Gene was very ill. I asked Michael to join me and we created *Deep Space Nine*. I kept Gene abreast of the broad strokes on it, but he was really not quite well enough to get involved in any way. And then, when Gene passed away [Gene died following a stroke on Thursday, 24 October 1991], things just sort of evolved as one would guess they would. But it was never, 'OK, here's the torch. It's yours now.'

STAR TREK Magazine: What's the one thing you're proudest of when it comes to ST:TNG?

BERMAN: I'm answering that in terms of my pride. My pride was that, after Gene died, we did everything we could to keep the show fluid, but to keep Gene's vision as the major target of what we were doing, and to keep the quality up. And I think we managed through all seven seasons of the series to accomplish that. There's something very rewarding about doing a television show that means so much to people. As successful as we were, there were series that had three, four times the audience that *TNG* had – but it wasn't the same kind of audience. Our audience was remarkably

"...after Gene died, we did everything we could to keep the show fluid, but to keep Gene's vision as the major target of what we were doing..."
Rick Berman

Rick Berman (left) and Gene Roddenberry (right) on the Bridge set of the *U.S.S. Enterprise* NCC 1701-D during filming of the pilot, *Encounter at Farpoint.*

dedicated to the show and there were a lot of people for whom *TNG* was a weekly appointment, and it really meant a great deal to families. It was wonderful to get the kind of feedback that we got of how much *TNG* meant to people.

STAR TREK Magazine: Looking back, is there anything you wish you could have changed about ST:TNG?

BERMAN: I wish we'd been on a broadcast network. As successful as we were in syndication, and as hands-off as Paramount distribution was for us, I don't think the show ever got the chance to be recognised and be awarded in a way it deserved to be. I think we had some remarkable actors who should have gotten all kinds of nominations and they never did because there was a certain lack of seriousness paid to television shows that were in syndication as opposed to being broadcast on one of the major networks.

STAR TREK Magazine: Who are the unsung heroes of ST:TNG? Who didn't get the credit they deserve?

BERMAN: I think that one of those people was definitely Bob Justman, who came in and helped set up this incredible piece of machinery that lasted for 18 years. He was sort of the sole survivor of the original series, who worked with us through that first season. He taught me a tremendous amount and was a wonderful, dedicated man. Peter Lauritson, in a very unsung fashion, ran the post-production of every one of these shows, often doing two shows at once. He did two shows at once for at least seven

years, and the movies. His ability to run the post-production, the editing, all the visual effects, the sound, the music – it was just remarkable.

I stay in touch with a lot of our people and all of them who are working on other shows now cannot believe how problematic post-production on shows can be compared to what they experienced when they were working on one of the *Star Trek* series. And I think that was due in a very, very large part to Peter's dedication and talent.

STAR TREK Magazine: And, finally, how do you feel about ST:TNG today?

BERMAN: It holds a very, very special meaning for me because it was the first show. I was starting out in big-time television at the same time all the actors were, and they were all pretty much my age. We became very close, and to this day I'm still in touch with Brent Spiner, Jonathan Frakes and Patrick Stewart, and with LeVar Burton, Michael Dorn, Marina Sirtis and Gates McFadden. We're all close friends. We see each other on a regular basis, and I feel a huge affection towards them and towards that experience. It was the only TV show that I was involved with that went on to make movies, and it was the most successful. So it holds a lot of firsts and a lot of bests for me.

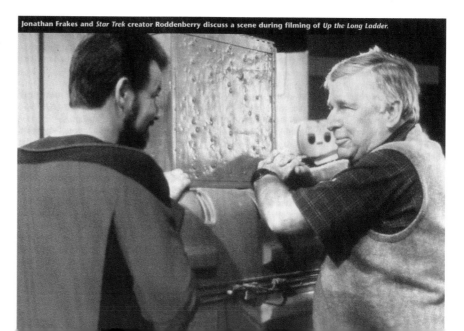

Jonathan Frakes and *Star Trek* creator Roddenberry discuss a scene during filming of *Up the Long Ladder.*

MAKE IT SO!

K. Stoddard Hayes reveals how *Star Trek: The Next Generation* reinvented the *Star Trek* universe...

How do you recreate a cult TV series for a new generation, without alienating a devoted fan base or losing what is essential to the original? That was the problem faced by Gene Roddenberry and his team of writers and producers, when Paramount asked them to create a new *Star Trek* series 20 years after the original. The solution was *Star Trek: The Next Generation*, one of the most successful syndicated series ever made.

The success of *ST:TNG* began with keeping the format that had worked so well for *Star Trek*: an impressive starship, a diverse cast, an idealistic future, and a mission to explore a galaxy full of adventure. But it was the ways that the formula was changed to bring *Star Trek* into the 1980s, were what made *ST:TNG* so special.

The biggest change was to move the story 100 years farther into the future, so that the writing team could invent almost any new story scenario without

The holodeck was introduced in *Encounter at Farpoint* as a new recreational technology, and quickly became a major story device.

Q-Pid

Elementary, Dear Data

Episodes tackled issues as varied as genetic engineering, the rights of artificial life forms, military honour, addiction, family conflict, torture and even homophobia.

conflicting with the continuity of *Star Trek: The Original Series*. The Federation appears much more powerful in 2363 than it did in 2268, and its explorations have progressed much farther out into the Alpha Quadrant. And 100 years of progress is the best of all reasons to incorporate a shipload of exciting technological advances into *ST:TNG*'s awe-inspiring new *Galaxy* class *U.S.S. Enterprise* NCC 1701-D.

The trademark *Star Trek* technologies – sensors, transporters, weapons, shields – all became bigger, better and more sophisticated in *ST:TNG*. Medicine, especially, has advanced until ship's doctors seem near miracle workers in their ability to heal the sick and injured and even revive the dead (but only when the plot requires!). However, the technologies that became *ST:TNG*'s signature were two new inventions using the transporter's matter-energy conversion.

The replicator, a huge step forward from the original *U.S.S. Enterprise*'s food processors, can produce not only food, but almost any physical artefact at a moment's notice. While every fan might wish to have this magical technology in their homes, the writers got an added bonus: a simple explanation for how the crew could obtain any exotic prop or costume the story demanded. The holodeck was introduced in *Encounter at Farpoint* as a new recreational technology, and quickly became a major story device. It allowed the writers to take the *U.S.S. Enterprise*'s crew almost anywhere in space and time, without having to explain how they got there – thus saving *ST:TNG* from having a preposterous number of time travel incidents!

While holodeck holidays may be good for crew morale, only danger creates drama and suspense. So the holodeck also became the technology most likely

to malfunction. Beginning in the first season episode, *The Big Goodbye*, which traps Picard in his Dixon Hill simulation, holodeck adventures ranged from accidentally creating a sentient holodeck character (*Elementary, Dear Data*), to populating an entire holodeck program with Data doubles (*A Fistful of Datas*). Holodeck-style simulated realities also appeared in several memorable episodes that occur outside the holodeck, such as *Q-pid*, *Future Perfect*, *Frame of Mind* and fan favourite *The Inner Light*.

It was not only the *U.S.S. Enterprise*'s technologies that changed: so did the command and personnel structures. The ship carries not only a full crew complement, but also their non-military families: husbands, wives and children, who bring new dimensions to the story – most notably the introduction of a teenager as a regular character. And since the Captain is far too valuable to risk on front line duties, the landing parties, now called Away Teams, became the responsibility of his Executive Officer.

Most important, *ST:TNG* gave fans old and new, a cast of memorable characters as different from each other and from the original crew as the 24th Century is from the 23rd. Nearly 20 years on, all of these characters and their actors have become pop culture icons almost as recognisable as the original *Star Trek* players.

The First Officer, Commander William T. Riker inherits Kirk's mantle of cowboy, adventurer, Away Team leader, and ladies man (fittingly, he's also the first character who mentions Kirk's name). Soft spoken Chief Engineer Geordi La Forge is the quiet guy who always comes through; his visual disability provides some story opportunities while his VISOR's specialised vision serves almost as a superpower. His friendship with Data provides enough humour and drama to make it one of *Star Trek*'s best relationships.

Star Trek's first female Chief Medical Officer, Dr. Beverly Crusher, the usual brilliant scientist, brings in the challenges of single motherhood, and a lurking romantic attraction to her Captain. Her son, kid genius Wesley, introduces some coming-of age themes, and his career as a Starfleet cadet gives us a firsthand glimpse into the training of all Starfleet officers.

While *ST:TOS* had Spock to observe the human condition, *ST:TNG* gives us three characters to comment on humanity. The half-Betazoid Deanna Troi complements Dr. Crusher's medicine with her counselling, and in a franchise known for its male friendships, her friendship with Crusher provides some welcome girl time. Lieutenant Worf is Starfleet's first Klingon officer, and through him Klingon culture becomes the most fully developed *Star Trek* alien culture of all. And the android Data, like his dramatic predecessor, Spock, is frequently perplexed by human foibles, but in contrast to Spock, Data's dream is to become as human as possible.

Most important, the *U.S.S. Enterprise*'s new Captain, the urbane and cerebral Jean-Luc Picard, sets the tone for *Star Trek*'s new incarnation. Nowhere is the difference between old and new more clearly embodied than in the two Captains: Kirk and Picard – the cowboy and the scholar. We imagine Kirk, so quick with his fists and his phasers, as coming from a society that is still taming the wilderness at its frontiers. In contrast, an officer like Picard could only come from a great, secure and peaceful civilisation. As much diplomat as soldier, he's always inclined to reason his way through a difficulty, and lives by courtesy, dignity and respect for alien ways. Though Picard has a little cowboy in him still, he's rarely called upon to use that side of his character in the universe he inhabits.

In its seven year run, *ST:TNG* expanded the *Star Trek* universe exponentially. Recurring characters like Chief O'Brien, Barclay and Guinan made an enduring impact. The Klingons and the Romulans developed complex and distinctive cultures over a series of stand-alone episodes that unfolded over several seasons. And dozens of new alien species appeared, including some who would inspire *Star Trek*'s future, like the Trill, the Ferengi, the Cardassians and the Bajorans. Then there was Q, the dramatic descendant of Trelane of Gothos. Not only was he mischievous, egotistical, charming, and nearly omnipotent, Q introduced Picard and his crew to a race of cyborgs from a remote part of the galaxy – and *Star Trek*, and science fiction, were never the same.

ST:TNG's signature bad guys, the Borg, have become one of the most universally recognisable *Star Trek* aliens. From the moment they appeared, they were the scariest – and not because they're cyborgs. What's terrifying about the Borg is that they take away our individuality. In this, they provide, once and for all, the definitive answer to *Star Trek*'s enduring question, "What does it mean to be human?" It

means to be a unique individual, with a distinct personality, and above all, freedom to make one's own destiny.

True to Gene Roddenberry's ideals, the crew of the new *U.S.S. Enterprise* always worked together in harmony. Yet there was always plenty of conflict in this much wider galaxy, because every *ST:TNG* story had to be about something more important than just fixing a broken holodeck. Episodes tackled issues as varied as genetic engineering (*The Masterpiece Society*), the rights of artificial life forms (*The Measure of a Man*, *The Offspring*), military honour (*The First Duty*, *The Pegasus*), addiction (*Symbiosis*, *The Game*), family conflict (*The Icarus Factor*, *Brothers*, *Sins of the Father*), torture (*Chain of Command*) and even homophobia (*The Outcast*).

For some, especially the most devoted *ST:TOS* fans, *ST:TNG* proved too serious, cerebral and idealistic; there was a little too much harmony, especially when the new crew resolved their issues with the bad guys in the same spirit. These viewers thought Kirk's shoot-first style was a lot more fun to watch, and they missed the banter, the space opera stylings and the occasional outright silliness of the original series. Yet for most, the civilised ideals of 24th century Federation were precisely what made the show worthwhile. *ST:TNG* proved appealing enough to attract a large and enduring audience, and that was what mattered for the series and the future.

By becoming a huge success in syndication, *ST:TNG* cleared the way for three more *Star Trek* series, as well as new movies, a huge market in tie-in merchandise, and perhaps most important, a new golden age of science fiction television. *ST:TNG* proved, in defiance of network and studio wisdom, that intelligent, literate science fiction could thrive on television. Hence when television writers and producers brought other intelligent, literate series proposals to the studios, they could point to *ST:TNG*'s success. Without *ST:TNG*, there might have been no *The X-Files*, no *Buffy*, *Babylon 5* or *Stargate: SG-1*. In a very real sense, *ST:TNG* gave us the universe.

A Fistful of Datas

The Outcast

STAR TREK: THE NEXT GENERATION
TOP 10!

Everyone has their favourite *Star Trek* episode – but here's a rundown of the very best *Star Trek: The Next Generation* episodes, as voted for you, our readers, in our recent Anniversary poll...

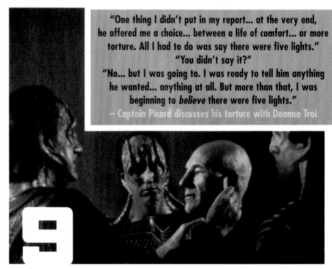

> "One thing I didn't put in my report... at the very end, he offered me a choice... between a life of comfort... or more torture. All I had to do was say there were five lights."
> "You didn't say it?"
> "No... but I was going to. I was ready to tell him anything he wanted... anything at all. But more than that, I was beginning to *believe* there were five lights."
> – Captain Picard discusses his torture with Deanna Troi

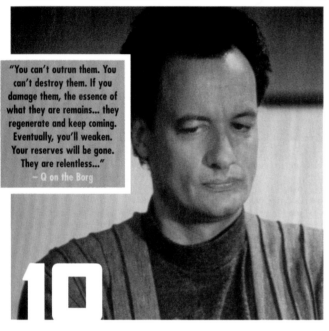

> "You can't outrun them. You can't destroy them. If you damage them, the essence of what they are remains... they regenerate and keep coming. Eventually, you'll weaken. Your reserves will be gone. They are relentless..."
> – Q on the Borg

10
Q Who

First US broadcast: 8 May 1989	**Guest Cast:**
Director: Rob Bowman	John de Lancie – Q
Writer: Maurice Hurley	Colm Meaney – Miles O'Brien
	Lycia Naff – Sonya

The story: Picard's arch-nemesis, Q, hurls the *U.S.S. Enterprise* to the far end of the galaxy where they're forced to fight their first, deadly battle with the Borg. Only Picard's admission that he needs Q's help saves the starship, which the delighted superbeing returns to the Alpha Quadrant. Of course, there's a twist to the tale – now the Borg know about humanity they're certain to come after them. Pondering this, Picard – clearly rattled by the whole experience – tells Guinan: "Perhaps we needed a kick in our complacency..." It certainly gets kicked as the series progresses!

Top Ten material because: Combined with a re-appearance of Q (John de Lancie) this first appearance by the Borg, a race first hinted at in *The Neutral Zone*, is simply chilling. *Star Trek* fan or not, this is simply a brilliant science fiction story which helped convince the world at large that *Star Trek* was truly back.

Scene to watch: The reaction as the Borg simply corkscrew a section of the *U.S.S. Enterprise* out of the ship – leading to a battle that leaves 18 crew members dead.

Points of interest
- The Borg cube and the look of the drones is different to that used later in the series
- Emmy Award-winning actress Lycia Naff, who guests stars in this episode and *Samaritan Snare* as Sonya Gomez, was apparently cast as a possible love interest for Geordi La Forge, but that storyline was never pursued. Her character features in Pocket Books SCE novels, as second-in-command of the *U.S.S. Da Vinci*.

9
Chain of Command

Original US Broadcast: Part I – 14 December 1992; Part II – 21 December 1992	**Guest Cast:** Ronny Cox – Captain Jellico
Directors: Robert Scheerer (Part I) Les Landau (Part II) Writers: Frank Abatemarco Story by Ronald D. Moore (Part I); Frank Abatemarco (Part II)	Natalija Nogulich – Admiral Nechayev John Durbin – Gul Lemec Lou Wagner – Solok Heather Lauren Olson – Jil Orra (Part II) David Warner – Gul Madred (Part II)

The story: Captain Picard, Doctor Crusher and Worf are sent on a top secret mission to destroy a cache of metagenic weapons – genetically engineered viruses that destroy all living things in their path – as tensions mount between the Federation and the Cardassians. Meanwhile, the belligerent Captain Jellico takes command of the *U.S.S. Enterprise*. But Picard's mission turns out to be a Cardassian trap and he is tortured by Gul Madred, in an attempt to get him to reveal the Federation's plans to deal with any Cardassian attack...

Top Ten material because: Patrick Stewart and David Warner prove a compelling double act as Picard is tortured to breaking point. The performances are some of the best *ST:TNG* has to offer, but equally enjoyable is Riker's battle with the arrogant Captain Jellico. Not only is this one of the series' best stories, the Cardassians are used at their best.

Scene to watch: The scenes between Picard and Gul Madred are priceless, but Picard's determination to stand up his torturer is clear when he eats a taspar egg – a raw, living, pulsating, gelatinous blob...

Points of interest
- *Chain of Command* was developed to establish the Cardassians as the main villains of the then forthcoming *Star Trek: Deep Space Nine*. This episode aired just before *Emissary*, the *ST:DS9* pilot, screened.
- Patrick Stewart reviewed tapes supplied by the human rights charity, Amnesty International, which he supports, to prepare for his grim torture scenes.

[*STAR TREK: THE NEXT GENERATION* ▲]

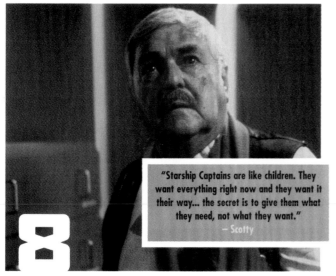

"Starship Captains are like children. They want everything right now and they want it their way... the secret is to give them what they need, not what they want."
– Scotty

8

Relics

Original US Broadcast: 12 October 1992
Director: Alexander Singer
Writer: Ronald D. Moore

Guest Cast:
James Doohan – Montgomery Scott
Erick Weiss – Ensign Kane
Stacie Foster – Engineer Bartel
Ernie Mirich – Waiter
Lanei Chapman – Ensign Rager
Majel Barrett – Computer Voice

The story: Rescued from a looped transporter beam aboard the *U.S.S. Jenolen*, Captain Montgomery Scott struggles to find his way in the 24th Century, until he and Geordi La Forge have to save the *U.S.S. Enterprise*, trapped in a huge Dyson Sphere.

Top Ten material because: A classic crossover episode with little sentimental nonsense, an incredible alien spaceship and Montgomery Scott and Geordi La Forge working together. What more could you want?

Scene to watch: Scotty on the holodeck-recreated Bridge of the original *U.S.S. Enterprise*, pondering his future, at a complete loss in the 'modern' world.

Points of interest
• Dyson spheres – a star system's entire contents rebuilt in a globe around its star – were first proposed by Freeman Dyson in 1959.
• Scotty's dialogue suggests that Captain Kirk was alive at the time he boarded the *U.S.S. Jenolen*, which is at odds with events seen in *Star Trek Generations*.
• Instead of rebuilding the entire original Bridge set for the holodeck scenes, a Captain's chair and helm/navigation console built by *Star Trek* fan Steve Horch was used, with almost everything else shot using blue screen techniques, utilising footage from the *Star Trek: The Original Series* episode *This Side of Paradise*.
• The Aldebran whisky featured in the Holodeck scenes was actually Hi-C Ecto Cooler, a licensed drink inspired by *The Real Ghostbusters* film.

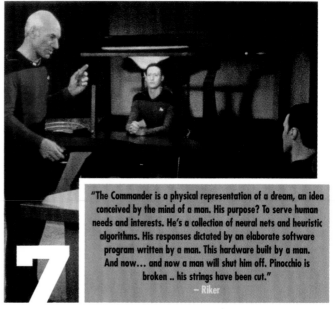

"The Commander is a physical representation of a dream, an idea conceived by the mind of a man. His purpose? To serve human needs and interests. He's a collection of neural nets and heuristic algorithms. His responses dictated by an elaborate software program written by a man. This hardware built by a man. And now... and now a man will shut him off. Pinocchio is broken .. his strings have been cut."
– Riker

7

The Measure of a Man

Original US Broadcast: 13 February 1989
Director: Robert Scheerer
Writer: Melinda Snodgrass

Guest Cast:
Brian Brophy – Commander Bruce Maddox
Clyde Kusatsu – Admiral Nakamura
Amanda McBroom – Captain Philipa Louvois

The story: A Federation commander wants to disassemble Data for study. Picard and Data object, sparking a hearing that will settle the question: is Data a sentient being?

Top Ten material because: If there's a staple of American television it's court room drama and this episode lives up to the best of the genre, particularly given Riker's role as the prosecutor. Surely one of Data's finest hours.

Scene to watch: The moment Riker switches Data off is a classic, challenging any call for the android's right to self-determination.

Points of interest
• Writer Melinda Snodgrass, whose credits include *Sliders*, *Profiler* and *Odyssey 5*, also gets fictional credit in *ST:TNG* – she's mentioned as being captain of the 22nd Century vessel the SS *Hokule'a* in *Up the Long Ladder*.
• When Riker views Data's file on his computer, Data is listed as "NFN NMI Data" – "No First Name" and "No Middle Initial."
• Data's book of Shakespeare, given to him by Picard, features an inscription from one of the sonnets, "When in disgrace with fortune in men's eyes, I all alone beweep my outcast state."

COOL FACTS

• The characters of William Riker and Deanna Troi are based on Decker and Ilia from *Star Trek: The Motion Picture*.

• Geordi La Forge is named after a real *Star Trek* fan named George La Forge. George La Forge died from muscular dystrophy in 1975. Sidney Poitier was one actor considered for the role.

• Q is named after Janet Quarton, responsible for founding *Star Trek* fandom throughout Europe in the early 1970s.

• Denise Crosby originally tried out for the role of Counsellor Troi – and Marina Sirtis tried out for the role of Security Chief Tasha Yar.

• Gene Roddenberry's full name was Eugene Wesley Roddenberry... in creating Wesley Crusher, Gene used his own middle name and based the character on what he wanted to be like when he was young.

> "All our technology and experience:
> our universal translator, our years in space — contacts
> with more alien cultures than I can remember...
> "I have encountered 1,754 non-Human races during
> my tenure with Starfleet."
> "... and we still can't even say 'hello' to these people."
> —Troi talking with Data

Darmok

Original US Broadcast: 30 September 1991
Director: Winrich Kolbe
Writer: Joe Menosky. Story by Philip Lazebnik and Joe Menosky

The story: Captain Picard's attempts to communicate with an alien race, the Tamarian, is frustrated by their language, based on local metaphor to communicate ideas which the Universal Translator cannot understand.

Top Ten material because: It's a mystery just how a race could build spaceships if they use metaphor as the basis for language – how would they communicate mathematics and physics? But Writer Joe Menosky can always be relied upon to provide a clever script that's still something anyone can follow, and he excelled with this season five entry into the ST:TNG canon.

"It was a brilliant metaphor for not only the difficulty implicit in communicating with another form of life," feels Star Trek consultant Andre Bormanis, "but just how hard it is for us to communicate with each other; even if we speak the same language."

Scene to watch: The moment when Picard finally understands what the alien Dathon is trying to tell him as they fight a deadly creature, to the Tamarian's clearly visible delight.

Points of interest
• The episode title is inspired by the metaphors used by Dathon, "Darmok and Jalad at Tanagra" – a reference to a situation where people must unite to defeat a common enemy.
• This episode has been used by linguistics teachers to help students understand how languages work and evolve – there's even a Darmok dictionary!
• The use of a metaphor-based language is pretty unique in science fiction, although the Ascian language used in Gene Wolfe's The Citadel of the Autarch has some similarities.

TAMARIAN FOR BEGINNERS!

"Kiteo, his eyes closed" ("You don't get it")
"Shaka, when the walls fell." ("Failure")
"Temba, his arms wide." ("Gift", or "to Give".)
"Sokath, his eyes uncovered" ("He understands!")
"The river Temarc, in winter" ("Stop!")
"Kiazi's children, their faces wet." ("It's nothing.")

▪ Industrial Light and Magic (ILM) provided special effect shots for Encounter at Farpoint, but no other shows. They are credited in every episode because of the extra stock footage occasionally used for U.S.S. Enterprise NCC-1701-D fly-bys and other scenes, and when the starship enters warp.

▪ If you look closely at the U.S.S. Enterprise during the fly-by in the show's original opening credits, you can see someone walking past the windows. According to designer Mike Okuda, it's Captain Picard.

> "Captain Bateson... do you know what year it is?"
> – Captain Picard

Cause and Effect

Original US Broadcast: 23 March 1992
Director: Jonathan Frakes
Writer: Brannon Braga

Guest Cast:
Kelsey Grammer – Captain Morgan Bateson
Patti Yasutake – Nurse Ogawa
Michelle Forbes – Ro Laren

The story: The U.S.S. Enterprise is caught in a "casuality loop" and is heading for eventual destruction – collision with another starship, until crew members begin to realise something is very wrong and try to change events.

Top Ten material because: Classic time travel problems with a very deadly twist, as the starship crew slowly realise the déjà vu they're all experiencing is no coincidence.

Scene to watch: Apart from the stunning destruction of the U.S.S Enterprise just minutes into the story? The look on the face of a bemused Captain Bateson of the U.S.S. Bozeman, when Captain Picard asks him the date.

Points of interest
• The U.S.S. Bozeman is named after Braga's home town of Bozeman, Montana.
• Kirstie Alley was approached to guest star on this episode, reprising her role as Lieutenant Saavik – first seen in Star Trek II: The Wrath of Khan – but a fee could not be agreed.

[*STAR TREK: THE NEXT GENERATION*]

* Although not seen in later seasons – possibly for budgetary reasons – the *U.S.S. Enterprise* NCC-1701-D has the ability to separate into saucer and warp drive sections in case of an emergency situation, as revealed in *Encounter at Farpoint*. When separated, the saucer section is capable of only impulse speed, while the warp drive section can be used as a battle vessel.

"If you remember what we were, and how we lived... then we'll have found life again."
– Eline to Kamin (Picard)

"We wanted to see if you had the ability to expand your mind and our horizons... and for one brief moment, you did."
– Q to Picard

4 All Good Things...

Original US Broadcast: 23 May 1994
Director: Winrich Kolbe
Writer: Ronald D. Moore & Brannon Braga

Guest Cast:
Denise Crosby – Natasha 'Tasha' Yar
Andreas Katsulas – Tomalak
Clyde Kusatsu – Admiral Nakamura
John de Lancie – Q
Colm Meaney – Miles O'Brien
Patti Yasutake – Nurse Ogawa

The story: Picard is set a temporal conundrum by Q, who insists the last seven years have all been part of his celestial tribunal. The Captain finds himself pinballing across three different time periods to try to prevent the destruction of humanity, spanning the maiden voyage of the *U.S.S. Enterprise*, the present and the distant future.

Top Ten material because: Seven years of *ST:TNG* come to an end in a thoroughly enjoyable story pitting Picard against Q one last time, a cameo from Denise Crosby and a host of possible futures for the crew – including Data as the holder of the Lucasian Chair for physics at Cambridge.

Scene to watch: Too many to count, but Picard joining the rest of the Bridge crew for a game of cards for the first time sums up the bond between this future "family."

Points of interest
• By the end of the series, only Picard and Riker appear in every episode
• *All Good Things...* won an Emmy for Outstanding Individual Achievement in Special Visual Effects.
• Talking about the origins of *All Good Things...* co-writer Ronald Moore, interviewed for the Season Seven *ST:TNG* DVD release, revealed he wanted to do an episode where Q went insane and the universe started falling apart as a result – but it never happened.

3 The Inner Light

Original US Broadcast: 1 June 1992
Director: Peter Lauritson
Writer: Morgan Gendel and Peter Allan Fields. Story by Morgan Gendel

Guest Cast:
Scott Jaeck – Administrator
Jennifer Nash – Meribor
Richard Riehle – Batai
Margot Rose – Eline
Daniel Stewart – Young Batai
Patti Yasutake – Nurse Ogawa

The story: Hit by a transmission beam from a probe, Captain Picard is apparently transported into, and lives the entire life, of Kamin, a man on a planet suffering from drought.

Top Ten material because: Quite simply, one of *ST:TNG*'s finest hours, with Patrick Stewart delivering a bravura performance as a simple iron weaver named Kamin. Experiencing 30 years in just 20 minutes, it's a well told, wonderfully delivered tale with a powerfully emotional performance from Stewart.

Points of interest
• Richard Riehle, who plays Batai, Kamin's son on Kataan, is actually Daniel Stewart, Patrick Stewart's son.
• *The Inner Light* won the 1993 Hugo Award for Best Dramatic Presentation, the first television show to be honoured by science fiction's best since the 1968 *Star Trek* episode *City on the Edge of Forever*.
• The episode title springs from the eponymous George Harrison composed Beatles song, featured on the original release of the *Lady Madonna* single.

"Let's make sure history never forgets the name... 'Enterprise'."
– Captain Picard

"I am Locutus, of Borg. Resistance is futile. Your life, as it has been, is over. From this time forward, you will service... us."
– Captain Picard

2

Yesterday's Enterprise

	Guest Cast:
Original US Broadcast: 19 February 1990	Denise Crosby – Natasha 'Tasha' Yar
Director: David Carson	Christopher McDonald – Richard
Writer: Ira Stephen Behr, Richard	Castillo
Manning, Hans Beimler and Ronald	Tricia O'Neil – Rachel Garrett
Moore. Story by Trent Christopher	
Ganino & Eric A. Stillwell	

The story: A time warp sends the *U.S.S. Enterprise* NCC-1701-C into the future – and history is changed with devastating consequences.

Top Ten material because: It's no wonder *Star Trek* returns again and again to time travel when it comes up with stories like this. Not only do we see a darker, more menacing future for the Federation but we also finally discover the fate of a previous *U.S.S. Enterprise* and get a welcome, enjoyable guest appearance from Denise Crosby. A definite classic.

Scene to watch: The moment when the 'alternative' Captain Picard refuses to surrender to the fast-approaching Klingons.

Points of interest
- The featured alternate timeline Starfleet uniforms were designed with a functional and more military look.
- In a final scene, Geordi is still wearing an alternate timeline costume – although that future is no more.
- *Yesterday's Enterprise* remains one of the highest-rated *ST:TNG* episodes ever on first transmission – over 13 million viewers.

1

The Best of Both Worlds
Parts I and II

	Guest cast:
Original US Broadcast: 18 May	Elizabeth Dennehy – Lieutenant
1990/24 September 1990	Commander Shelby
Director: Cliff Bole	Colm Meaney – O'Brien
Writer: Michael Piller	George Murdock – Admiral J. P. Hanson

The story: When the Borg destroy a colony, the *U.S.S. Enterprise* heads the Federation attack against them – but new weapons are needed to be effective in the assault. When Picard is captured the Borg gain the upper hand, wiping out much of Starfleet at the battle of Wolf 359 – and head for Earth to 'assimilate' the planet.

Top Ten material because: Not just the favourite *ST:TNG* story, this is many fans' favourite *Star Trek* story and well deserved that is, too. The Borg at their worst, a kicker of a cliffhanger as Picard becomes Locutus, and a race against time to defeat the Collective. What more do you need?

Scene to watch: The chilling moment when Riker realises Picard may be lost to them, and orders the *U.S.S. Enterprise* to open fire on the Borg.

STAR TREK

Ian Spelling

Star Trek VI: The Undiscovered Country warped into theaters in 1991, promoted as the final big-screen voyage of the original Star Trek cast. And it was. But by 1993, the second wave of Star Trek couldn't have been burning brighter. Star Trek: The Next Generation was nearing the end of its remarkably successful run and Star Trek: Deep Space Nine was beginning its own seven-year success story. Plus, Star Trek conventions around the world drew thousands upon thousands of fans.

And so it surprised no one when Paramount turned to Rick Berman, executive producer of ST:TNG and ST:DS9, and asked him to develop a feature film toplined by the cast of The Next Generation. It also

shocked no one that Berman elected to pursue a pass-the-baton adventure that starred Patrick Stewart, Brent Spiner, Jonathan Frakes and Marina Sirtis, but also William Shatner, Walter Koenig and James Doohan.

"It was a first for a lot of us," Berman recalls. "It was a first feature film for me and for the cast of The Next Generation, at least as their Next Generation character. We were being asked to do a Next Generation movie and we knew already that Next Generation would be ending after seven seasons. We were doing Deep Space Nine and were already at work on Voyager. There were a lot of things going on. The idea of doing a feature film was both scary and exciting. When you do seven years of a television show – or at that point we'd

FEATURES

already done six years of *The Next Generation* – you're always constrained. You're constrained by budgets and you're constrained by time, and here we were in a position where we were going to be constrained by neither, at least not in the same way that we'd been used to. We were going to be able to do something on a large scale. So it was extremely exciting from that point of view."

The biggest challenge on *Star Trek Generations* boiled down to coming up with a story that would propel *The Next Generation* beyond the confines of the small screen, and would feel genuinely like a film rather than an episode shown on a larger canvas. Berman elicited Paramount's blessing to write the

script before worrying about securing the services of a director. Actually, Paramount felt comfortable with the notion of developing two scripts, so Berman discussed the idea with several familiar *Trek* scribes: Michael Piller, the tandem of Brannon Braga and Ron Moore, and also Maurice Hurley. "Michael, unfortunately, was not interested in being in any kind of a competitive situation," Berman says. "Michael's feeling was that if he was going to be asked to write a movie script he would do it, but that he was not going to be in a situation where more than one person would be writing a script and somebody else's script might be chosen. So we developed a script with Ron and Brannon and we developed a script with Hurley and, as we all know, the

> "THE IDEA OF DOING A *NEXT GENERATION* FEATURE FILM WAS BOTH SCARY AND EXCITING."

> **"FIRST CONTACT WAS JUST A WONDERFUL EXPERIENCE AND AS THE FILM EVOLVED, WE JUST KNEW THAT WE HAD SOMETHING GOLDEN."**

Pictures clockwise: *Star Trek: First Contact*; The Borg Queen, played by Alice Krige

script by Ron and Brannon was the script that we moved forward with. Brannon and Ron and I worked on the story. We worked on it with the people at Paramount, to a point where everybody was pleased.

"Our idea, my idea originally, was I felt it was important to bring members of the original cast into the story to pass the torch. Now, obviously, because there was a century time difference we had to come up with a story that would allow that to happen. And we did. We created an idea that could take advantage of some or all of the original cast, depending on how things would work out. Then, when it came time to select a director, after everybody was happy with the script, the first person we agreed we would go and talk to was Leonard Nimoy. Leonard was not pleased with the script. He wanted to do some pretty dramatic work on redeveloping the script and there was a lot of differing of opinions on what evolved at that point, but let it be said there were disagreements and the end result was that there was a bit of a falling out and Leonard's involvement in the project did not happen. The next person that I spoke to about directing the project was David Carson, who I had worked with on a number of episodes of *Next Generation* and who had also directed the pilot of *Deep Space Nine* for me. Bill Shatner agreed to appear in the film and then the question became 'Which other cast members from the original series would we put in?' We needed other members of the cast and we knew we were not going to get Leonard."

Berman and company then set about making the film, in which a little something called the Nexus provided the device for bringing together Captains Picard and Kirk in an effort to thwart the plot of mad, time-tripping scientist Soran (Malcolm McDowell). The

shoot itself was, to quote Berman, "difficult." Much of it was filmed on location on the top of a mountain in Nevada, in tremendous heat. The cast and many of the crew members were physically drained, having leapt straight from season seven of the show into the ambitious two-hour series finale, *All Good Things...* and then into *Generations*. And then, even after *Generations* wrapped production, the difficulties continued. "When we tested the movie everyone seemed to agree that the ending was quite soft," Berman remembers. "We decided to go back in to rework the ending and reshoot the ending. With Herman Zimmerman's brilliant work as our production designer, we managed, in a record amount of time, to rebuild this set up on top of this mountain out in the desert in Nevada, and to build this huge collapsing bridge where Captain Kirk met his final demise. We ended up reshooting, I would say, the last 10 minutes of the film. *Generations* was a great learning experience for everyone."

Star Trek Generations debuted on November 18, 1994, and while something short of a blockbuster, it performed well enough domestically and overseas to ensure a return engagement. That return engagement, of course, would turn out to be *Star Trek: First Contact*, the most successful *Star Trek* movie and the first *ST:TNG* adventure with no connections to previous films. In the story, penned by Braga and Moore, Picard and crew dip back in time in order to stop the dreaded Borg from annihilating Earth of the future. Along the way they encounter Dr. Zefram Cochrane (James Cromwell), a brilliant but boozy scientist who is about to pilot his ship the Phoenix into history as the first spacecraft to achieve warp speed. *First Contact* seamlessly blended action, drama and laughs, let the *ST:TNG* cast shine,

made time for the main guest actors (Cromwell, Alfre Woodard and especially Alice Krige as the sexy and sadistic villainess, the Borg Queen) to make their respective marks, and featured entertaining cameos by fan favorites Robert Picardo, Dwight Schultz and Ethan Phillips.

"In terms of the writing of *First Contact* I felt very comfortable working with Ron and Brannon, and we decided to lead with what we felt most comfortable with, a time travel story and a Borg story," Berman notes. "Those were two things that we'd been involved in and knew a lot about, and we felt a bit wiser having gone through one motion picture. We also felt very comfortable going with Jonathan Frakes as our director. He had done some excellent work as a director on the show and he earned the shot at directing the film. The story was something that came together beautifully. It was something that just evolved. The whole idea, the premise of basically having to go back and fix something, of having to go back and meet Zefram Cochrane and have him not be the person we all thought he was, to have him be quite a reluctant hero and to, in a sense, have our people turn him into the hero we know him to be, was just a delight to work on.

"The casting process was wonderful. The process of the art direction and how everything went... it all just went beautifully. *First Contact* was just a wonderful experience and as the film evolved we just knew that we had something golden. I remember when the film was tested for the first time. We went in and waited in Sherry Lansing's office, and then the research people came in

with their little cards and the results, and there were smiles on everyone's faces. We had just hit a home run and everything worked perfectly. It opened, I think, to $31 million, and this was back in 1996. That was a whole lot of money for an opening weekend back then. It was gigantic, and it opened equally big in England. Everything about the film was extremely successful. It was just a delight to work on from beginning to end."

Released November 22 1996, *First Contact* went on to elicit arguably the best reviews of any *Star Trek* feature to date, or at least since *Star Trek IV: The Voyage Home*. It grossed just shy of $100 million in the U.S. and just over $50 million elsewhere around the world. And it set the stage for *Star Trek: Insurrection*.

Berman and company took a real gamble on *Insurrection*, a thinking fan's *Star Trek* tale, light on action and deep on ideas and words. Penned by Michael Piller, *Insurrection* follows the *Enterprise* crew as they explore why Data malfunctioned on the seemingly peaceful home world of the Ba'ku. They discover that the area of space around the Ba'ku home world is full of metaphasic radiation particles with Fountain of Youth-like properties that keep the Ba'ku people healthy and eternally youthful. As such, darker forces wish to harvest the particles, forcing the *Enterprise* crew to take on not only a high-ranking Starfleet officer – Admiral Dougherty (Anthony Zerbe) – of questionable character, but also Ru'afo (F. Murray Abraham), a Son'a with a chip on his shoulder and a yen to be young again.

"What happened with *Insurrection* is not unlike the situation we faced when doing the *Star Trek* shows," Berman says. "When you've done one show that's set on a spaceship, the next one, especially if there's going to be an overlap, you put on a space station. You can't have two of them on a spaceship. The next one, though, can be back on a spaceship, and that's how you got from *Next Generation* to *Deep Space Nine* to *Voyager*. In the same way, after dealing with the Borg and time travel in *First Contact* we couldn't do that again. And because Brannon was busily at work on *Voyager* and because Ron was busily at work on *Deep Space Nine* neither of them was in a position to get involved with the third of these films, and I went to Michael. He was interested in working with me on a movie, but Michael was a very serious writer and Michael was not looking to write anything frivolous or fun."

Insurrection, which opened December 11 1998, ultimately met with critical indifference and its box office numbers reflected that. It beamed down $70 million domestically and another $42 million internationally: not disastrous, but not great, especially taking into account the budget: $60 million, nearly $15 million more than its far more lucrative predecessor. On the other hand, plenty of hardcore *Star Trek* fans laud *Insurrection* as one of the best big-screen journeys, arguably the closest of them all to the spirit of Gene Roddenberry's creation. "I agree that it was classic *Star Trek* and one of the reasons for that was Michael," Berman says. "We ended up making a film that still dealt a great deal with principle, with conflict, with conflict within Starfleet. It had romantic themes. It was true to *Star Trek* in a way that Michael felt was essential to his story. We had some wonderful actors in it. I thought F. Murray Abraham was terrific. Herman

Zimmerman did amazing work, building an entire village about 60 miles north of L.A. We also shot up in the Sierra Nevada mountains. So we had some really remarkable locations and set work. It was not a perfect movie, but I think it had a great deal to say and there were some fun moments in it."

Next up would be *Star Trek Nemesis*. In the film, Picard and his crew take on a powerful Reman named Shinzon (Tom Hardy), a figure who speaks of peace but actually seeks vengeance. Shinzon, it turns out, is Picard's clone, who is rapidly degenerating. Thus, he's lured the *Enterprise* into a trap and kidnaps Picard in order take from Picard what he needs in order to survive and complete his personal mission – to destroy Earth. Meanwhile, in a thematic parallel, the discovery of a Data-like prototype android called B-4 (Spiner) ups the ante, as B-4 has been programmed to serve as a Shinzon spy. Berman explains that the aim with *Nemesis* was to deliver something as different from *Insurrection* as *Insurrection* was from *First Contact*.

"*Star Trek* was going through some changes," Berman says. "*Deep Space Nine* had ended. *Voyager* had ended. *Voyager*'s ratings had not fared all that well. *Enterprise* was on the air (and struggling). I think that the studio was not in a big rush. Patrick Stewart was kind of busy. There was a sense I was getting from that studio that perhaps the next film we produced might be better off if we did it with a new cast. I felt, right or wrong, that because we were introducing a new cast with *Enterprise* that to introduce a new cast almost simultaneously was not a good idea. I felt since it had been a while, four years, I believe, since the audience had seen Picard and company, that we should give the cast of *The Next Generation* another shot.

"I WOULD SAY THAT MY BIGGEST AND GREATEST DISAPPOINTMENT IN ALL OF THE MOVIES WE MADE WAS *NEMESIS* BECAUSE I THINK *NEMESIS* WAS A FAR BETTER FILM THAN YOU'D BELIEVE FROM THE WAY IT WAS RECEIVED."

Pictures clockwise: The Viceroy, played by Ron Perlman, Shinzon's Reman advisor from *Star Trek: Nemesis*; *First Contact*; *Nemesis*

"There are a lot of things I'm leaving out that had to do with negotiations and a variety of negotiating points with a number of cast members that get very complicated and difficult. You're dealing with roles that you can't have casting sessions for. There's only one person who can play Picard or Data or Worf, and because of that you have very complex negotiations. And I'm not just talking about money. I'm talking about negotiations that deal with everything from money to participation in story and in script, participation in [approving] other people who were involved in the project. It gets very, very complicated, and as each film evolved those negotiations with a variety of the different people involved in the projects got more and more complicated. Some of that had to do with why there was a long hiatus between *Star Trek IX* and *Star Trek X*. I felt strongly that the tenth film should be another film with the *Next Generation* cast. In retrospect, perhaps I was wrong, but I still feel it was the right decision."

Brent Spiner introduced Berman to his friend, acclaimed screenwriter John Logan. Subsequently, Berman, Spiner, Stewart and Logan held numerous meetings together. Logan, at that point, had already written *Gladiator* and a number of other films. Plus, Berman hastens to add, Logan represented that true rarity:

an A-list Hollywood screenwriter who had a remarkable understanding of *ST:TNG*. "He became a close friend and remains a close friend to this day," Berman notes. "John wanted to write this movie. So he was not only an Academy Award-nominated writer, but he absolutely had a passion for these characters. Paramount could not have been more thrilled to have him do it. They also felt strongly that it was time to get a director also from outside of the *Star Trek* family. Jonathan was working on another project, so it seemed like a good time to do that. I was encouraged to consider Stuart Baird. Stuart Baird was a world-renowned film editor (who most recently edited *Casino Royale*), but he'd also directed *Executive Decision* and *U.S. Marshals*. I met him and he was self-effacing and absolutely charming, and he knew his stuff. I've always found, at least in television, editors make very good directors. They know exactly what they need. And he seemed to have an understanding of what went into all of this.

"The one thing that film editors don't necessarily have is an understanding of how to deal with actors, which is also true in television. So, after being encouraged by Paramount, which I believe had pretty strong reasons to give this gentleman a directing job, we hired Stuart. The process of developing the story had started, really, before Stuart was hired. There was a good deal of conflict during the shooting. There was conflict between the actors and the director, more so than usual. We had, for the first time, a director who knew virtually nothing about *Star Trek*, which caused some struggle. Our actors are all used to working with directors who know *Star Trek* inside and

Pictures clockwise: Soran from *Star Trek Generations*; *Nemesis*; *Generations*; Shinzon from *Nemesis*, played by Tom Hardy

out, whether it's David Carson or Jonathan Frakes or directors who did the shows over the years. And that was not the case here."

Nemesis arrived in theaters on December 13 2002, and landed with a loud, ominous thud. The film opened, shockingly, second behind an unheralded Jennifer Lopez romantic comedy, *Maid in Manhattan*, and it vanished quickly from theaters, grossing a lethargic $43 million at home and just $23 million abroad. *Nemesis* marked the last silver screen trek for the *Next Generation* cast and heralded the end of Berman's rein as overseer of the *Star Trek* movie franchise.

"I would say that my biggest and greatest disappointment in all of the movies we made was *Nemesis* because I think *Nemesis* was a far, far better film than you'd believe from the way it was received," Berman says. "I have heard many people blame the outcome of *Nemesis* on a variety of different phenomena, and I don't buy any of it. I heard the studio be blamed for picking a date of release so close to [the latest] *Lord of the Rings* movie. I don't think that's a valid complaint because if that were true we would have done better in other countries where it did not open close to that film and it did not do any better in those countries. I don't know what to blame it on. The reviews of the film were, I would say, 80 per cent miserable, as were the opening weekend numbers. It went against the tracking, the quite scientific approach the studios use to determine how a film is going to do. The film did nowhere near as well as the tracking results had predicted.

"I still believe that *Nemesis* was a very good film and I, to this day, don't quite understand what went wrong. John is a remarkable writer. I thought Stuart did a good job. I know the film has some flaws to it, but it bothers me and it puzzles me that it didn't do better than it did."

something more than just the narrative sequences in it. One of the things I was happy with was that, through meetings with the writers and producers, we developed a 'B' story for Picard that is very private, personal and a very intense emotional story that runs parallel to the main action story. For me, that was the most satisfying element of the pre-production on the movie.

"Of course, David has quite a bit of experience directing NEXT GENERATION episodes," Stewart says. "I was thrilled when I heard Malcolm was doing it. Malcolm and I have a history that goes back almost 30 years."

Both, of course, took the stage as members of the famed Royal Shakespeare Company. Stewart is also a veteran of numerous BBC television productions including I, Claudius; Tinker, Tailor, Soldier, Spy and Smiley's People. Among his film credits are Excalibur, Lifeforce, Dune (as Gurney Halleck), Lady Jane, L.A. Story and Gunmen. Two forthcoming films—Jeffrey and Let It Be Me—offer change-of-pace roles for Stewart. In recent years, Stewart has won even more acclaim performing a one-man show version of Charles Dickens' A Christmas Carol (on

Patrick Stewart

Captain Jean-Luc Picard

By MARC SHAPIRO

Patrick Stewart is once again Captain Jean-Luc Picard as STAR TREK: THE NEXT GENERATION's crew makes its big-screen debut.

The film not only re-teams Stewart with his regular co-stars but with the series' executive producer Rick Berman, writers Brannon Braga and Ronald D. Moore and director David Carson as well as old friend Malcolm McDowell.

For Stewart, it's an intriguing move from one medium to another. "I always felt that the biggest challenge in making the first NEXT GENERATION movie was to make the best film that we could first and to make the best STAR TREK movie second," he says. "I didn't want something so elitist that it could appeal only to fans or to those people who have been watching the series. I wanted it to be a movie that someone who had never heard of STAR TREK could sit down and enjoy and not feel excluded. In advance, I felt that would be the biggest challenge.

"During the months prior to filming, my attention shifted to the character of Picard and in creating a storyline for the Captain which had

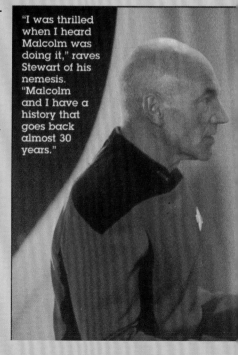

"I was thrilled when I heard Malcolm was doing it," raves Stewart of his nemesis. "Malcolm and I have a history that goes back almost 30 years."

"I've been aware that there are fewer days ahead than there are behind."

Broadway and elsewhere and available as an audiobook).

His tenure in the STAR TREK Universe began while on a working vacation in Los Angeles in early 1987.

"I was reading some scenes at a lecture at UCLA and STAR TREK producer Robert Justman happened to be enrolled in a course which required he take that lecture," Stewart recalls.

Admitting he is at a loss to explain why he was asked to read for the role of Picard, Stewart does note, "Authority figures have weighed strongly in the roles I have played in the past. I can only suspect that the sense of authority that I have brought to my previous roles must have rubbed off on my approach to acting. I was aware of drawing on some very authoritarian attitudes when I read for the part of Picard. I can only feel that the STAR TREK producers picked up on that.

"When I was a very young actor, I believed that a performance meant stepping on a stage and telling the audience *everything*. With each episode, I tried with the writers to work in something new about Picard, something that expands the audience's knowledge of who this man is. I don't know much more about him than they do. If I'm doing my job properly, the audience will know things about Picard that I *don't* know and never will know. If acting is the endeavor

it should be, it *must* be open to the possibilities for the audience to have insight into the character. The audience can see things that are *not* planned to be there."

Stewart's bravura performances on STAR TREK: THE NEXT GENERATION earned great acclaim from fans and critics alike. While commanding the *U.S.S. Enterprise*, Stewart also made his directorial debut, helming five episodes ("In Theory," "Hero Worship," "A Fistful of Datas," "Phantasms" and "Preemptive Strike"). Although his first episode ("In Theory") remains his favorite, making the Holodeck Western saga "A Fistful of Datas"

was the most fun. "Working from sun-up to sundown on the Western lot with three cameras rolling," Stewart says, "was the most exciting day of my life."

Seven years later, with STAR TREK: THE NEXT GENERATION leaving first-run production, the acclaimed saga eases onto the big screen, offering Stewart and company an unexpected luxury. "Time," he says. "Instead of being involved in a shooting day [for the TV series] that would have us putting seven to 10 pages on film, we were putting two to two-and-a-half pages each day. Everything, consequently, was able to be done more slowly, more carefully and involved many more rehearsals and takes. There was

"There'll be no more Picards."

no moving on until everybody involved felt we had gotten it as well as we could. Beyond that, the big thing was that we were able to take the show out of the studio and into some spectacular locations that give the movie an appropriately scenic and epic feeling."

For many fans what especially makes STAR TREK GENERATIONS special is the on-screen teaming of the two Captains from two different generations. That's a feeling Stewart shares. "It had been an argument of mine from the early days of THE NEXT GENERATION movie that it *should* be a film that should include as many of the original STAR TREK

members as we could get," he observes. "I felt having members of the original cast would provide the opportunity to present something really intense and dramatic. I felt that having the two Captains share screen space was something audiences would enjoy seeing. I didn't know Bill Shatner very well, but I was lucky enough to spend some time with him on a plane ride back from an industry convention. The two of us spent 60 minutes in the air and, in that hour, we got to know one another. We talked about our lives, personal things and what STAR TREK had meant to our careers. I was delighted to find out what a sensitive, intelligent and gentle man Bill was.

fairly intense feelings to be communicated. Fortunately, we had a whole day to shoot this scene."

Then, there were the Holodeck ship and the horseback ride in the Nexus, two sequences which tested Stewart's athletic ability. "I also remember a scene in which Jonathan [Frakes] and I were attempting to walk a dignified straight line on board another U.S.S. Enterprise which is a sailing ship. It was pitching and rolling, and it was quite funny. I also recall a riding sequence with Bill and me on horseback. I ride, but I'm not a championship-caliber horseman like Bill is. I felt a certain amount of pressure on me that day to match his riding skills. But he was very

supportive of the difference in our skills, which many actors would not have been."

Gene Roddenberry created both STAR TREK sagas. And Patrick Stewart believes the events of STAR TREK GENERATIONS would suit the late writer/producer. "I think he would have been pleased with the connection that happened between Bill and myself," the actor announces. "He would have been satisfied to see Kirk and Picard sharing the screen together. If he's looking down from that great writers' building in the sky, I'm sure he would find everything that we did was appropriate. I certainly felt it was."

"I doubt this will be the last ship to carry the name Enterprise."

And so, when the time came for us to work together, I felt it would be a good experience and it was. We had a great deal of fun."

The film's major difficulties came, perhaps not surprisingly, on location. "The whole final dramatic climax of the movie, which we shot on the top of a 500-foot mountain of rock in the Nevada desert, contained conditions that were extremely grim," Stewart notes. "The temperature was in the hundreds and there were hot winds and dust blowing all the time. The location was extremely dangerous, but the resulting scene should look tremendous.

"Early in the movie, I have a scene with Counselor Troi in which Picard has just undergone a tremendous, personal, emotional shock. The shock makes him examine how he has lived his life. The scene called for some

"The biggest challenge in making the first NEXT GENERATION movie was to make the best film we could," reveals Stewart, here with director David Carson.

Top & centre: The *U.S.S. Enterprise* NCC-1701-B in space dock, just prior to its fateful maiden voyage.
Left: The *U.S.S. Enterprise* NCC-1701-D in the Veridian system.

STAR TREK®
GENERATIONS™

Time marches on, ignorant of the little games played to dissuade it. Pavel Chekov and Montgomery Scott await the arrival of an orbital skydiving friend.

Captain James T. Kirk, once and future savior of the galaxy, stands again on the Bridge of an *Enterprise:* the *1701-B*—albeit reluctantly.

The first maxim of the starship Captain should be "Be Prepared," as Captain John Harriman learns when the ill-equipped *U.S.S. Enterprise* must attempt a rescue mission.

A frantic Dr. Tolian Soran is rescued from the transport ship *Lakul.* For a man saved from certain death, his only desire is to return to where he was.

One of the survivors of the *Lakul* is a familiar face on another *U.S.S. Enterprise*—Guinan. The rescue has left the *U.S.S. Enterprise N.C.C.-1701-B* stuck in a gravimetric field that threatens to draw the ship into an energy ribbon.

There's only one hope for the *U.S.S. Enterprise*—an anti-matter explosion at the nose of the ship. And only one man can plant the charge—Kirk.

Kirk's ploy works. The *U.S.S. Enterprise* is able to pull out of the field, but not before the ribbon destroys the fore section of the ship—and Kirk.

In their rightful places at the helm of the sea-faring *S.S. Enterprise*, Captain Jean-Luc Picard and First Mate Will Riker begin a grueling ritual...

...the dunking of the newly promoted Lieutenant Commander Worf. The elaborate ceremony, and the dousing of the doctor, is interrupted by a message for the Captain.

Picard has received bad news. Low hangs the head of this sorrowed man.

No matter how he feels or what he's going through, a Captain must be strong for his ship, a ship which now races to the wounded Amargosa observatory.

In his ongoing quest to be as human as possible, Data enlists the help of his friend Geordi La Forge to install the emotion chip.

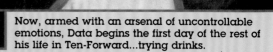

Now, armed with an arsenal of uncontrollable emotions, Data begins the first day of the rest of his life in Ten-Forward...trying drinks.

Some people just have a knack for surviving. Soran is one of them. They say, time is the fire in which we burn, and Soran *must* return to the observatory, for his time is running out.

While scanning the Amargosa observatory for clues, and weathering Data's incessant laughter, Geordi finds a solar probe with a trilithium core—and Soran.

No man can choose his family, we are saddled with the luck of the draw. Picard was one of the lucky ones...until now. His brother Robert and nephew Rene, the last of the Picard line, perished in a fire.

Disaster. The Amargosa star is breaking down, thanks to a quantum implosion triggered by a solar probe. The resulting shock wave will destroy everything within the entire system.

Desperate men do desperate things, as Soran teaches Riker, Worf, La Forge and Data with his phaser. Mere seconds before the observatory explodes, Soran escapes with Geordi as his prisoner.

Soran's saviors are a pair of wily Klingon vultures, Lursa and B'Etor. The power to destroy a star has been promised to them, but only when Soran is ready.

The emotion chip has been fused into Data's brain and cannot be removed. Geordi's fate weighs heavy on the android, who cowered in fear.

Every criminal has a motive and Guinan is the only one on the *U.S.S. Enterprise* who knows what it is—the Nexus. Whatever Soran does, it is to return to the joy of the Nexus.

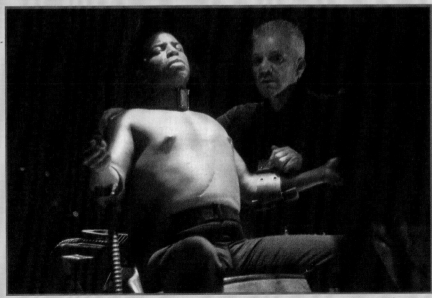

We are all prisoners of something. Before his VISOR, Geordi was a prisoner of blindness, now he is a prisoner of Soran—who takes a special interest in Geordi's artificial sight.

Picard's last chance for stopping Soran is a face-to-face confrontation. In exchange for Geordi, Picard beams to the Klingon ship and is then beamed, weaponless, to the planet's surface.

In Stellar Cartography, Picard and Data track the course of the Nexus. It will enter this sector in 48 hours, and Soran has been extinguishing stars to draw the Nexus to him.

The Klingon sisters play their ace in the hole, Geordi's VISOR. They can see whatever Geordi sees, including Engineering displays that tell the frequency of the ship's shields.

The *U.S.S. Enterprise* is rocked by a hail of Klingon torpedoes. Worf and Data conclude that the only possible retaliation is to engage the Klingons' cloaking device from afar, causing their shields to drop.

The battle of wits has begun. It ends when either Soran enters the Nexus a happy man or Picard "convinces" him to give up, by any means necessary.

Oblivious to the destruction of the Klingon ship overhead, Soran's attention—and aim—is drawn to Picard, who has managed to sneak *under* the energy field.

If Picard knew that the *U.S.S. Enterprise* was going up in flames, perhaps his drive would be sapped, but there are more lives at stake than his crew's—and Soran *must* be stopped.

Even as the courageous Captain and the mad scientist grapple, the energy ribbon enters the atmosphere and rips across the mountaintop, taking Picard and Soran with it.

Welcome to the future that could forever be yours, Jean-Luc Picard. A warm house. Loving children. *Christmas.* But it's not real. Soran *is* real, and must be stopped—and only one man can help.

There's more than one Captain of the *U.S.S. Enterprise* stuck in the harmony of the Nexus—James Kirk is here as well, but it will take some convincing to make him want to leave paradise.

Starfleet captains are a rare breed. Even when surrounded by all that life has to offer, they want more...a chance to save the galaxy one last time. Captain Kirk is back in the saddle again.

Back on the mountaintop—before the Nexus arrived—Soran is again ready to do battle with Picard, who now has an ace up his sleeve.

And that ace is Kirk. While Picard disables the solar probe that drew the Nexus here before, Kirk takes on the 24th Century with both fists.

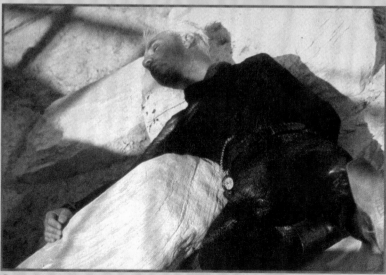

Soran is defeated and millions of lives are saved—at the cost of Kirk's. Fear not, for James Kirk learned long ago that the needs of the many outweigh the needs of the few...or the one.

Back on the Bridge of the once-mighty flagship, Picard takes stock of the damage, to both the ship...and to himself. It is time for both to move on...but there will be another ship named the *U.S.S. Enterprise.*

Top, centre & right: U.S.S. Enterprise
NCC-1701-D and Lursa & B'Etor's *Bird of Prey*
engage in head to head combat with
horrific results.

William Shatner

B ittersweet is a perfect characterization," says William Shatner, trying to find the right words to describe his feelings about his involvement in *STAR TREK GENERATIONS*, in which the actor reprises his role as the legendary Captain James T. Kirk one final time. "It had never occurred to me that there would be another *STAR TREK* film that I could be part of, after *STAR TREK VI: THE UNDISCOVERED COUNTRY* came out.

"I was glad to be asked to do *GENERATIONS*. I looked forward to working with Patrick Stewart and I had a little bit of a hand in guiding my part in the script. But when we did actually began shooting the film, there was this slowly dawning realization that this would be the *last* thing I was going to do in *STAR TREK*."

Of course, the actor has done so much in the famed *STAR TREK* Universe, and for his efforts, he has become an international star. Shatner has parlayed his immense fame into a stunningly busy and varied career that has found him acting in films and television, hosting a TV reality program, bylining bestselling fiction and non-fiction books, breeding championship Saddlebred horses, lending his name to numerous charitable organizations and, in what he describes as his personal career highlights, directing *STAR TREK V: THE FINAL FRONTIER* and creating the syndicated *TekWar* telemovies and the upcoming cable *TekWar* TV series starring Greg Evigan as futuristic private investigator Jake Cardigan. "I love the idea that I've created, written, acted in, directed and [in the case of *TekWar*] produced

By IAN SPELLING

some things," marvels Shatner. "That kind of gives me a shiver."

Born and raised in Montreal, Canada, Shatner always envisioned himself being an actor and, resisting his parents' urging that he join the family clothing business, he pursued the craft with a passion. As a teenager, Shatner acted in several Canadian Broadcasting Company (CBC) productions, then attended McGill University, from which he graduated with a business degree. He was soon working for the Montreal-based Mountain Playhouse as an assistant manager. Not much later, Shatner graduated from the office to center stage, and he eventually spent three years with the Canadian Repertory Company in Ottawa. More opportunities came his way when he understudied with the Stratford (Ontario) Shakespeare Festival. A critically-acclaimed performance in *Tamberlaine* led to a move to New York City and Broadway stage appearances, which in turn, led to various roles in live television drama.

The actor wasted little time in making a name for himself on the small screen, earning praise for his work on *Playhouse 90*, *Studio One* and now-classic episodes of *The Twilight Zone*, including the legendary "Nightmare at 20,000 Feet," in which he—and only he—saw a gremlin ripping apart the wing of the airplane on which he was a very reluctant passenger. Stage roles followed in *A Shot in the Dark*, *The World of Suzie Wong* and *L'Idiote*. Shatner relocated to Los Angeles, earning rave reviews for his work as Alexei in the film version of *The Brothers Karamazov*. Subsequent films included the Oscar-winning drama *Judgment at Nuremberg*, as well as *The Explosive Generation* and *The Intruder*.

"The first thing you learn as Captain is how to cheat death."

"I was out saving the galaxy when your grandfather was still in diapers. And frankly, I think the galaxy owes me one."

Once more into the *STAR TREK* Universe comes William Shatner, ready to take on all comers as Captain James T. Kirk in *STAR TREK GENERATIONS*.

Shatner notes. "He still would be very important in my future life and work."

Shatner, of course, has appeared in every *STAR TREK* film, while making the time to breed his horses at his Belle Reve Farms in Lexington, Kentucky; host *Rescue 911*, which has helped save hundreds of lives; and write (with Chris Kreski) the best-selling memoir *Star Trek Memories*

hen came Gene Roddenberry's *STAR TREK*. Jeffrey Hunter had portrayed Captain Christopher Pike of the Starship *Enterprise* in the *STAR TREK* pilot, "The Cage," but there was to be a new hero, Captain James Tiberius Kirk, in the second pilot commissioned by NBC, "Where No Man Has Gone Before." And into his boots stepped Shatner. For three years, from 1966-1969, Shatner trekked across the 23rd Century, journeying with Mr. Spock (Leonard Nimoy), Dr. Leonard McCoy (DeForest Kelley) and the rest of the *U.S.S. Enterprise* crew, where no man had gone before. He provided the voice of Kirk for a season's worth of animated *STAR TREK* adventures; starred in the TV series *Barbary Coast* and the long-running cop action-drama *T.J. Hooker*; the films *Big, Bad Mama, Kingdom of the Spiders, The Kidnapping of the President, Airplane II: The Sequel* and *Loaded Weapon I*; and such specials as the PBS drama *Andersonville* and the ecologically-minded cable mini-series *Voice of the Planet*.

Slowly, the repeats of *STAR TREK* grew in popularity, as their often timeless and creative stories held the attention of original fans and captured the imagination of an entirely new generation of Trekkers. By the late 1970s, the world was ready for a *STAR TREK* revival and the demand was to be met with a new series, *STAR TREK II*, which was intended to reunite the original cast. Then, *Star Wars* came out and suddenly, the series was transformed into *STAR TREK: THE MOTION PICTURE*, which proved to be a launching pad for the *STAR TREK* film franchise. "Regardless of what I was doing, or where my career was at the moment, I knew Kirk was not far behind me,"

With his companions— Walter Koenig and James Doohan—at his side, Shatner passes the torch to another generation.

Since the original *STAR TREK* series in 1966, Shatner has never left the public eye. The publicity hounds have even followed him to the 23rd Century.

"I was glad to be asked to do *GENERATIONS*," states Shatner. "I looked forward to working with Patrick Stewart."

to be called *Underground*.

Returning to *STAR TREK GENERATIONS*, Shatner says of the film, in which James Doohan and Walter Koenig also appear, respectively as Scotty and Chekov, that it's literally and figuratively the passing of the torch from the original cast to the actors of *STAR TREK: THE NEXT GENERATION*. "I refer to Picard as Captain of the *Enterprise*

and its sequel, *Star Trek Movie Memories*. As if that weren't enough, Shatner recently returned to the stage for a limited run as Harry Houdini in a 1993 Buck's County Playhouse production of *Harry and Arthur*; appeared as a wily murderer in a *Columbo* TV movie opposite Peter Falk; and guest starred in an episode of *seaQuest*. He's writing, producing, directing and acting in his *TekWar* series for the USA Network and helping to create an interactive CD-ROM *TekWar* game. Shatner also serves as a frequent guest at *STAR TREK* conventions; continues to byline the ongoing series of *TekWar* novels, the sixth of which, *TekPower* is out now, with a seventh on the way; and is

"When we began shooting the film, there was this slowly dawning realization that this would be the *last* thing I was going to do in *STAR TREK*," says Shatner.

developing a project involving *STAR TREK* telephone calling cards. If everything works out, he'll direct and co-star with his old friend Leonard Nimoy in an Agatha Christie-like mystery-thriller

on a couple of occasions in the film, and as those words came out of my mouth the reality was there," he reveals. "Patrick Stewart is now the Captain of the *Enterprise*. The irony, of course, was that the series was over for him, too, though he has the movies to come."

Although, as William Shatner puts it, "I really think *GENERATIONS* is the end for Captain Kirk," the actor is fully aware of the fact that both the character and *STAR TREK* will forever be a part of his life. "I'm sure it will," he says, with not a tinge of dissatisfaction in his voice, "and I don't challenge it."

"I refer to Picard as Captain of the *Enterprise* on a couple of occasions," reveals Shatner. "As those words came out of my mouth, the reality was there."

"Of course, if Spock were here, he'd say I was being an irrational, illogical human."

Whoopi Goldberg

By
IAN
SPELLING
& MARC
SHAPIRO

Guinan

"I liked the show, so I asked if I could be on it. As a matter of fact, I asked *twice*," remembers Goldberg of trying to get on *STAR TREK: THE NEXT GENERATION*.

As a child growing up, Whoopi Goldberg remembers sitting before the television set, avidly watching *STAR TREK*. She appreciated what the show had to say and how it said it, and she relished the fact that the show, unlike virtually any other of its era, prominently displayed the talents of a black actress, Nichelle Nichols. Further, Nichols' character, the communications officer Lt. Uhura, was a proud woman of color, respected by her peers, and counted upon to do her job as well as anyone of another race, creed or, for that matter, sex. To the young, impressionable Goldberg, the fact that there was a black actress with a featured role on a 1960s series and an African-American shown to be a vital part of mankind's future, was quite inspiring.

By age eight, Goldberg was performing in a variety of stage plays in and around New York, including Broadway. Relocating to the West Coast in 1974, the actress was soon performing drama and improvisation, then starred in *Spook Show*, a popular one-performer show, that took Goldberg across America and all throughout Europe. Already well regarded in industry circles, Goldberg earned public recognition for a Mike Nichols-directed staging of an acclaimed one-woman show in which Goldberg portrayed numerous characters that ranged from hysterically funny to touchingly sad. Her first album, a recording of that show, went on to be rewarded with a Grammy as Best Comedy Recording of the Year. Those successes led to her casting as the homely-on-the-outside, but beautiful-on-the-inside lead character in Steven Spielberg's 1985 adaptation of Alice Walker's *The Color Purple*.

For her effort, Goldberg earned a Best Actress Oscar nomination and she followed up *Color Purple* with several comedies, among them *Jumpin' Jack Flash*, *Burglar* and *Fatal Beauty*, and the dramas *The Telephone* and *Clara's Heart*. Suddenly, in 1988, there was the sight of Goldberg as the hostess of Ten-Forward, the meeting place of the Starship *Enterprise* during the second season of *STAR TREK: THE NEXT GENERATION*. She had returned to a childhood inspiration, on a recurring basis, as the mysterious El-Aurian Guinan, who dispensed various exotic foods and beverages, offered great advice to the crew, particularly to her friend Captain Jean-Luc Picard, and also sported outrageously colorful outfits.

"I did it because, frankly, I couldn't get any other work then," admits the actress. "I liked the show, so I asked if I could be on it. As a matter of fact, I asked *twice*. The first time, I sent a message to LeVar Burton asking him to tell the producers that I would *really* like to be on the show. He got the message to the producers and they said, 'Yeah, right. Whoopi wants to do *STAR TREK*.'"

> "Soran? That's a name I haven't heard in a long time."

Then... nothing.

"One of the cast members [Gates McFadden] left the show and I heard about it, so I approached the show's producers again and said, 'Listen, I don't know if you know it or not, but I've been trying for a long time now to get on this show.' They said LeVar had told them about it and they thought he was kidding. I told them I can't do all the episodes but I would like to do some of them. 'Can I have the job?' They finally said, 'Sure, we'll build you a bar.' And they built me Ten-Forward. I got to go in and be really sage and wear great hats. I also got to hang out with some extraordinary people, like Patrick Stewart, LeVar and Jonathan Frakes."

Linking the past to the future is Whoopi Goldberg, Guinan of *STAR TREK GENERATIONS*.

G uinan, named after the famed bartender Texas Guinan, who operated a saloon during the Prohibition, made her debut in "The

"If you go into that nexus, you're not going to care about Soran or the *Enterprise* or me."

Child," then appeared in several subsequent second and third season *STAR TREK: THE NEXT GENERATION* episodes, including "The Outrageous Okona," "The Measure of a Man," "Q Who?" "Booby Trap" and "Deja Q."

Even after she hit new personal highs with the smash hits *Ghost*—for which she won an Oscar as Best Supporting Actress—*Soapdish*, *The Player*, *Sister Act* and *Made In America*, Goldberg made time in her schedule to trek in such episodes as "The Best of Both Worlds II," "The Loss," "In Theory," "Redemption I & II," "Ensign Ro," "I, Borg," "Time's Arrow I & II" and "Suspicions." Though she didn't appear in any episodes during *STAR TREK: THE NEXT GENERATION*'s seventh season, a period during which she filmed *Sister Act II: Back in the Habit* and *Corrina, Corrina*, she does rejoin the cast for *STAR TREK GENERATIONS*.

In the film, Goldberg plays three versions of Guinan: There's the 24th Century one with which Trekkers are familiar; the 23rd Century one beamed, along with several of her race—including *STAR TREK GENERATIONS*' main villain, Dr. Soran—from the Eden-like Nexus; and the Guinan "echo" who lives within the Nexus and guides Picard to the only man who can help stop Soran: Captain James T. Kirk.

Goldberg knows that her career and the incredible celebrity she has

Of her time spent in the 24th Century, Goldberg states, "I've done it as a tribute to my love of the show."

achieved in recent years is far from the norm, especially for a woman, and an African-American one at that, in Hollywood. "I don't know if I'm the one who should be commenting on the situation," she says. "I can't complain about the amount of work that's out there. I am black. But I didn't become black yesterday. I'm black and I'm getting the work and I'm doing some good things, but I realize many black actors and actresses are not being given the opportunities. The industry has got to stop thinking in terms of black and white and has to start thinking in terms of who is right, regardless of color, for the role."

There seem to be no limits to Goldberg's energy. Despite her relentless film schedule, which includes the upcoming *Moonlight and Valentino* with Kathleen Turner and *Boys on the Side*, she has found time to host the 1994 Academy Awards ceremony; co-host Comic Relief, the HBO fund raiser for the homeless; provide one of the voices (along with Stewart and classic *STAR TREK* star Leonard Nimoy) for the Macaulay Culkin part-animated/part-live-action holiday release *The Pagemaster*; toil on behalf of a variety of cause-related organizations including the Starlight Foundation and groups battling AIDS; and be mother and grandmother to her family.

Whether or not Whoopi Goldberg appears in *STAR TREK: THE NEXT GENERATION* films remains to be seen, but whatever happens, *STAR TREK* will always remain a part of her life. "I've done it as a tribute to my love of the show. I liked the idea of being in space," she says. "I know I'm never going up [for real] in anybody's rocket ship. I know this, because I hate to fly. Gene Roddenberry's vision always included a multiethnic group of people. I thought that was pretty amazing. Being on *STAR TREK* has been a great way to sort of expand on the universe and be a part of it."

"They say, time is the fire in which we burn."

By RANDY &
JEAN-MARC LOFFICIER

Malcolm McDowell

have the capability to believe it's the greatest thing that you've ever done," McDowell says, noting that he doesn't have a favorite role or believe he's typecast as a villain. "Every film has its little reasons why you love it, even dumb films. And I've done some real clunkers. But I don't regret *anything* I've done. I never regret anything, because having the capacity to fail is very important. That's how you grow, it keeps your feet on the ground."

The 50-year-old actor's first job was not on stage, or in front of a camera, but in his father's pub in Leeds, England, serving drinks. He then became a traveling salesman for a coffee company. Determined to pursue acting, McDowell took classes and, after months of hard work, was accepted by the Isle of Wight Repertory Company.

Then, McDowell became a member of the famed Royal Shakespeare Company (where he met both Stewart and Warner) and began appearing on British television. His first movie role was in 1967's *Poor Cow*, starring Terence Stamp.

Director Lindsay Anderson noted McDowell's abrasive charisma and chose him to play Mick, the lead in *If...* (1968), a bizarre tale of the students' revolt at a British boarding school. The association between actor and director led to two further sequels in what is sometimes termed the "Mick Trilogy": *O, Lucky Man!* and *Britannia Hospital*.

Between *If...* and *O, Lucky Man*, McDowell appeared with Robert Shaw in *Figures in a Landscape*, *The Raging Moon* and, eventually in 1971, in Stanley Kubrick's provocative adaptation of Anthony Burgess' *A Clockwork Orange*. The character of young, amoral, ultraviolent Alex

Dr. Tolian Soran

As a man of two different times, Dr. Tolian Soran may be the greatest antagonist the *STAR TREK* Universe has ever known. Not only does he face two Captains of the Starship *Enterprise* in deadly confrontations, but for a time, Soran wins.

And who better to play this enigmatic obsessive, this villain without parallel, but an actual old friend of Patrick Stewart's? Prolific British actor Malcolm McDowell—who had first worked with Stewart in several Royal Shakespeare Company theatrical productions almost 30 years ago—essays the role. And, as is McDowell's custom, he plays the villainous Soran for all he's worth.

McDowell is no stranger to villainy

or for that matter, science fiction. He was the brutal Alex of *A Clockwork Orange*, the nasty British mercenary in charge of *Blue Thunder* and the feline killer from *Cat People* (1982). But he has also been a hero, most notably portraying the time-traveling H.G. Wells who battles a nefarious Jack the Ripper (fellow RSC veteran and Stewart friend David Warner) in the classic *Time After Time* (1979).

"Every time you do a film, you

brought worldwide fame to McDowell, and turned him into one of the leading stars of the British cinema almost overnight.

Other films followed: Richard Lester's *Royal Flash*, *Voyage of the Damned*, and *Aces High*. In 1979, taking on *real* villainy, McDowell etched a memorable portrait of Nazism in *The Passage*. "That movie contained some of the best work I've ever done," he announces. "I managed to

"Now, if you'll excuse me Captain, I have an appointment with eternity and I don't want to be late."

Even Klingons have reason to fear Soran, the unpredictable El-Aurian who will stop at nothing to reach the Nexus.

pack into a dozen scenes the whole period of Nazi tyranny in a convincingly evil way."

I n *Time After Time*, as the gentle and bemused Victorian H.G. Wells, McDowell's refined, upper class accent was perfect. "I used to talk like the Beatles," says the actor, demonstrating his abilities by repeatedly changing accents in mid-conversation. "But now I'm like a chameleon. I drive down the M1 [British motorway] and my accent changes depending on where I am. If

"In the end, time is going to hunt you down...and make the kill."

I'm in London, I'll speak cockney. In *Cross Creek*, I played the great editor, Maxwell Perkins with an American accent. The point is to make people believe you. How you do that is up to you."

McDowell has made moviegoers believe him as all sorts of other characters in such films as *Get Crazy*, *Arthur the King* (as legendary King Arthur in a TV movie), *Sunset* and the upcoming *Tank Girl* (as the villain). Teaming on stage with Lindsay Anderson for the director's off-Broadway restaging of John Osborne's *Look Back in Anger* was a personal highlight. "It was a kind of crossroads for me as an actor," McDowell explains. "At the end of the play, the whole audience was in tears. I could hear them sobbing, and that gave me an unbelievable thrill!

"I've got a long way to go. I've got

at least 20 more years and I haven't done my best work yet, by far. I've always tried to base my career on longevity, rather than on a flash in the pan, because, at the beginning, that's what happened to me. I was a big success in three films in a row, and then the British film industry collapsed overnight!"

After all these years, time spent both in and out of the news, the actor has a philosophical view of critics and box-office success. The reception accorded him as Dr. Soran in *STAR TREK GENERATIONS* just doesn't bother him.

"I've done my work the best I could, and if you don't like it, tough," Malcolm McDowell says. "I made up my mind *not* to read reviews. Ever since I did that, I've had some great reviews, and I can't read them, which is unfortunate! But I felt great, because I don't get emotionally involved in a picture anymore. I'm an actor—and what I do is up on the stage or on the screen—and it's the best work I can do."

Jean-Luc Picard wasn't prepared for the two-faced terror that Malcolm McDowell brought to *STAR TREK GENERATIONS* as Soran.

113

STAR TREK
GENERATIONS

PREVIOUSLY ON *STAR TREK:*

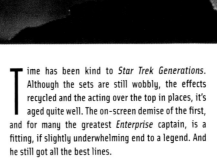

1. Data's emotion chip was retrieved from his brother Lore and installed in *Brothers*.

2. The Duras sisters became a regular pain in the side of the *Enterprise* crew in *Redemption*.

3. Guinan's travels before joining the *Enterprise-D* included late 19th Century San Francisco in *Time's Arrow*

Time has been kind to *Star Trek Generations*. Although the sets are still wobbly, the effects recycled and the acting over the top in places, it's aged quite well. The on-screen demise of the first, and for many the greatest *Enterprise* captain, is a fitting, if slightly underwhelming end to a legend. And he still got all the best lines.

Generations seemed to mark a return to a *Star Trek* where ideas and philosophy were as important as phasers and alien women. A theme of mortality and the ever-ticking clock runs through every strand; there are theories on the nature of reality and much more emotional depth, especially for Picard. Occasionally touched upon in *Star Trek: The Next Generation*, here it is expanded to allow Picard to mourn the family he's lost, as well as the family he never had. Feeling the weight of mortality and the guilt of having no children to whom he can pass on his legacy, leads him to a Dickensian paradise when he is pulled into an alternate reality in the Nexus. Kirk too feels time catching up to him and the urge to right the wrongs in his personal life. From the opening scene where he is incredulous that Sulu had time to procreate, to the nagging feeling that he should be making a difference somewhere – all roads lead to the inevitable collaboration with Picard, and Kirk's eventual appointment with eternity. Both men choose duty over their personal lives, and both seem content that history will bear them out. As Picard says: "What we leave behind is not as important as how we've lived."

Emma Matthews

CAPTAIN JEAN-LUC PICARD
Patrick Stewart

"In Star Trek: First Contact, despite the Borg connection, we see Picard being very much the Captain."

Captain Picard and the crew of the U.S.S. *Enterprise* versus the *Borg*. That's the plot of *Star Trek: First Contact* in a nutshell. It sounds so promising, so right and, with Patrick Stewart back in command as the authoritative and very Human Jean-Luc Picard, so rife with the likelihood of acting fireworks. After all, Picard had quite a history with those relentless humanoids on *Star Trek: The Next Generation*. No doubt, Stewart sees the opportunities the film offers him and Trekkers alike.

"It's a great adventure, quite dark at times, and necessarily so, it being a story that features the Borg," enthuses Stewart. "I feel especially pleased in terms of what we do with Picard. He spent a lot of *Star Trek Generations* on a downer (because his brother, nephew and *Kirk* all died). In *Star Trek: First Contact*, despite the Borg connection, we see Picard being very much the Captain. We see him on the Bridge of the U.S.S. *Enterprise* and in command, which is where he should be and what he should be doing."

Picard may be Stewart's signature role, but

it's merely one of many he has tackled. Born in Mirfield, a small town in the English county of Yorkshire, Stewart always knew the thespian life was the life for him. After studying at the Bristol Old Vic Theatre School, he was well on his way. He was soon performing in touring stage shows and eventually became a member of the Royal Shakespeare Company. Roles followed in assorted BBC television productions, among them *I, Claudius,* the classic cold war thriller *Tinker, Tailor, Soldier, Spy,* and *Smiley's People.* Early film credits included *Lady Jane, Excalibur, Lifeforce* and *Dune.*

In 1987, Robert Justman, the producer of *ST:TNG* with Gene Roddenberry, caught Stewart doing a scene reading in Los Angeles and invited him to audition for Picard. "Authority figures have weighed strongly in roles I've played in the past, and I can only suspect the sense of authority I brought to my previous roles must have rubbed off on my approach to acting," Stewart has said. "I was aware of drawing on some very authoritarian attitudes when I read for Picard. I can only feel that the *Star Trek* producers picked

up on that."

Stewart won the part and the rest is history. Not content to rest on his laurels, Stewart has consistently proven himself an actor to be reckoned with in projects outside the *Star Trek* Universe. During his *ST:TNG* hiatuses, Stewart appeared in the films *L.A. Story* and *Gunmen,* starred in a one-man production of *A Christmas Carol* (staged in London, Manhattan and Los Angeles), and directed a limited-run play called *Every Good Boy Deserves Favour,* which featured, among others, Gates McFadden, Brent Spiner and Colm Meaney.

Since *ST:TNG* beamed off the air, Stewart has appeared in the films *Star Trek Generations, Jeffrey,* and the upcoming thriller *Safe House,* and a comedy, *Smart Alec.* On television, Stewart starred in *The Canterville Ghost* and hosted *Saturday Night Live.* Furthermore, Stewart's memorable voice can be heard in many US television commercials and CD-ROMs. Perhaps the actor's high-point came in summer 1995, when he starred as Prospero in a free staging of *The Tempest* which proved so popular it transferred to Broadway for a sold-out, several month run.

Clearly, Stewart knows he has *ST:TNG* to thank for much of the success he has enjoyed. "I can only say what I've said so often before: I'm very, very proud of *ST:TNG,* and of having been a part of it," Stewart comments. "And I am very thankful for everything it has done for me and for my career." ■

Ian Spelling

The Story

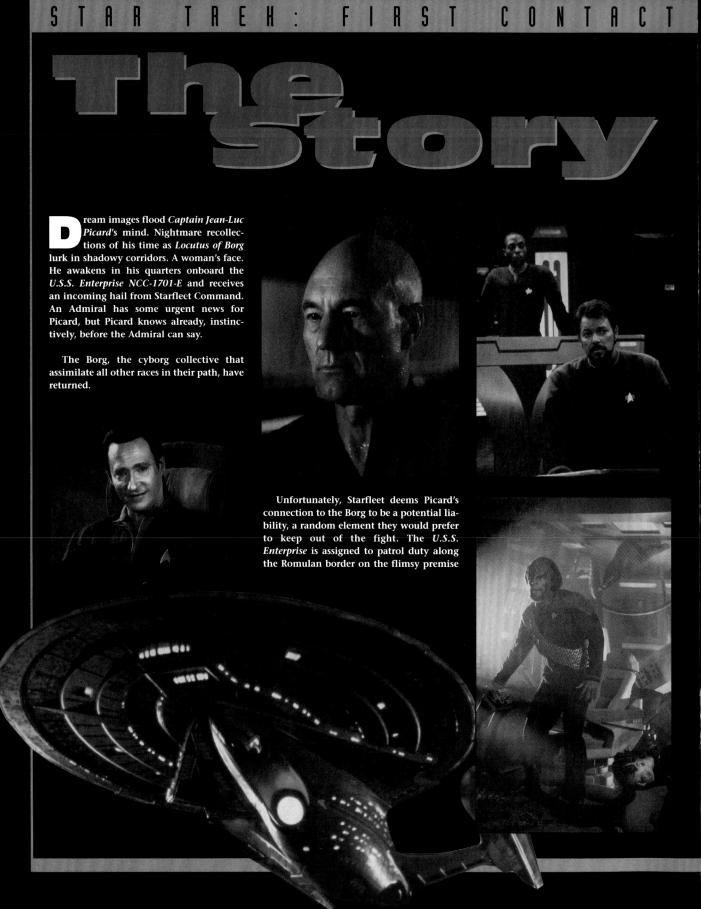

Dream images flood *Captain Jean-Luc Picard's* mind. Nightmare recollections of his time as *Locutus of Borg* lurk in shadowy corridors. A woman's face. He awakens in his quarters onboard the *U.S.S. Enterprise NCC-1701-E* and receives an incoming hail from Starfleet Command. An Admiral has some urgent news for Picard, but Picard knows already, instinctively, before the Admiral can say.

The Borg, the cyborg collective that assimilate all other races in their path, have returned.

Unfortunately, Starfleet deems Picard's connection to the Borg to be a potential liability, a random element they would prefer to keep out of the fight. The *U.S.S. Enterprise* is assigned to patrol duty along the Romulan border on the flimsy premise

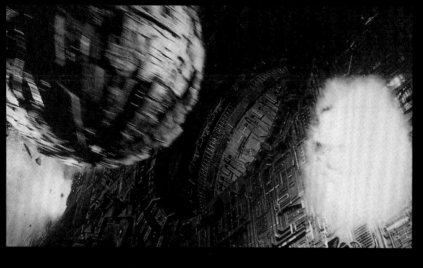

that the *Romulans* may try to take advantage of the Borg situation.

As the *U.S.S. Enterprise* crew listen on long-range subspace channels, they hear ship after ship going down in the wake of the Borg onslaught. They unanimously agree to disregard their orders and rush to the scene. The starship arrives in time to witness the *U.S.S. Defiant*, under *Worf's* command, on the verge of being destroyed. The *U.S.S. Defiant's* crew is beamed aboard, and Picard engages the Borg. His special insight allows Starfleet to gain the upper hand, and the Borg ship explodes, but not before ejecting a smaller, spherical ship which speeds towards earth.

As it appears to flee, the spherical Borg ship creates a temporal vortex. Heading inside, the earth outside begins to change – turning blackened, metallic, a Borg world! It becomes obvious that the Borg sphere has somehow altered earth's past. With little choice, the *U.S.S. Enterprise* follows it through into the temporal vortex before the changes to the timeline can affect the ship and its crew...

The *U.S.S. Enterprise* arrives in Earth's atmosphere on 6 March 2063, the day before the first warp flight and subsequent first contact with an alien species. The Borg sphere is firing repeatedly at an area in Montana. The *U.S.S. Enterprise* manages to destroy it, but not before it does sizeable damage to a complex below.

An Away Team consisting of Picard, *Commander Data, Doctor Crusher* and

Counselor Troi learn that this is the site where Zefram Cochrane, inventor of the warp drive, is constructing his ship, the Phoenix. Unfortunately, the ship, which is built from a leftover Titan Missile, is heavily damaged. Cochrane's assistant, Lily Sloane, is wounded, and Crusher insists on transporting her to sickbay aboard the U.S.S. Enterprise, accompanied by Picard and Data.

On the ground, Cochrane is located. Geordi La Forge and Commander Riker have no choice but to take Cochrane into their confidence. When he is not convinced, they show him the U.S.S. Enterprise through a telescope. Cochrane is told that at 11 o'clock tomorrow, his warp signature will be detected by a ship passing through this sector. That incident will be First Contact with an alien species.

Unfortunately, Cochrane estimates that it will take weeks for him to make repairs to the Phoenix. As First Contact must occur tomorrow for history to remain unchanged, Geordi and Riker assist in the repairs, the benefit of their 24th Century know-how expediting the process.

Back aboard the U.S.S. Enterprise, the crew discover that before the Borg sphere exploded, it was able to transfer something on board. With frightening speed, the Borg take over engineering, converting it into a central hive chamber, beginning to expand outward. Soon, they have taken everything below Deck 22, and power is shut down. When sickbay is overrun, Crusher and Sloane manage to escape with the aid of the

ship's newest feature, an Emergency Medical Holographic Doctor.

Picard leads an attack force with Worf and Data. Although Worf is able to rescue Crusher, Data is captured by the Borg, and Picard and Sloane are trapped, cut off behind enemy lines.

As events transpire in the *U.S.S. Enterprise*, the Zefram Cochrane with whom Geordi works shows himself to be increasingly unlike the Cochrane of history. Although he is remembered as the father of their way of life, the catalyst towards a peaceful Federation, Cochrane himself is a gold-digger, a self-serving capitalist who only wants warp drive for the riches it will bring him. This Cochrane is noticeably uncomfortable with the mantel that history will place on his shoulders.

Inside Engineering, Data is strapped to a table where the Borg attempt to assimilate him. He comes face-to-face with the Borg Queen. Not a separate entity from the collective, she claims to be the collective in its entirety. Although Data can now turn his emotional chip on and off, making his assimilation difficult, the Borg Queen offers

him something extremely seductive – flesh.

Meanwhile, Picard and Sloane use a Dixon Hill holodeck program to aid in their escape from the pursuing Borg. Reaching the bridge, they learn that their enemy plans on converting the deflector dish into an interplexing beacon and sending a message to the Borg of this century, alerting them to the Earth's presence and ordering an immediate invasion.

Picard, Worf, and a crew member named Lieutenant Hawk attempt to stop the Borg in the only way they can. They set out in space suits to climb down the deflector dish and destroy the interplexing beacon. After an intense fight in zero gravity, they cut the deflector dish loose, but the Borg seem to have won control of the ship. The crew feel that the only solution is to set the auto-destruct, but Picard will not stand for it. His

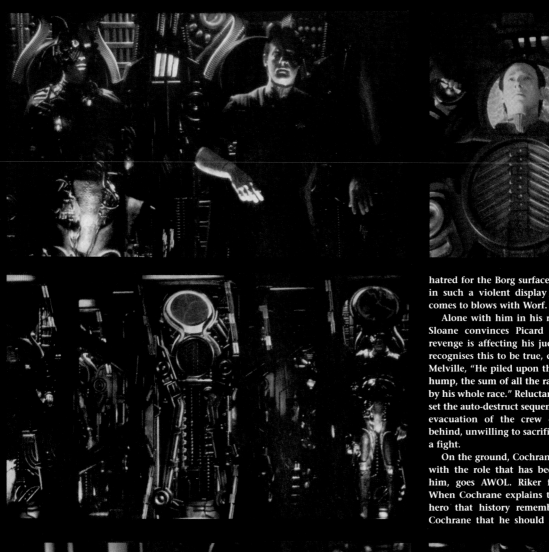

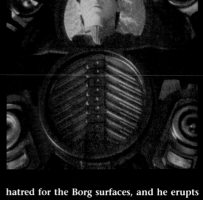

hatred for the Borg surfaces, and he erupts in such a violent display that he almost comes to blows with Worf.

Alone with him in his ready-room, Lily Sloane convinces Picard that desire for revenge is affecting his judgement. Picard recognises this to be true, quoting Herman Melville, "He piled upon the whale's white hump, the sum of all the rage and hate felt by his whole race." Reluctantly, he agrees to set the auto-destruct sequence, ordering the evacuation of the crew – but he stays behind, unwilling to sacrifice Data without a fight.

On the ground, Cochrane, overwhelmed with the role that has been prepared for him, goes AWOL. Riker finds him first. When Cochrane explains that he isn't the hero that history remembers, Riker tells Cochrane that he should not try to be a

way, Data thrusts the Borg Queen into the escaping coolant, killing her, but also melting away all of his own new skin. The Borg Queen dies, and the collective falls apart around her.

The *Phoenix* returns from its first successful jump into warp. On the ground, the *U.S.S. Enterprise* Bridge crew watch from a safe distance as a beautiful alien ship descends to earth and visitors step out onto the ground. As Cochrane steps forward to greet the extraterrestrials, one of them holds up a hand, and parts his fingers in the ceremonial greeting of the Vulcan. History is right on schedule... ∎

hero, only a man, and allow history to make up its own mind. A wise quote, which, it seems, will later be voiced by Cochrane himself. Cochrane returns and together with Geordi and Riker begins the launch of earth's first warp driven ship.

In the engine room, Picard confronts the Queen, and, in exchange for Data's freedom, offers himself as Locutus – the perfect partner for the Queen. But Data has been altered. Now, he is mostly flesh with skin and hair and the resulting feelings and frailties. It seems he has fallen under the Borg Queen's snare, and she no longer needs Locutus for a mate. She directs Data to destroy Cochrane's ship as it prepares to go to warp.

At the moment when all seems lost, Data turns, smashing a coolant tube and releasing a substance that burns away the biological components of the Borg. As Picard climbs out of harm's

COMMANDER WILLIAM RIKER

Jonathan Frakes

Jonathan Frakes laughs.

"Complaints?" he asks, repeating the question just posed to him. "Not one."

And why should he? Not only does Frakes act in *Star Trek: First Contact*, but he realised a dream by directing the film as well. "It is a dream come true," Frakes enthuses. "I wasn't sure I was going to get the job, actually. Time was passing and I didn't think it would happen. As you can only imagine, I was surprised when I got it. We have a terrific script, the entire cast back in action, a wonderful director of photography (Matthew Leonetti) and great sets. We're all doing everything we can to make a good, entertaining movie."

If Frakes' track record as a director is any indication, *ST:FC* should be a winner. After all, the 'Directed by Jonathan Frakes' title card has been attached to such episodes as *The Offspring* from *Star Trek: The Next Generation*, *Meridian* from *Star Trek: Deep Space Nine*, and *Parturition* from *Star Trek: Voyager*. Certainly, Frakes has come a long way in a career that began at Penn State University, in his native Pennsylvania, and continued at Harvard University. It was at the Loeb Drama Center at Harvard that Frakes studied drama before trying his hand at the craft professionally in New York. There, he performed in such off-Broadway productions as *My Life in Art*.

Later, Frakes made the jump to Los Angeles and to television, appearing in such shows as *Falcon Crest, Hill Street Blues* and *The Doctors*. Other credits brought him into first contact with actors he still associates with today. During *Paper Dolls*, Frakes worked with *ST:DS9* star Terry Farrell. While making *Dream West*, he came face-to-face with *ST:FC*'s Borg Queen, Alice Krige. On the *Bare Essence* set, he encountered his future wife, actress Genie Francis, with whom he has a young son, Jameson.

In 1987, Frakes landed the role of William Riker on *ST:TNG* and he has been Picard's loyal Number One ever since. The series also set the stage for Frakes' directing career. "I just get tickled by directing. I don't know

"I just get tickled by directing. I don't know why I waited until so late in life to get hooked on it."

why I waited until so late in life to get hooked on it," he says. "It's really become addictive. It's a wonderful job. I get great joy when things come together on a shot, when the acting is good, the camera movement is good and the energy is right. Those are the moments when all the elements are in place, and *that* is why people direct."

Once *ST:TNG* left the airwaves, Frakes not only directed episodes of *ST:DS9* and *ST:VOY*, but also US television series such as *University Hospital* and *Diagnosis: Murder*, as well as the CD-ROM game, *Star Trek: Klingon*. As an actor, Frakes turned up on *ST:DS9* (*Defiant*), *ST:VOY* (*Death Wish*) and *Super-man: The New Adventures of Lois and Clark*, in which he shared the screen with his wife. He also lends his voice to the evil Xanatos on the current hit animated series, *Gargoyles*, along with fellow *ST:FC* crew members

Marina Sirtis, Brent Spiner and Michael Dorn. Beyond acting and directing, Frakes hosted the documentary television series, *The Paranormal Borderline*.

Frakes is very much indebted to *Star Trek*, his co-stars, the show's producers, and to Trekkers. And he knows it. It's why he continues to direct *Star Trek* episodes, why he occasionally pops up on a current *Star Trek* show, why he participated in the ground-breaking launch of *Star Trek: The Experience*, a theme park ride opening soon in Las Vegas, Nevada, and why he attends so many *Star Trek* conventions. "I'm a very lucky man, very lucky," Frakes says. "My involvement with *Star Trek* has given me a lot of opportunities I never thought I would have. I'm extremely grateful. I can't begin to tell you how grateful I am." ∎

Ian Spelling

A Borg is Born

"At the very beginning, somewhere around February or March of '95" says co-screenwriter Ronald D. Moore, speaking of the conception of *Star Trek: First Contact*, "[Executive Producer] Rick Berman started talking about the next picture to Brannon [Braga] and me. He wanted to do a time travel picture, and he wasn't sure what the story would be or who it would involve. Brannon and I wanted to bring the *Borg* in as villains and do a big action thing. We basically just married those two."

In that way, the basic idea of *Star Trek: First Contact* was born. The next step was to find the Borg's motivation. "It's easy to get to that because their whole thing is to assimilate Humanity and destroy the future. If they can't beat us in the present, they'll go back in time and solve their problem."

Once this basic idea was accepted, Berman, Moore and Braga had to settle on a time period. "We talked extensively at one point about the Italian Renaissance, because that was a period where a lot of scientific discoveries were being made and mankind was coming out of the dark age into an age of enlightenment. Ultimately, it just seemed too removed for the audience, plus, it's a period where some of the costumes might be a problem. We didn't want to see everybody running around in tights, although part of me kind of wishes that we had tried it a little further. Fighting the Borg, a highly technological race, in a low-tech environment, is kind of cool."

After this, the writers discussed various time periods, finally deciding that most of our past has been milked thoroughly by various science fiction series. They chose instead to travel to a past that was still in our future. "In the *Star Trek* history that's already been established, we knew that certain things happened within the next hundred years. There was a third world war, warp drive was invented, first contact was made with an alien race, and most of Humanity's problems started getting solved pretty quickly. The Borg could go back and destroy that piece of mankind's history, at a point where mankind was coming out of a second dark age and about to embark on a journey to the stars. It would be interesting to see the birth of *Star Trek*. That first contact with an alien race is the beginning of Roddenberry's *Star Trek* future."

Initial drafts had *Captain Picard* down on Earth, with *Riker* in charge of protecting the ship from a Borg invasion.

"On the surface of the planet, Picard met up with Lily, who in the early drafts was called Ruby. She was living in a town nearby called Resurrection. That's why the early drafts were called *Star Trek: Resurrection*. In those drafts, *Zefram Cochrane* was basically in a coma. Beverly took him to a hospital, and she had to perform old surgery on him. There were also some futuristic militia groups roaming the countryside that Picard had to fight. Then Picard flew the warp ship himself at the end."

But *ST:FC* wasn't born yet. Neither the writers nor Patrick Stewart were quite happy with the story. "We said, 'Wait a minute! This is about the Borg, for crying out loud! It's weird that we have a picture where Picard is not dealing with the Borg, since he's the one character on the show who has the biggest backstory.' We went 'Duh! What if we just swap Riker and Picard, throw the emphasis upstairs, put Riker down on the planet's surface, wake up Zefram Cochrane, play that for more of a light adventure, and forget about the militias? Make [Cochrane] the B-story, then go upstairs and have Picard facing his greatest nightmare. The Borg are back and they want him and they want his ship.'" ∎

Interview by Lou Anders

> *"Fighting the Borg, a highly technological race, in a low-tech environment, is kind of cool."*

BRANNON BRAGA

Writing from Scratch

Star Trek Generations had to satisfy a number of pre-existing requirements. It had to incorporate certain characters, and it had to serve as a bridge between original series *Star Trek* and *Star Trek: The Next Generation*. By contrast, when Executive Producer Rick Berman approached writers Brannon Braga and Ron Moore about writing a second *Star Trek* film, they began from a blank slate. As Braga explains, "The only dictum was to make this an *ST:TNG* adventure. The three of us knew at the time that we wanted to do the *Borg*, because we were anxious to see the Borg done on the big screen. We felt that they were a villain that still hadn't been fully explored. Time travel came into it because we felt we'd seen the Borg attack Earth in the 24th Century. They knew that they were defeated the last time, so we wondered what would happen if their plan was to go back in time to when Earth still had a lot of technology."

Braga explains the Borg strategy thus: "The Borg would turn to the most technologically advanced time with the least resistance." This time of maximum technology, minimum resistance happened to be the early 21st Century, on an Earth recovering from World War III, at a time when warp drive was about to be discovered. "We had a lot of different time periods, but what makes the time period that we chose unique is that it's never been seen and it's definitely a part of *Star Trek* lore, or at least will be now, after this movie! We thought it would be fun after 30 years of this franchise to see just how it all came to be and put that at stake, so that the audiences' rooting interest is the franchise itself. In a funny way what's at stake in this movie is *Star Trek* itself. If the Borg stop Cochrane from doing his first warp flight and they assimilate Earth, *Star Trek* will never be born. It had a nice self-reflective logic that I think really pays off.

"This movie is about Picard's quest for vengeance as much as anything else," Braga continues, "and his relationship with Lily Sloane, who is, ironically, the woman from the time of war, the 21st Century, the only one who can sense in him this blood lust –

"This movie is about Picard's quest for vengeance as much as anything else."

that's a *huge* arc in the movie." But is having Picard face his Borg nightmare retreading ground already covered in the *ST:TNG* fifth season episode *I, Borg*? "That's a valid point," says Braga. "I'd never even considered it, because we decided basically to ignore *I, Borg* and *Descent, Parts I & II*, because we wanted the Borg to return to their original collective state. I don't think anything was resolved in that show, though. *I, Borg* is more about *Hugh*. It's also about Picard's prejudice. He refuses to acknowledge Hugh as an individual. And even when he does it's begrudging. The bigger question is, is it a redux of *Family* [in which Picard returns home to try and

recover from the ordeal he faced in the now classic Borg story, *The Best of Both Worlds*]? That's *really* where the catharsis took place. Yeah, there's some concern there, but I think it's different. I think that in *Family*, he was basically a rape victim. He was dealing with anger, remorse and violation, but he was dealing with it in a more passive way.

"The movie is more of a *Moby Dick* kind of story. He's vengeful. This is a Picard that is bent on destroying the Borg once and for all, no matter what the cost, even if it means destroying his ship and his crew. It has a different flavour to it, so I'm not too worried." ∎

Interview by Lou Anders

L I L Y   S L O A N E

Alfre Woodard

Alfre Woodard is the new kid on the *Star Trek* block in the new film. The Oscar-nominated actress had never before ventured into cinematic space prior to beaming aboard the *U.S.S. Enterprise* as the tough, acerbic Lily Sloane, an associate of *Zefram Cochrane*, the creator of warp drive. Instead, Woodard was best known for her memorable performances in such films as *Cross Creek, How to Make an American Quilt* and *Grand Canyon*, all of which took place on Earth in the 20th Century. In *Star Trek: First Contact*, however, Woodard makes up for lost time by battling the villainous *Borg*, firing weapons and even getting quite close to none other than *Captain Jean-Luc Picard*.

"It was a great experience for me," enthuses Woodard. "I've always chosen things that interest or excite me. That's what I've done my entire career, really. I got sent the script for *ST:FC* and as I read it I was totally on edge. I was seeing it in my head. It was to the point where I was talking out loud, pulling for some of the characters or gasping at what some of the other characters were doing. When I got to the set, it was a joy as well. I loved working with Jonathan (Frakes), who's my godson, and with Patrick (Stewart). I'm glad I did the film."

Woodard remembers being a little girl who was always running, jumping and pretending to do the kinds of stunts she saw on the television series *I, Spy* and other shows of her youth. Those memories came in handy on the *Star Trek* set. "I had to run all over the place and get pretty dirty," she says, laugh-ing. "I got a few bumps and bruises, but that was OK, because I wanted it to look real. I did as many stunts as I could because I did-n't want to be a weenie. I didn't like the idea of a stunt woman doing the hard stuff, and then me just popping in there, looking all sweaty but having done nothing."

Born and raised in Tulsa, Oklahoma, Woodard attended Boston University before beginning on her path towards an acting career. She has since made her mark on stage, screen and television. Among her television credits are *St. Elsewhere*, on which she was an Emmy Award-nominated series regular. Guest-star roles on *Hill Street Blues* and in the *L.A. Law* pilot earned Woodard Emmy Awards. She has also starred in the television movies *Unnatural Selection* and *Mandela*, in which she portrayed Winnie Mandela opposite Danny Glover as the South African freedom fighter and president. Most recently, Woodard starred in a production of the popular Broadway play, *The Piano Lesson*, and she has completed filming the television movies *Member of the Wedding* and *Miss Evers' Boys*.

Filmgoers will remember Woodard, who lives with her husband and two children in Los Angeles, not only for the films mentioned above (*Cross Creek* won her an Academy Award nomination as Best Supporting Actress), but also for *Primal Fear, Crooklyn, Bopha!, Passion Fish, Blue Chips, Heart and Souls, Scrooged* and *Miss Firecracker*. Asked what Trekkers who might never have heard of Woodard should sample, Woodard suggests the drama *Passion Fish*, the comedy *Miss Firecracker*, and an upcoming feature called *Follow Me Home*, about four graffiti artists from Los Angeles – one Native American, two Latino and one black – who head to Washington, D.C. intent on painting the White House as only they know how.

"All of my films are different," Woodard explains. "*Passion Fish* is different from *Scrooged*, which is different from *Cross Creek*, which was very different from *Star Trek: First Contact*. And I like it that way!" ■

Ian Spelling

> **"I got sent the script for ST:FC and as I read it I was totally on edge."**

STAR TREK FIRST CONTACT

Andy Lane examines *Star Trek: First Contact* and finds some surprising roots for the eighth *Star Trek* movie...

PREVIOUSLY ON *STAR TREK*:

1. The crew of the *Enterprise* NCC-1701 encountered Zefram Cochrane at the end of his life in *Metamorphosis*

2. Jean-Luc Picard was assimilated to become Locutus of Borg in *The Best of Both Worlds* but was able to recover

3. Beverly Crusher was able to induce some self-awareness in the Borg nicknamed Hugh in *I, Borg*

4. Unlike the rest of the crew of the *Enterprise-D*, Worf had not transferred to the *Enterprise-E*, but was part of the crew of *Deep Space Nine*.

I f *Star Trek Generations* was the first movie to be based on the massively successful TV series *Star Trek: The Next Generation* then you could argue that *Star Trek: First Contact* was the first movie to be based on its sibling, *Star Trek: Deep Space Nine*. The fact that neither the space station nor the newly-created characters from *ST:DS9* appear is missing the point. In terms of style and content, *First Contact* has the spirit of *ST:DS9* permeating through every frame.

Despite the appearance of several guest stars from the Original Series, *Generations* replicates the ponderous, even-handed style of the show that spawned it in almost every way. *First Contact*, by contrast, is sleek and fast, centring around the problems caused by a massively traumatic event in the past of one main character – Captain Picard (Patrick Stewart) – and his temporary assimilation by the biomechanical hive-mind known as the Borg, and putting him and his crew through hell while he comes to terms with it. All the events of the movie loop back and connect to this. Rather than containing a battle, the entire film is about a battle – external and internal – which runs more or less from beginning to end, and about the stress that the apparent inevitability of death can cause. It's about grace under pressure, and that, in a nutshell, is what also sets *ST:DS9* apart from the other series.

Star Trek has always toyed with the idea of time travel and its resulting paradoxes, and *First Contact* returns to this theme with a vengeance. However, where, for instance, *Star Trek IV: The Voyage Home* had the crew deliberately travelling back into the past in order to retrieve something which was needed in the future, and trying not to change things while they were there, *First Contact* has them virtually dragged back by the time-travelling Borg (and thankfully the Borg forgot how to do that) in order to deliberately recreate a past that had already been comprehensively rewritten.

Key to the success of the film at the box-office was the relentless unstoppability of the Borg. The originals from the TV series were pasty-faced punk rockers dressed in black PVC; here they actually look like they're decaying in front of our eyes – a look that would, without any explanation, infect the various TV episodes in which they would subsequently appear. We even get to see the mechanism by which the Borg replicate themselves – rather than the surgical technique we had assumed, where limbs and organs are removed and various mechanical appendages grafted on in their place, the process involves a kind-of reverse vampirism, with tiny nano-robots injected into the body via a snake-like pair of tendrils and then reconstructing it from within, melding flesh and mechanism at a molecular level. Which unfortunately doesn't explain how the various Borg fixtures were removed quite so easily from Picard's body, back in the *ST:TNG* episode *The Best of Both Worlds, Part II*, any more than the surgical reconstruction theory does.

Jonathan Frakes directs with a speed and tautness that are, simply, amazing in someone who had only previously directed episodes of TV series. He is aided in this by a script, written by veteran *Star Trek* writers Ronald D. Moore and Brannon Braga, which gives each character something to do while recognizing that this is

ultimately Picard's film. His is the character arc that defines the whole thing. His is the journey we are meant to follow.

Having said that, there is a sub-plot which the film adopts, switching away from Picard's obsessive desire to eradicate the Borg when it becomes too intense. It's the need for Commander Riker (Frakes again) and the team under his command to persuade Zefram Cochrane to complete his first warp drive trial, which they know will bring the planet to the attention of a passing Vulcan ship and thus set up the future the way they remember it. Another example of the revisionist attitude towards the various TV series displayed by the film is the treatment of Zefram Cochrane – feted on TV as the heroic inventor of the warp drive but here an embittered drunk who more or less makes history by accident. Veteran actor James Cromwell puts in a good performance as Cochrane, and Alfre Woodard portrays his minder, and Picard's almost-love interest, Lily Sloane with single-minded enthusiasm, but the prize for most interesting performance has to go to Alice Krige as the Borg Queen. The idea that the Borg even needed a Queen was strange enough, but Krige provides her with a perverse sexuality that brings the film alive, even when she's acting as a disembodied head. In a sense, the film-makers have echoed with the Borg the evolution seen in the *Alien* movies, with a hive of glossy black killers with no personality of their own who inject a little bit of themselves into their prey suddenly given a Mother figure who they protect and who, in turn, protects them. The difference being, of course, that the Borg Queen can argue her own point in a way that the Alien Queen can't, almost turning the android Data against his friends with her persuasive (and probably mechanical) tongue.

The parallels with the *Alien* movies serve to draw attention to the thing that makes *First Contact* so

different from the other movies, and more like *ST:DS9*. *Star Trek* has always been granted citizenship of that country named "science fiction," but that country shares a border on one side with fantasy and on the other with horror. *Star Trek* has typically resided closer to the border with fantasy, with Starfleet personnel displaying what might seem like magical powers (pointing their fingers and making things disappear, disappearing themselves and appearing in other places) and, in turn, coming up against beings with magical powers much greater than theirs. *First Contact* is a deliberate relocation closer to the border with horror. The Borg are zombies, and the crew of the *Enterprise* have to hunt them down and kill them all before they, in turn, are zombified. The film really is that simple.

In its avoidance of simple solutions with no after-effects, and its concentration on one man's flaws, *First Contact* is closer to the ethos of *ST:DS9* than any *Star Trek* film before or since, but there are strangely few references to that show. The U.S.S. *Defiant* – stalwart of *ST:DS9* – makes an appearance and is badly beaten up by the Borg, prompting a character to refer to it as a "tough little ship" (a line requested by the production team on *ST:DS9*, who were unhappy at the way "their" ship had been trashed). Explicit and implicit references in the film are, strangely, aimed more at *Star Trek: Voyager*, which was in its third season when the film premiered. Robert Picardo recreates his character of the *Starship Voyager*'s holographic doctor for a short scene, and Ethan Phillips (the alien trader Neelix in *ST:VOY*) appears as a waiter in a holographic bar.

Ultimately, *First Contact* is unlike any of the other *Star Trek* films. It has a different feel, a different pace, a different engine driving it. The events of the film affect the characters in a way they don't in the other films. It's more visceral, less thoughtful.

And, for those very reasons, it's probably the best.

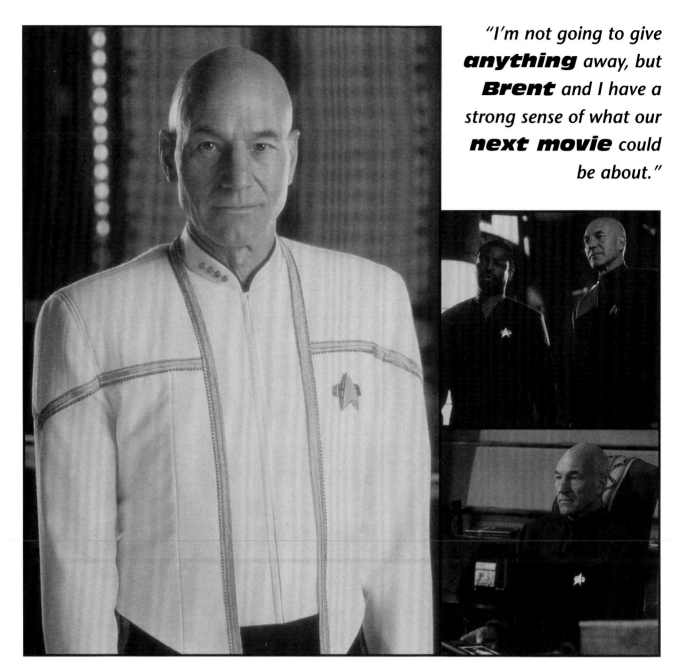

*"I'm not going to give **anything** away, but **Brent** and I have a strong sense of what our **next movie** could be about."*

Patrick Stewart

CAPTAIN JEAN-LUC PICARD

by Ian Spelling

Patrick Stewart, sitting in a chair on the set of *Star Trek: Insurrection*, smiles slyly and reveals a little secret: he and Brent Spiner already have an idea in mind for *Star Trek* 10.

"I'm not going to give anything away, but Brent and I have a strong sense of what our next movie could be about," Stewart taunts. "We've talked a lot about it while filming *Star Trek: Insurrection*. I never had a sense before, with the other movies, where we could go next with Picard in particular or *Star Trek: The Next Generation* in general. It may not happen, but assuming there is a next film, we have a very intriguing idea."

Neither the threat of *Borg* torture nor journalistic arm-twisting convinces Stewart to spill the beans about that *Star Trek X* idea. Better to focus on *Insurrection*. This time around, Captain Picard relinquishes command in order to aid the *Ba'ku*, a race whose planet's fountain of youth-like properties makes it of prime interest to turncoat Starfleet personnel, including *Admiral Dougherty* (Anthony Zerbe), and such alien races as the *Son'a*, led by *Ru'afo* (F. Murray Abraham). As Picard learns of the Ba'ku and their ways, he falls for *Anij* (Donna Murphy), a beautiful Ba'ku woman and one of the leaders of her people.

Stewart jokes that the *ST:TNG* cast, as always, is nothing less than superb. It's the guest cast that the actor believes may catch filmgoers off guard. "One of the great strengths of both *Star Trek Generations* and *Star Trek: First Contact* was our guest stars," he comments. "On *Generations* we had Malcolm McDowell. On *First Contact* we had James Cromwell, Alfre Woodard and Alice Krige. Each made tremendous, distinct contributions. We remembered that going into *Insurrection*. We knew it would be difficult to match the likes of McDowell, Cromwell, Woodard and Krige, but I think we have with Murphy, Zerbe and Abraham. These are powerful actors, each very impressive. And, of course, they all have theater backgrounds. Jonathan (Frakes) always refers to Donna as our 'double Tony Award-winner'. Their impact on *Insurrection* will be as effective as the contributions of the actors I've mentioned from *Generations* and *First Contact*."

Patrick Stewart was born in Mirfield, a small town in the English county of Yorkshire. After studying at the Bristol Old Vic Theatre School, he joined the casts of touring show companies and soon became a member of the Royal Shakespeare Company. Graduating from the stage to the screen, Stewart appeared in such BBC television productions as *I, Claudius* and *Smiley's People*. His early film credits include *Lady Jane, Excalibur, Lifeforce* and *Dune*.

But it was in 1987 that Stewart's life changed forever. Robert Justman, a *Star Trek*: The Original Series producer working with Gene Roddenberry to create something called *Star Trek: The Next Generation*, caught Stewart performing a scene reading in Los Angeles and suggested Roddenberry meet the talented British actor. Roddenberry did and the rest... well, you know the rest.

Stewart went on to forge Jean-Luc Picard into a memorable *Star Trek* hero, a man who's honorable, fierce in battle and fair in negotiation. A captain who earns the utmost respect from his loyal crew. During *ST:TNG*'s seven-year television run, Stewart made time for several non-*Star Trek* projects, including the play *Every Good Boy Deserves Favour*, a one-man production of *A Christmas Carol* (performed in London, Manhattan and Los Angeles), and the films *LA Story* and *Gunmen*.

Once *ST:TNG* completed its television run, Stewart embarked on a busy diet of stage, television and film work. He appeared in such theatrical productions as *The Tempest* and

Othello, and such television programs as *The Canterville Ghost*, *Saturday Night Live* and the mini-series *Moby Dick*. Stewart's film credits include not only *Generations, First Contact* and *Insurrection*, but also *Masterminds, Safe House, Dad Savage* and *Conspiracy Theory*. His commanding voice has been heard in numerous television commercials and specials, not to mention educational CD-ROM games and the animated movies *The Pagemaster* and *The Prince of Egypt*.

So what's next?

"I'm just about to start a new Arthur Miller play called *The Ride Down Mt. Morgan* at the Public Theater in Manhattan, and early next year I'm going to do *A Christmas Carol* as a mini-series for the same people who did *Moby Dick*," he reveals. "I'm also busy at my production company, *Flying Freehold*, developing projects. Paramount just optioned a book for us, *A Conspiracy of Tall Men*, which I hope to produce and act in next year. So, I'm pleased to say that my plate is very, very full." ●

Above left: *Geordi and Picard try to solve the mystery of Data's malfunction*

Left: *A troubled Picard tries to find a way to avert disaster*

Right: *Picard comforts Anij as they are held prisoner by the Son'a*

Below: *Accepting a gift from Regent Cuzar*

Star Trek: Insurrection

On the planet *Ba'ku*, children play in an idyllic village situated at the edge of a clear blue lake. Hidden behind a nearby rock face, a group of Starfleet officers and members of a race called the *Son'a* observe the village, while men in isolation suits walk unnoticed among its inhabitants. Suddenly, an explosion breaks the calm. The rock face shatters, uncovering the observation station and revealing the men in isolation suits.

On board the *U.S.S. Enterprise NCC-1701-E*, *Captain Picard*, *Deanna Troi* and *Dr Crusher* are dressing in formal uniform for a banquet to welcome the *Regent Cuzar* and his people. As they arrive at the banqueting hall, Picard bumps into *Lt. Commander Worf*, who was in the sector installing a new defence perimeter when he heard the *Enterprise* was nearby. Picard invites Worf to stay onboard.

Picard has to cut his meeting with the Regent Cuzar short due to a pressing matter he has to take up with *Geordi La*

Forge, who reports that *Data* has not returned from a mission on the planet Ba'ku, and that Starfleet Admiral Dougherty has requested Data's schematics.

Talking to Dougherty, Picard learns that Data is not responding to hails and is holding Dougherty's people hostage.

The crew of the *Enterprise* are forced to fire on a member of their own crew when Data, having reverted to his ethical and moral subroutines, attempts to protect the Ba'ku but destroy his own people.

Picard agrees to send Dougherty Data's schematics, but plans to 'stop off' at the sector on the way to the Goren System.

On board the Son'a ship, *Ahdar Ru'afo* is having a facial when Dougherty enters to explain what has happened on the planet surface. Suddenly, the Son'a ship is hit by a blast from Dougherty's own scout ship, with Data at the helm.

Meanwhile, on board the *Enterprise*, the crew are conducting research into the Son'a and the Ba'ku planet. When the *Enterprise* arrives at the co-ordinates of the Son'a ship, Picard pleads for his android's life, and manages to negotiate 12 hours to try to get Data off the planet. Worf and Picard take the captain's yacht to find Data's ship and, after a short

battle, manage to capture him before both ships plummet to the planet surface.

Picard, Troi and Crusher beam down to the Ba'ku village. Picard explains to the Ba'ku that they've come to 'rescue' the hostages, but they are met with contempt and resentment by *Anij* and the Ba'ku people, who have rejected technology in favour of a more natural lifestyle.

The *Enterprise* crew return to the ship with the hostages, and are promptly ordered to leave the planet immediately. But Picard has no intention of leaving the system and, armed with proof that it was the Son'a who caused Data to go rogue, returns to the planet surface to investigate. There, he and Data meet *Artim*, a young boy, who leads the officers to the place where he remembers seeing Data. They reach a lake, where Data takes some scans that reveal a submerged, cloaked Federation ship which houses a holographic representation of the Ba'ku village.

Returning to the *Enterprise*, Picard orders Worf to debrief the hostages a second time. Riker appears, clean-shaven, relaying a message from Admiral Dougherty that their 12

Having uncovered a cloaked ship beneath the lake, Data, Anij and Picard row out to investigate, only to find the ship houses a holographic representation of the Ba'ku village – an intended prison for the Ba'ku.

face an angry Picard who wants some answers about the holoship. Dougherty explains he's acting on orders from the Federation Council, telling Picard that the Son'a have found a way to collect metaphysic particles from the planet's rings, and how that could benefit thousands of people on Earth. Picard asks Dougherty to delay the procedure, but Dougherty refuses and demands that Picard leave.

Planning to leave for the planet surface on a personal rescue mission, Picard is discovered by his crew. After some discussion, it is agreed that Worf, Data, Crusher, Troi and Picard will beam down to the planet, while Riker and Geordi take the *Enterprise* out of Ba'ku space. The shuttle is spotted by Ru'afo, who aims to remove the Ba'ku from the planet, even

hours are up, but Picard will not be forced to leave. Dr Crusher tells him that the entire crew have elevated levels of endorphin production, and are in unusually good health. Returning to his quarters, Picard looks in the mirror only to discover that his skin has become tighter and more youthful...

Picard visits the village that evening, where the Ba'ku reveal that they came to the planet over three centuries ago when their world was threatened with destruction. The youthfulness of the people is the result of metaphysic radiation in the planet's rings. Picard realizes that the planet's youth-replenishing properties are endangering the Ba'ku from outsiders, and promises to help them.

Ru'afo and Dougherty pay a visit to the *Enterprise* only to

if it means eliminating the *Enterprise* crew...

On the planet, the *Enterprise* crew evacuate the villagers to safety in the mountains. Data places transport inhibitors around the village to prevent the Son'a from beaming down, but a Son'a ship destroys one of the inhibitors and over 50 villagers are beamed off the surface.

On board the Son'a ship, Ru'afo, Dougherty and Gallatin are angered by the actions of the *Enterprise* officers. They decide to use isolinear tags to lock onto the Ba'ku in order to beam them off the planet.

The people on the planet are now in the foothills of the mountains. Data manages to strike up a conversation with Artim while Picard and Anij, who are leading the procession, sit down to rest. As they flirt, Anij takes Picard's hand. They kiss, and Picard experiences a new emotional perspective.

A dozen Son'a ships suddenly appear over the horizon and start dropping flying drones which target the Ba'ku with isolinear tags. In seconds, people start to disappear. The Ba'ku panic and rush to hide in nearby caverns, but Son'a troops begin to land on the planet. As a fight breaks out, one Son'a is wounded, and when Dr Crusher scans him, she discovers something incredible. She shows Picard, but before they have time to discuss the readings, there is a blast near-

While Picard, Worf, Crusher, Data and Troi herd the villagers to safety on the planet, Riker captains the *Enterprise*-E in a mission to alert Starfleet to the impending threat to the planet Ba'ku.

by and a cave collapses in on Anij and Picard.

Meanwhile, on board the *Enterprise*, Riker and Geordi are being pursued by two Son'a ships. The Son'a detonate an isolytic burst which creates a tear in subspace, and the *Enterprise* is forced to eject the warp core to prevent them from sliding into it. In retaliation, Geordi collects metreonic gas which creates an explosion and destroys the ships.

Safely extracted from the rubble, Picard and Anij are making their way further up the mountains when a group of drones appears in front of them. Panic ensues as the drones open fire on the people. Picard and Anij are tagged and dematerialize...

They find themselves on board the Son'a ship, where they are greeted by Dougherty, who tells Picard he can avoid a court-martial if he orders the Ba'ku to surrender. The captain will not comply, however, even when Ru'afo announces that he plans to strip the planet's rings, despite the consequences to the Ba'ku people still on the surface...

Picard suddenly asks Ru'afo if he is prepared to kill his own people. He explains to an astounded Dougherty that the Ba'ku and the Son'a are the same race. Ru'afo, his secret exposed, reveals that a century ago a group of young Ba'ku tried to take over the colony and, when they failed, were exiled. Dougherty tells Ru'afo that the mission is over and he is leaving, but Ru'afo kills Dougherty and orders Gallatin to carry out the mining of the rings.

With three minutes to go before Ru'afo's particle collector is launched, the captain's yacht appears, firing seemingly harmless tachyon bursts at the ship. Data is at the helm. After a while, Ru'afo realizes that Data's actions are disrupting the Son'a's shields, and orders the yacht's destruction...

Suddenly, there is a flash on the bridge of the Son'a ship. The mining process has begun, but a Son'a officer soon real-

izes that nothing is happening – the ship's functions are off-line. They discover that Picard and Data have transported them to the holoship where the simulation is playing out...

Meanwhile, on board the Son'a ship, Gallatin secures the bridge from the Son'a crew. Ru'afo beams over to the collector and begins the countdown from there. Picard tries to destroy the collector but is unable to and, realizing the launch sequence has begun again, beams himself over to the collector. On the Son'a bridge, the doors burst open and sol-

diers stream in, attacking Gallatin and Worf. The *Enterprise* arrives at the scene and rushes to Picard's aid.

Picard reaches the collector's control matrix, but the *Enterprise* is now under attack from the Son'a ship. Riker sets a collision course for the ship, forcing the Son'a to veer off side. Meanwhile, on the collector, Picard and Ru'afo have been fighting and a shot has been fired, causing explosions on the collector. With the countdown at nine seconds, the *Enterprise* arrives. There is an explosion at the far end of the collector and a fireball approaches. The *Enterprise* races towards Picard, attempting to beat the fireball and, as the explosion reaches the captain's position, he is beamed off less than a second before Ru'afo is hit by the explosion. The collector is blown apart by the explosion and destroyed, and Worf and the Ba'ku are beamed over to the *Enterprise*.

The *Enterprise* crew return to the planet to bid farewell to the Ba'ku people. Anij and Picard say good-bye, and, as the crew prepare to beam up, realize that Data is missing. The android is playing in a haystack with Artim and some other children. Data takes leave of his new-found friend, Picard and Anij exchange a final look, and the crew depart. ●

The crew take one last look at the peaceful, natural world of Ba'ku as they depart for Federation space, mission accomplished.

Tales of the Script

Star Trek: Insurrection script-writer Michael Piller discusses the origin of the story

MICHAEL PILLER

> "Once the **characters** are **inside** you I don't think they go **away**."

Michael Piller is back, although he might argue that he never really left.

Piller is of course one of the writer-producers considered responsible for helping to transform *Star Trek: The Next Generation* into the successful, respected show it became over the years. He also co-created and co-produced both *Star Trek: Deep Space Nine* and *Star Trek: Voyager*, and wrote some of the most acclaimed episodes of both shows.

The writer-producer essentially left the *Star Trek* fold a few years ago in order to pursue projects of his own, among them the popular but short-lived action-adventure series *Legend*, which starred Richard Dean Anderson and John de Lancie of Q fame. Although Piller serves as a consultant on *ST:DS9* and *ST:VOY*, he has not been a day-to-day presence on the set since his departure, and he had nothing at all to do with the

ST:TNG film series... until now, that is. Piller is the man responsible for penning the script for *Star Trek: Insurrection*.

"What's the right metaphor to use?" Piller asks aloud, as he tries to answer the question of what it was like to write again for characters he once knew so intimately. "Once the characters are inside you I don't think they go away. I was quite ready to come back. It was time." As for the difference between writing for the big screen as opposed to the small screen, Piller comments that "You're starting with a movie screen and you have to fill it. There are certain expectations that everybody starts with in terms of action and set pieces, if

by Ian Spelling

These pages: *Piller's return to the* Star Trek *universe gave him the chance to write for some characters with whom he had not been intimate since his time on* ST:TNG, *and one or two more familiar ones...*

you will. But aside from all of that, aside from the fact that as a given you have millions of dollars to spend properly [scripting a movie], it really isn't very different in terms of the writer's process. I still start with the same questions. What is this movie going to be about? What makes it interesting for me to write it? What is the quality of Human nature that I want to explore here? That's where I always start from."

Michael Piller was born in New York and graduated from the University of North Carolina at Chapel Hill in 1970. He then worked as a television journalist in Chicago, New York and North Carolina. While in Chicago, he began to produce local news programs. He quickly grew restless and relocated to

Los Angeles in order to try his hand at the entertainment industry. He found work as a CBS censor, then started to write scripts for such shows as *Cagney & Lacey* and *Simon & Simon*, and was soon working as a producer-writer on *Miami Vice* and *Hard Time on Planet Earth*.

It was while working on *Planet Earth* that Piller met then-*ST:TNG* producer Maurice Hurley, who put him in touch with Gene Roddenberry. Shortly thereafter, Piller was assigned to write the episode *Evolution*, and Rick Berman soon invited Piller to join *ST:TNG* as a co-executive producer supervising the show's writing staff.

Piller wrote scripts of his own and did uncredited rewrites

on a good many others. Among the most well-regarded episodes bearing Piller's by-line are *The Best of Both Worlds, Part 1 & 2, Unification, Part 1 & 2* and *Ensign Ro*. When the time came to launch *Star Trek: Deep Space Nine*, Piller joined with Berman to create and produce the series, as well as write multiple episodes, including the series pilot, *Emissary*, and *The Siege*. He then teamed up with Berman and Jeri Taylor for *Star Trek: Voyager* two years later, with Piller contributing such scripts as that for the pilot, *Caretaker*, and Q's first visit to the Delta Quadrant, *Death Wish*.

Right now, Piller is busy with a variety of projects. He's still hoping to sell a major US television network his idea for a series about the first television set on the block, and he recently sold a 'spy-action-comedy-adventure' concept to the US cable television network Showtime. He's also developing other ideas to pitch to the television networks, and is working on a book about the screen writing process in general and his experience with *Star Trek: Insurrection* in particular. In the meantime, he, like everyone else who appreciates *Star Trek*, is awaiting the response to *Star Trek: Insurrection*.

"I've seen a rough cut of the film, and it works," he enthuses. "[At the time of this interview] I haven't seen any of the special effects or heard any of the music. It's been screened for the studio and I don't know how that went, but what I have seen is a solid movie. So, I'm quite pleased." ●

"[*Jonathan Frakes* is] the king of *flattery* and the greatest camp *counselor* you could ever *fantasize* about."

Donna Murphy

A N I J

by Ian Spelling

"To be totally honest," admits Donna Murphy, **"I'd only seen fragments of episodes of the different *Star Trek* shows. I was a little more familiar with *Star Trek: Deep Space Nine* and *Star Trek: Voyager* because I've known other actors who've been on those shows. As a kid I'd seen parts of episodes of the original show. I just didn't watch that much of anything regularly on television.**

Left: *Anij consoles some frightened children in the caves on Ba'ku*

Above right: *A trust forms between Anij and the Starfleet captain she at first felt threatened by...*

Right: *... which soon grows into something much deeper*

Below: *Picard helps Anij to defend her world from the Son'a onslaught*

"I have friends who are *big* Star Trek fans, especially of *Star Trek: The Next Generation*. As an actor I was aware of the actors on the newer *Star Trek* shows, but I was ignorant, quite frankly, about the genre and about the specifics of the world Gene Roddenberry created, that has grown and grown and grown through the years."

Ignorant until now, that is.

Murphy, of course, dives head first into the *Star Trek* universe with her turn as Anij, the 300-plus-year-old Ba'ku woman who melts *Captain Picard*'s (Patrick Stewart) heart in *Star Trek: Insurrection*. To prepare for her audition, Murphy remembers, she read the passages of the *Insurrection* script made available to her and also rented *Star Trek Generations* and *Star Trek: First Contact*. Once she won the role of Anij, Murphy delved deeper into *Star Trek* history, renting episodes of both the original *Star Trek* series and *ST:TNG*.

And what did Murphy take away from her immersion into the 24th Century? "I came away with a feeling that *Star Trek* was fantasy with a consistent kind of approach to the philosophy behind it, if that makes any sense. What I mean to say is that *Star Trek* is *about* something," she explains. "There's a core belief system behind it and every show and movie tries to express that and build on that."

Murphy speaks enthusiastically of her own *Star Trek* experience. She reports that she and Patrick Stewart got on famously and that the relationship between Picard and Anij

is "sensual, romantic and intimate." She calls director Jonathan Frakes "the king of flattery and the greatest camp counselor you could ever fantasize about." And the actress points to all the firsts that making *Insurrection* resulted in: her first trip on a helicopter, her first time shooting scenes in a water tank (and using a water gun to douse Stewart and Brent Spiner), and her first film that will involve such merchandising elements as official magazines, action figures and trading cards. "I can tell you this," the actress notes, "I'm very glad I made the decision to do *Star Trek: Insurrection!*"

Donna Murphy was born in Corona, New York, and raised in both Hauppauge, New York and Topsfield, Massachusetts. She knew early on that performing would be her calling and wasted no time in pursuing a career as an actress. It wasn't long before she landed work as an understudy during the Broadway run of *They're Playing Our Song*. To make money during the slower times, Murphy worked as a singing waitress and sang advertising jingles. Her big break came when she assumed the lead role from Betty Buckley in the Broadway production of *The Mystery of Edwin Drood*.

Murphy has been employed steadily ever since. She's a regular on the Broadway stage and has won Tony Awards for Best Actress in a Musical for both *Passion* and *The King & I*. Appropriately enough, Murphy can be heard on the cast recordings of *Passion* and the *King & I*, as well as on Leonard Bernstein's *New York*.

For the small screen, Murphy's credits include *Someone Had To Be Benny*, an hour-long program for which she won a Daytime Emmy Award and a CableAce Award, the TV movie *The Day Lincoln Was Shot* (in which she portrayed Mary Todd Lincoln), and guest starring roles on the series *Murder One*, *Ally McBeal*, *The Practice*, *Remember Wenn* and *Nothing Sacred*. Her films include the thriller *Jade* and the upcoming release *The Astronaut's Wife*, with Johnny Depp and Charlize Theron.

"Right now, I'm looking for my next big theater project," Murphy says. "I do hope to do more films, too. Really, the fun for me is going back and forth between the stage and the screen." ●

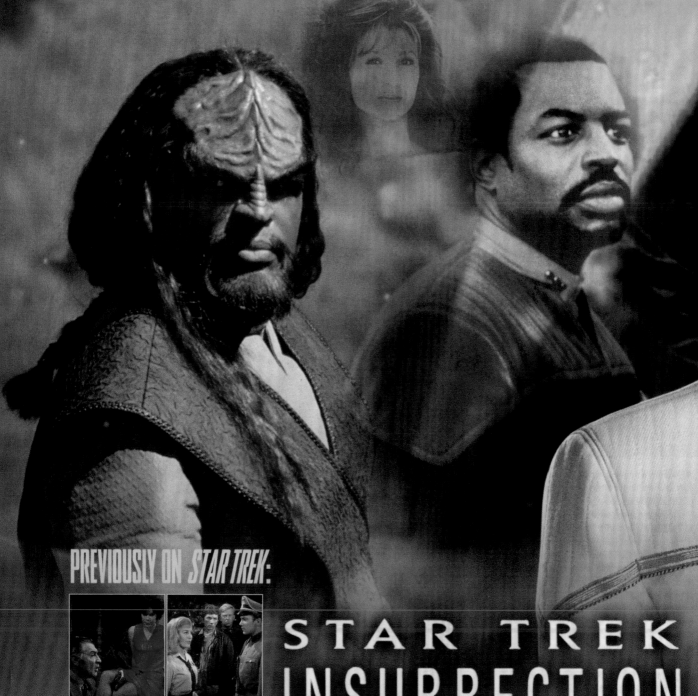

PREVIOUSLY ON *STAR TREK*:

1. The *Enterprise NCC-1701* encountered societies that had been unduly influenced in *A Piece of the Action*...

2. ...and *Patterns of Force*...

3. ...while Jean-Luc Picard and the crew of the *Enterprise-D* battled a violation of the Prime Directive in *Homeward*.

STAR TREK
INSURRECTION

Star Trek: Insurrection isn't a great movie, but it's terrific *Star Trek*, a refreshing change of pace after *Star Trek: First Contact*, and perhaps the most undeservedly overlooked of all 10 films. In fact, of the four *Star Trek: The Next Generation* adventures, *Insurrection* comes closest to capturing the spirit of the franchise's original concept. Scripted by Michael Piller and directed by the returning Jonathan Frakes, *Insurrection* finds Picard and company stumbling upon a Fountain of Youth-like planet – and a whole mess of trouble – when they beam down to check on a malfunctioning Data. Danger lurks in, around and even above this paradise thanks to corrupt Starfleet higher-ups and an alien character keen on reversing the ravages of time.

Insurrection plays like a top-drawer, unproduced *ST:TNG* episode. It's loaded with trippy sci-fi concepts (metaphasic radiation), lush cinematography, good old-fashioned Prime Directive debates (forced relocation, yea or nay?), and so earthy-crunchy are the Ba'ku they'd feel right at home in a first season original series episode. There's also a bit of action, the sight of the reunited Riker and Troi together in a bathtub, and dashes of humor, most of which work, including an outlandish Gilbert & Sullivan sing-along between Picard and Data. On the other hand, even diehard fans cringe during the scenes in which Data frolics in the hay with a Ba'ku boy or Worf deals with a case of Klingon puberty. Oscar winner F. Murray Abraham plays the aforementioned alien, Ru'afo, and he not only chews the scenery with abandon, but his scenes with Patrick Stewart amp up the tension as words give way to a wild chase and fight to the death as the film builds to a climax. Bottom line: Gene Roddenberry would've loved *Insurrection*.

Ian Spelling

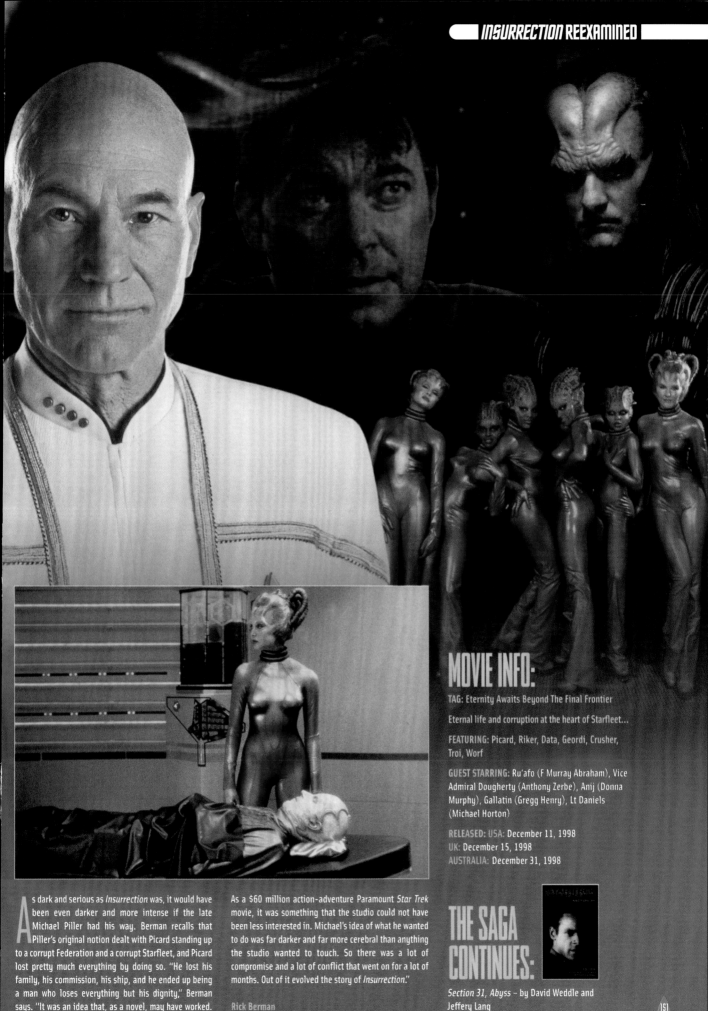

MOVIE INFO:

TAG: Eternity Awaits Beyond The Final Frontier

Eternal life and corruption at the heart of Starfleet...

FEATURING: Picard, Riker, Data, Geordi, Crusher, Troi, Worf

GUEST STARRING: Ru'afo (F Murray Abraham), Vice Admiral Dougherty (Anthony Zerbe), Anij (Donna Murphy), Gallatin (Gregg Henry), Lt Daniels (Michael Horton)

RELEASED: USA: December 11, 1998
UK: December 15, 1998
AUSTRALIA: December 31, 1998

A s dark and serious as *Insurrection* was, it would have been even darker and more intense if the late Michael Piller had his way. Berman recalls that Piller's original notion dealt with Picard standing up to a corrupt Federation and a corrupt Starfleet, and Picard lost pretty much everything by doing so. "He lost his family, his commission, his ship, and he ended up being a man who loses everything but his dignity," Berman says. "It was an idea that, as a novel, may have worked.

As a $60 million action-adventure Paramount *Star Trek* movie, it was something that the studio could not have been less interested in. Michael's idea of what he wanted to do was far darker and far more cerebral than anything the studio wanted to touch. So there was a lot of compromise and a lot of conflict that went on for a lot of months. Out of it evolved the story of *Insurrection*."

Rick Berman

THE SAGA CONTINUES:

Section 31, Abyss – by David Weddle and Jeffery Lang

151

JEAN-LUC PICARD

FAMILY VALUES

Although the film is packed with action, the story has a very familial feel for our good Captain Jean-Luc Picard, played by **Patrick Stewart**. First, his *Enterprise* family is breaking up, then he meets a brother he never knew he had, as **Abbie Bernstein** discovers...

amily has always been a complex issue for Jean-Luc Picard, exerting a subtle and powerful influence on his life – even if this is not always immediately evident in an overview of his many years as one of the most famous and history-making captains in the annals of not only Starfleet, but the Federation itself.

A chronicle of Picard's career would suggest that he has found fulfilment married to his duty as the captain of the *U.S.S. Enterprise NCC-1701-D* and *E*. In one sense, this is no doubt true – although not given to displays of emotion, Picard considers the crew his family and he has always put them, his ship and his mission before any personal considerations.

However, he is not immune to regret for what might have been. Once asked if he ever wished for children, Picard replied, "Wishing for a thing does not make it so."

Picard's devotion to Starfleet caused a rift with his biological family. Picard's father, Maurice, disapproved of technology in general and was disappointed when Picard entered Starfleet, instead favouring Jean-Luc's brother Robert, who inherited the family vineyard in France. In contrast, Jean-Luc Picard graduated from Starfleet Academy and progressed to the position of first officer and commander on the Federation ship *U.S.S. Stargazer*, which he eventually captained. When

the *Stargazer* was lost, an inquiry ruled Picard blameless in the matter. He was given command of the *Enterprise-D* in 2363.

During his tenure as captain, Picard has had various experiences of being a family man – *Star Trek: The Next Generation* episodes *The Inner Light* and *Family* and *Star Trek Generations*, among them – but with the emergence of Shinzon, a young man who bears Picard's DNA, in *Star Trek Nemesis* he is confronted not only with his exact copy, but one that's gone bad too!

Actor Patrick Stewart has enjoyed this little encounter with his younger, badder self: "[Screenwriter] John Logan has given me some fun

"[*Star Trek Nemesis*] is significantly more action based... It is a combination of action and perhaps psychological warfare."

'EXCLUSIVE PIC!'

things to say and to do, but also, in the three or four critical scenes between myself and Shinzon, he has written a subtlety into their relationship and into the psychology of those scenes, which is very distinctive and very typical of John." We haven't seen this side of Picard before, Stewart promises: "It's different in tone."

As he told *STAR TREK Monthly*: "[*Star Trek Nemesis*] is significantly more action-based... It is a combination of action and perhaps psychological warfare... I think what we have with *Nemesis* is really quite distinct... The story has some excellent surprises in it, unexpected turns and twists."

As well as facing himself, so to speak, a familial connection is continued throughout the film, with Captain Picard set to lose some of his *Enterprise-E* family to other ships. Such is the bond between the senior staff, that Picard even makes the best man's speech at the wedding of Counselor Deanna Troi and Commander William Riker.

Stewart jokes that he feels the movie doesn't go far enough in exploring the bonds between Picard and his crew: "When you look at it, clearly that was a bad error of judgement, not to have us all at the wedding night. I've always said this is an ensemble, but for some reason I don't fully

understand, we were not in the bed [with Riker and Troi]. We weren't even in the suite."

In real life, family is very important to Stewart. "One of my children made me a grandfather two years ago, and the other one will make me a grandfather in December. I told them, 'I will tell you when I am ready to be a grandfather.' But it doesn't work that way," he laughs. He recalls flying from Los Angeles to England on the occasion of the birth of his first grandchild and receiving a cell phone call upon arrival. "When I heard those words, 'Congratulations, you're a grandfather,' I just broke down in tears." ■

Hell is DARK

THE *STAR TREK NEMESIS* PLOT

Here is a very diluted synopsis of the 10th movie in the *Star Trek* filmography – well, we don't want to give everything away! Major plot points are revealed in this section, so don't read if you haven't seen the film and don't want the surprises ruined...

EXCLUSIVE PIC!

The film opens with the Romulan Senate in full session. One of the senators must rush off to another appointment, but leaves behind a box. A few minutes later and the box opens; there is a flash of light and all of a sudden the Senate is dissolved – literally!

The story then moves to Earth, where a special celebration is happening – the marriage of Deanna Troi and William Riker. Captain Picard is looking stressed, after all the best man's speech has fallen

to him. After he speaks eloquently about his two colleagues and friends, the party kicks into gear, with friends old and new enjoying the celebration.

Meanwhile, back on Romulus, the new Praetor Shinzon is revealing some of his plans for the Federation to the Romulan commanders, whose support helped him seize power. They are unhappy about being kept in the dark, but as Shinzon tells them: The time they have dreamed of is at hand. The time of the conquest of the Federation.

Back on board the *U.S.S. Enterprise NCC-1701-E*, the crew is preparing to celebrate the Rikers' wedding on Betazed, which traditionally means they will all have to appear naked! While *en route*, the ship picks up a positronic signal coming from a nearby planet, which can mean only one thing – the existence of another android like Data. With transporters unable to penetrate the atmosphere, Captain Picard, Data and Worf take a shuttle down to the planet and use a new piece of starship

EXCLUSIVE PIC!

1. A young Shinzon meets his Reman mentor.

2. The Romulan Senate meets.

3. Captain Picard gives his best man's speech at the Rikers' wedding reception.

4. Geordi discovers a strange signal coming from a nearby planet.

5. Worf, Data and Picard make a shocking discovery, before being attacked by alien bandits.

6. Geordi reassembles B-4.

7. Picard receives his orders from Admiral Janeway.

hardware, the *Argo*, a land vehicle, which is perfect for the desert landscape. They discover an exact replica of Data, scattered in pieces around the planet, but before they can make an assumption about its origins, alien bandits attack them. After an exciting race, they make it back to the shuttle and blast off back to the *Enterprise-E*. Geordi and Data reassemble the android and it reveals itself to be called B-4. It is a prototype to Data, and a rather simple one at that – a calculator with legs.

On the bridge, Picard receives a priority one transmission from Starfleet headquarters. It's Admiral Kathryn Janeway with orders to redirect the *Enterprise-E* to Romulus – the new Praetor wishes to put an end to hostilities between the Romulan Star Empire and the Federation. As Captain Picard says: "It seems we're truly sailing into the unknown." The naked wedding celebration will have to wait!

When the ship arrives at Romulus, it is met by the *Scimitar*, a gigantic Warbird that dwarfs the *Sovereign*-class Federation starship. Picard, Riker, Troi, Worf and Data beam over, where they meet Shinzon, the Viceroy and the rest of the Remans, who, because of their homeworld, are sensitive to bright light. Shinzon extends the hand of peace, but at the same time seems fascinated with Troi, the first human (or more specifically, half-human) female he has ever seen. He also reveals his origins – he's a clone of Jean-Luc Picard, genetically created to replace

the Federation's Picard with a Romulan agent. When the plan was abandoned, he was forced into exile on the planet Remus, where he became a Reman slave in the dark pits of its mines. Picard is shocked and tells Shinzon there is much to discuss before departing.

Later that night, the Rikers are settling in to enjoy their wedding night, when things turn sour. Using a telepathic link created by the Reman Viceroy, Shinzon is attempting to violate Troi, body and soul. She fights back, breaking the mental link.

Meanwhile, the Romulan commanders, especially Donatra, are starting to express doubt over

Shinzon's plans. Will he really be able to destroy the Federation? And what will happen to the Romulans, so long the oppressors of the Remans? While they ponder their future, B-4 suddenly becomes active on the *Enterprise-E* and starts to download information from the computer. Picard is also starting to express concern over Shinzon's motive for peace, especially when he discovers that the *Scimitar* is exuding Thaloran radiation, an extremely dangerous and volatile substance, banned in the Federation.

Troi is relating her story to Picard in Sickbay, when he suddenly dematerializes… only to appear

onboard the *Scimitar*. With the Reman ship cloaked and undetectable by scanners, Shinzon reveals his plan to kill Captain Picard. It seems that Shinzon is not a perfect copy after all, and needs to replace his DNA with Picard's.

B-4 turns up, having broken into the *Enterprise-E* computer and discovered the whereabouts of all Federation starships in the quadrant. However, it's really Data in disguise and he helps Picard escape in a stolen *Scorpion*-class attack fighter. Once safely aboard their starship, it zips to warp to meet up with the rest of the fleet to prepare for Shinzon's attack on Earth – he

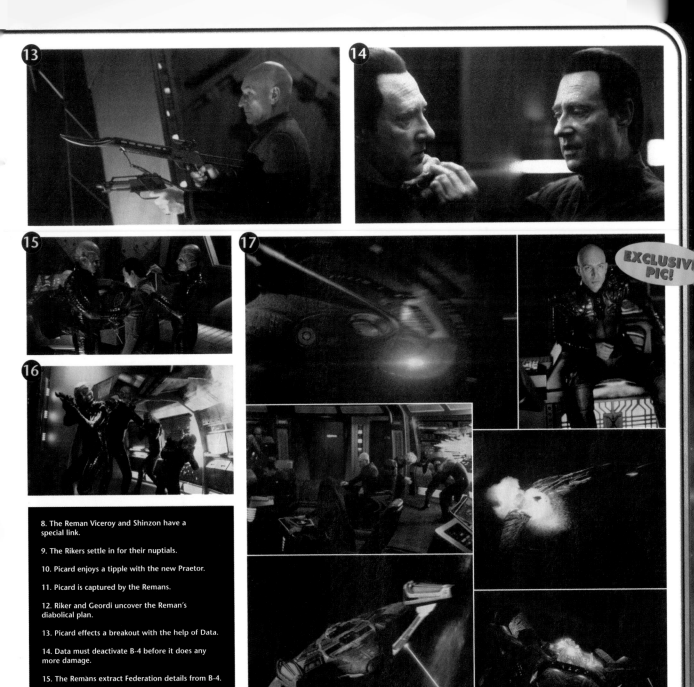

EXCLUSIVE PIC!

8. The Reman Viceroy and Shinzon have a special link.

9. The Rikers settle in for their nuptials.

10. Picard enjoys a tipple with the new Praetor.

11. Picard is captured by the Remans.

12. Riker and Geordi uncover the Reman's diabolical plan.

13. Picard effects a breakout with the help of Data.

14. Data must deactivate B-4 before it does any more damage.

15. The Remans extract Federation details from B-4.

16. The Remans board the *Enterprise-E*.

17. Let the battle commence!

intends to use the Thaloran weapon to kill all life on the planet.

To save time, the *Enterprise-E* cuts across a rift in space. It's a tactical error though as the comm system is disabled while the ship is in the rift. Immediately, the cloaked *Scimitar* attacks. The *Enterprise-E* is helpless against the Reman ship's attacks and looks doomed, until two Romulan Warbirds decloak and attempt to help. It seems the Romulans have made their choice.

A huge space battle follows, with the *Scimitar* looking dominant. Its ability to fire while cloaked is a distinct advantage and it's not long

before the Warbirds are crippled too. Deanna is their only hope – she must telepathically link to the Reman Viceroy to discover his ship's position. She locks on quantum torpedoes and fires, disabling the *Scimitar*'s cloak and evening the odds a little.

Reman soldiers board the *Enterprise-E*, led by the inflamed Viceroy, and Riker and Worf take command of the security teams to defend the ship. The fight is fierce, and the Viceroy attempts to escape via a Jefferies tube, but Riker heads him off and, in the darkness of the ship's tunnels, the two are left to fight to the death.

Meanwhile, the *Scimitar* is being repaired and its cloak is almost working again. In a desperate attempt to keep the odds even, Captain Picard orders ramming speed and the *Enterprise-E* charges at the Reman ship. Picard then beams over to prevent Shinzon from activating the Thaloran generator and thus killing them all, but with power available for a single transport, it's a one-way trip.

Will this really be the end of Picard, or does Data have one final trick up his sleeve? ∎

FULL ENGLISH

Brit director **Stuart Baird** is bringing something new to the *Star Trek* breakfast table, a franchise he readily admits he had little knowledge about pre-*Star Trek Nemesis*. **Ian Spelling** enjoys a taste of what's to come...

When he was tapped by *Paramount Pictures* to direct *Star Trek Nemesis*, Stuart Baird recalls, he was tasked with the following challenge: to break the mould a little bit without breaking the tea set. So, just how tricky a mission was that to pull off? "Well, that analogy is about right," Baird says with a laugh.

"*Star Trek Nemesis* is a *Star Trek* movie. It had to be. The characters are *Star Trek* people. The ethos, the philosophy, is definitely *Star Trek*. What I was bringing to it, or trying to bring to it with my sensibilities and my cameraman [Jeff Kimball] and some of the other people that I brought in, was a fresh look at it. Without breaking the mould, we wanted to give it a little more of an edge, a slightly darker feel to it.

"As I'm directing, a part of me is going to be there, and since I'm not a part of the *Star Trek* past and I didn't know the show at all, something new had to come out of that. I'm another element in the equation."

Star Trek Nemesis tracks the action and the emotions that ensue when Captain Picard comes face to face with Shinzon, a Picard clone with a Napoleon complex and the power to bring about the demise of Picard, the *U.S.S. Enterprise NCC-1701-E* and the entire Federation. Another key facet of the story finds Data coming face to face with, in a sense, a clone of his own. The B-4 is an android fashioned in Data's image, but never quite finished. Data, not too surprisingly, takes it upon himself to try to complete the B-4, even

though it's being used as bait to lure Picard and his crew to their deaths.

All of the various events – not to mention the wedding of Riker and Troi and the career aspirations of his long-loyal crew – weigh heavily on Picard as he contemplates the loss of those he loves and questions, as he looks into Shinzon's jealous and enraged eyes, the life he's led and the life he might have led.

A look at Baird's credits – the Englishman directed the features *US Marshals* and *Executive Decision* and edited *The Omen*, *Superman I* and *II*, *Outland*, *Ladyhawke*, *Demolition Man* and *Tomb Raider*, among others – would suggest that he's the right man for the *Star Trek Nemesis* job. On the other hand, it's been said that editing has

> **"I've given it my 110 per cent. I've given it everything I've got both as a director and as an editor. It's very exciting. It's very touching. It's got a good story, and it's very emotionally involving."**

everything and nothing at all to do with directing a film.

"You're right," Baird acknowledges without hesitation. "Editing has everything and nothing to do with it. Editing gives me a great sort of security. I have a strong sense of how something is going to go together, how I will structure it. But directing is getting performances, getting emotion out of those performances, and it's also getting the footage you need in order to put together the film.

"A lot of directors have been editors to begin with, and a lot of them haven't. I don't know if it necessarily makes you a better director, having been an editor. The editing craft doesn't help you learn how to get performances from a group of actors. Directing is about telling the story, and bringing out the emotions in the script through the performances of the actors."

Baird worked closely with the *Star Trek: The Next Generation* regulars to help them fine-tune their performances to meet the specific demands of the *Star Trek Nemesis* story. The director reports that he also collaborated from start to finish with executive producer Rick Berman, who's guided the *Star Trek* franchise for more than 15 years, and John Logan, the Oscar-nominated screenwriter and long-time *ST:TNG* fan who penned the *Nemesis* script.

In the end, Baird believes all the pieces fell into place accordingly and that he indeed broke the mould without trashing the tea set beyond recognition. "I think that *Star Trek Nemesis* is going to be good," he says. "I think it works. The people who've seen it at the studio seem to think it works. I think the studio feels confident about it in terms of the pacing and storytelling. We haven't screened the picture yet for an audience. I usually like to test my films with regular moviegoers. Maybe we'll do one screening just before release, to make sure that we've got it right.

"I've given it my 110 per cent. I've given it everything I've got both as a director and as an editor. It's very exciting. It's very touching. It's got a good story, a quite intricate story, and it's very emotionally involving. I would say that *Star Trek Nemesis* is a very full and hopefully very entertaining one hour and 50 minutes." ■

ROMULAN REDEEMER

He's the self-confessed Trekkie who was given the chance to realize a dream by creating his own *Star Trek* story — and he's brought his favourite *Star Trek* baddies to the party. **Abbie Bernstein** talks to Praetor **John Logan**...

"There are two kinds of *Star Trek* people," *Star Trek Nemesis* screenwriter John Logan asserts, talking on the set of the latest *Star Trek* movie. No, he's not talking about the distinction between casual and hardcore fans, *Star Trek: The Original Series* or *Star Trek: The Next Generation* fans, or anything so trivial. "There are Klingon people and there are Romulan people.

"I love Worf and I particularly love Dornie [Michael Dorn], and I loved Suzie Plakson as K'Ehleyr and I even liked the Alexander subplot, but I'm not a Klingon person. When you go back to the Roddenberry paradigm of the Klingons being Communist Russia and the Romulans being the Communist Chinese, to me the Communist Chinese were much more interesting, because

there's a sophistication, there's an elegance, there's a sort of lethal serpent-like quality to the way they conduct their politics that, for me, is just fascinating. I've always thought the Romulans were underused."

It's logical, then, that when the Oscar-nominated co-writer of *Gladiator* got the chance to pitch a *Star Trek* film to producer Rick Berman, the Romulans would loom large in the plot. "One of my first ideas when I came in to see Rick was the Remans and the Romulans, because I find them just beautifully seductive, more than the Klingons, who are strong and powerful and blood-pumping. The Romulans are more self-contained and also more verbally eloquent and interesting. And they have hygiene, which is

good. I've probably offended the half of you who are Klingon people."

Although Romulans are crucial to the plot of the new film, the nemesis of the title is actually a human with ties to Romulus' sister planet Remus. "I wanted a young, sexy male villain," Logan says, "we'd never had that before. I wanted a personal connection that Picard couldn't look away from."

Logan, who began his career as a playwright and has written films including *Any Given Sunday* and the recent *The Time Machine*, was professionally brought into *Nemesis* by his friend Brent Spiner, but he's felt a personal connection to *Star Trek* for most of his life. "I was the ultimate Trekkie – I was Captain Kirk for every single Halloween. You either get [*Star Trek*] or you don't. It's a world that is about

compassion, morality and ethics. You find people who get it and they become important in your life."

Visiting the set was a definite perk of the job for Logan. "They couldn't keep me away. Every time I was in LA on other business, when I should be writing, but, no, I visit *Trek*! This is the reward, this is the dream. Finally, you get a chance to sit in Picard's chair, you know?"

Most of the *Star Trek* actors didn't actually sit in the writer's chair, but all had suggestions. "I had meetings with each one of them," Logan says. "Because it would be the height of arrogance on my part to say to Marina Sirtis, 'I know Deanna better than you do – let me tell you how she'd react.' And my job as a writer is to be a cannibal of their ideas. They've lived with these people for 15 years."

In addition to bringing Logan in initially, Spiner shares story credit with him and Berman. "Brent is actually most useful in problem-solving things that had nothing to do with Data," Logan reveals. "Brent was my great go-to guy. For example, at one point, Data and Picard are trapped on the villain's ship. And I called Brent and said, 'I have no idea how to get them out! I've written myself into an absolute corner.' And Brent would sit by his pool and I'd come over and he would just pitch ideas."

As for Stewart's contribution to the script, Logan says: "In terms of Picard's response to the world, and the responsibility [Stewart] feels to Picard, he played a major part in what Picard actually does in the story and the actual narrative

of the story. Because Patrick, like me, takes this seriously. Not in a pompous way, but he believes there is something important about this *Star Trek* story, and we have a responsibility not only to the fans like me, but just to the people who go to see movies to do something appropriate to that story, which is somehow ennobled, which is somehow life-affirming, which offers redemption. And he was very strong in making sure this story did that.

"And we are dealing with huge emotions in this movie. You can see a production of *King Lear* set around the table, and it can still take your breath away because the ideas and the passions behind it are so overwhelming. I hope that's what we're doing with *Nemesis*." ■

BAD TO THE GENOME

As Picard's evil clone, Shinzon is a genetic recipe for disaster, but is he really all bad? **Abbie Bernstein** poses the question to actor **Tom Hardy**...

Perhaps one of the few fates worse than being conceived and bred for a vicious purpose is to have even that bleak destiny torn away, leaving a man with no identity of his own.

So it was for Shinzon, a biologically human child reared on Romulus. Brought into being as part of a long-range Romulan scheme for galactic domination, Shinzon as a child was sent to be worked to death in the dark mines of the planet Remus when the anti-Federation plan was abandoned. The Romulan Senate forgot about their 'project', who toiled ceaselessly in the endless night alongside the fearsome but powerful Remans.

It's on Remus that Shinzon met the future Reman Viceroy (Ron Perlman), who took it upon himself to protect and guide Shinzon, not only training the boy to tap into his innate confidence and gift for leadership, but also instilling in the human a sense of comradeship with the downtrodden Remans. Over time, his thirst for vengeance grows against both the immediate Romulan oppressors and the Federation that has allowed the original Picard to grow and prosper as an individual.

Of course, Shinzon has an altogether more personal reason for trying to strike out at the Federation, and in particular their peace envoy,

one Captain Jean-Luc Picard. It's their conflict that is really at the heart of the film, with Picard having to face the dark side of his own personality, to combat a person he could have been. After all, Shinzon is a younger version of himself – their lives have just been affected by circumstance. As he says in the film: "I can see as well as you can. I can feel everything you feel. In fact, I can feel exactly what you feel." Later he adds: "Look in the mirror, see yourself."

Actor Tom Hardy, who plays Shinzon, thinks the character is largely shaped by his tragic formative years. "He's a product of society," the actor explains. "I don't think that anybody who's told

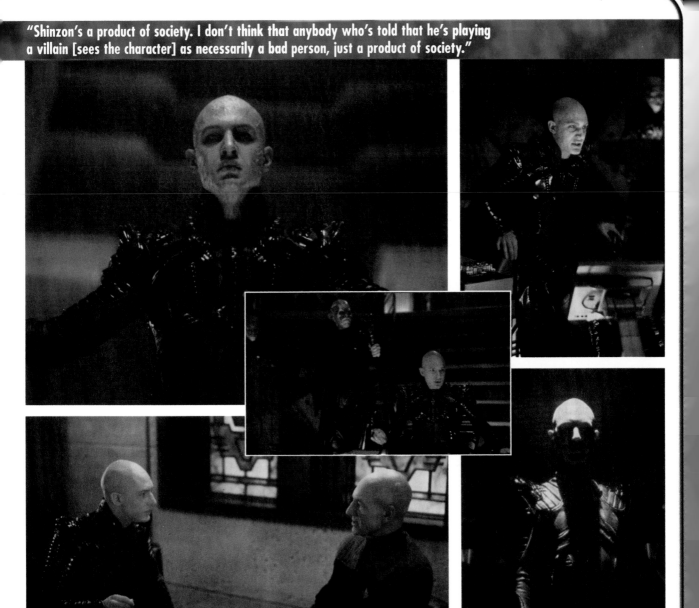

that he's playing a villain [sees the character] as necessarily a bad person, just a product of society."

As a performer, Hardy is a product of the Drama Centre London, which he joined in 1998. He left to begin a tradition continued with Shinzon – playing military men onscreen. His first on-camera role was as a US Army private during World War II in the acclaimed miniseries *Band of Brothers*. He followed this up with playing a real-life US Army specialist, Lance Twombly, in director Ridley Scott's intense war film *Black Hawk Down*, and then a member of the Foreign Legion in *Simon: An English Legionnaire*, for which Hardy had to have his head shaved. Videotaping his preliminary screen test for

Star Trek Nemesis in Morocco while still working on *Simon*, the already clean-scalped look evidently stood him in good stead, as it emphasized the link between Shinzon and Picard.

Hardy says he didn't know much about *Star Trek* before signing on for *Nemesis*, having seen little of it and being therefore unfamiliar with the universe: "I watched Captain Kirk and Spock a bit when I was a child, but no, not really."

Unlike the actor who plays him, Shinzon has studied Jean-Luc Picard thoroughly. The new Romulan Praetor has unusual insights into the Starfleet captain that may give him an advantage in their conflict, although Shinzon is also operating under the intense

pressure of a deadline in the most literal sense. Shinzon also possesses the kind of pride that comes to those who have already achieved the seemingly impossible, an asset that makes him bold but one that may also lead him to underestimate his nemesis...

Becoming an integral part of such a well known series proved a little daunting for Hardy: "There's always a sense of, 'Oh my God,' whenever you step into anything that's new. And I wouldn't say it's been easy." But he adds: "I don't look at this as being about career. I love doing good work. When I see a script that's a fantastic script, then it excites me. If something excites me, then I'm going to enjoy it." ∎

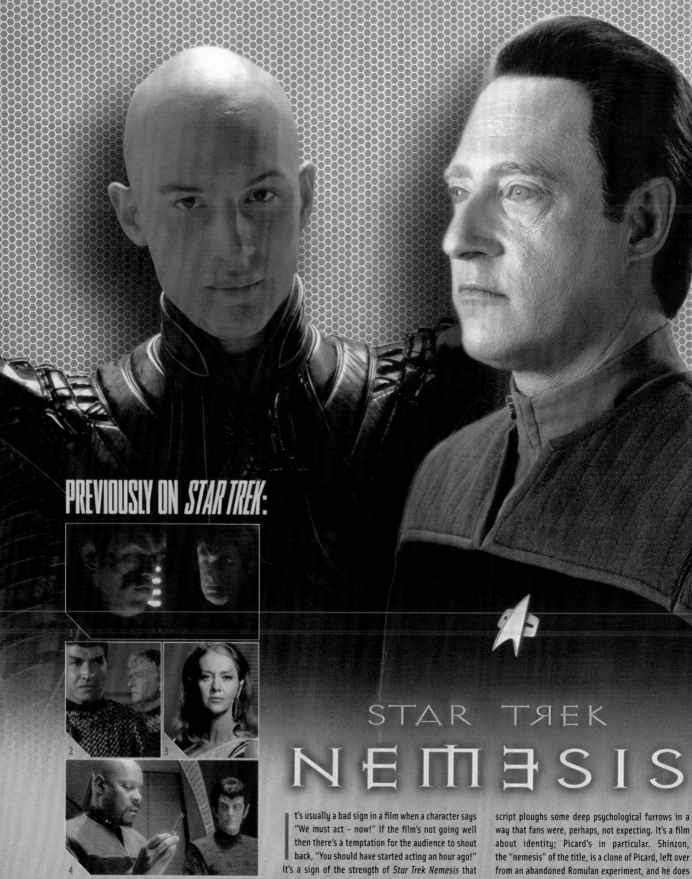

PREVIOUSLY ON *STAR TREK*:

1. The Romulans had plagued the Federation since the 22nd Century, preparing for war in *The Aenar*

2. They reappeared in *Balance of Terror*...

3. ...while Kirk and Spock went undercover in *The Enterprise Incident*.

4. During the Dominion War, they signed up with Starfleet and sent workers – including Remans – to help with the war effort

STAR TREK
NEMESIS

It's usually a bad sign in a film when a character says "We must act – now!" If the film's not going well then there's a temptation for the audience to shout back, "You should have started acting an hour ago!" It's a sign of the strength of *Star Trek Nemesis* that actor Ron Perlman can say that line with as straight a face as he can manage, wrapped as he in one of Michael Westmore's more unusual creations, and nobody watching the film feels inclined to weigh in with the obvious retort.

With both a writer and a director who had never worked in the *Star Trek* universe before – for the first time since 1982's *Star Trek II: The Wrath of Khan* – *Nemesis* deliberately breaks away from the cozy style that had been set up by previous films. John Logan's script ploughs some deep psychological furrows in a way that fans were, perhaps, not expecting. It's a film about identity; Picard's in particular. Shinzon, the "nemesis" of the title, is a clone of Picard, left over from an abandoned Romulan experiment, and he does not know who he is, what his heritage is or where he belongs. He can only find himself by killing his own reflection. And Picard – the most centered man in the Galaxy – staring into Shinzon's eyes, sees a ghost of a memory: himself as a younger man. When Shinzon dies, it is for Picard like watching his own death, and Patrick Stewart's acting in that scene alone makes the film worth watching.

Andy Lane

MOVIE INFO:

A Generation's Final Journey Begins

Picard versus his younger self – the ultimate battle...

FEATURING: Picard, Riker, Data, Geordi, Crusher, Troi, Worf, Wesley, Guinan

GUEST STARRING: Shinzon (Tom Hardy), Viceroy (Ron Perlman), Commander Donatra (Dina Meyer), Admiral Janeway (Kate Mulgrew), B-4 (Brent Spiner)

RELEASED: USA: December 9, 2002
UK: January 3, 2003
AUSTRALIA: January 17, 2003

THE SAGA CONTINUES:

Much like *Insurrection* might have been a vastly different film had the studio indulged Michael Piller in his intention of penning a decidedly more serious screenplay, Berman reports that the same could be said of *Nemesis* and John Logan. "John is a classicist," the former *Star Trek* producer explains. "He's very well-read. He's a man of the theater. He wanted to deal with a relationship between Picard and a clone of Picard. This went through many, many stages. There were times where it was going to be Patrick playing both parts, himself and the clone. There were times it was going to be a young boy. It went through many, many different versions before it became what it became. Patrick was very involved in the story development. Brent was involved in the story development. John – and this was true with *Gladiator* and this was true with *The Aviator* – if we had shot his first draft of the script it would have been four hours long. John writes very, very quickly, he writes beautifully, and he writes very, very long. He wrote some remarkable Shakespearean-like scenes between Picard and Shinzon that probably would have run 25 minutes each had they not been pared down."

Rick Berman

A Time for War, A Time for Peace – by Keith R.A. DeCandido; *Death In Winter* – by Michael Jan Friedman; *Taking Wing* – by Michael A. Martin and Andy Mangels

MAKING

At the end of *Star Trek Nemesis*, the crew of the *U.S.S. Enterprise* went their separate ways: Will Riker to captain the *U.S.S. Titan*, alongside his wife Deanna; Beverly Crusher to head up Starfleet Medical, while Jean-Luc Picard continued to captain the *Enterprise* with a lot of new faces in his command crew. Pocket Books have published three stories so far chronicling the adventures of the *Titan*, and last year saw *Death in Winter*, which reunited Jean-Luc Picard and Beverly Crusher on board the *Enterprise*. As editor of the *Star Trek: The Next Generation* range, Margaret Clark oversees Picard's continuing exploits, with J.M. Dillard's *Resistance*, Keith R.A. DeCandido's *Q & A* and Peter David's *Before Dishonor* next in line for release... Words: **Paul Simpson**

IT SO

"What I try to do is be true to the overall arching theme of the show as it was on television," Margaret Clark explains. "*TNG* was really about the family of the ship and dealing with things onboard. I thought starting with a new crew would be an interesting way to bring conflict onto the ship without actually having to bring in a guest star which Picard has to butt heads with – except Admirals. He just has this things for Admirals. They don't really get along. Doesn't matter who they are, he's not really crazy about Admirals!

"The idea is that the *Enterprise* has recovered from its battle with Shinzon in *Nemesis*, and we have to deal with what the Federation is right now. Starfleet is still rebuilding from the Dominion War where so many officers were lost, so many peoples devastated and so many ships destroyed that we have a fleet that is fighting under-strength. But luckily the Romulan threat is slightly reduced, although not in one fell swoop, because that entire Empire has sort of stabilized. It's a rebuilding period for Starfleet and the Federation, and hopefully a period of going back to exploration, which

is what has been happening with the *Titan* books."

Although certain crew assignments were made at the end of *Nemesis*, the editors of the book range assigned the rest of the original *Enterprise* personnel to their new ships. "I said they couldn't have three people: Geordi, Worf and Beverly," Clark says. "Everyone looked at me and said, 'Beverly?' I said, 'Yes, I'm giving her back to Picard. Anybody else, feel free!' In a normal service area, you would not stay on the same vessel for 20 years. You would move around, and move up. On the *Enterprise*, you could only get promotion when

167

someone died, which is unfortunately what happened in *Nemesis*."

Clark felt that transferring Crusher back to Starfleet Medical was "a cop out," so in *Death In Winter*, she had author Michael Jan Friedman put them back together. "In the TV series, Patrick always had to have a lovely leading lady to play against, but it always seemed silly to me that the producers actually tried to step back from how to make a relationship work on a starship."

"YOU HAVE TO KICK THE TABLE OVER AND CHANGE ALL THE RULES TO MAKE THE BORG INTERESTING AGAIN. I ALWAYS WANTED TO TAKE THEM BACK: I THOUGHT WHEN I FIRST SAW THEM THAT MAURICE HURLEY CREATED THE MOST FANTASTIC THING. *TNG* NEVER HAD A PURE VILLAIN WITH NO REDEMPTIVE QUALITIES, BUT THEY WERE A SOULLESS MONSTER."

Although, like Picard, Clark wants the *Enterprise* crew eventually to be able to focus on exploration, there are other practical considerations to be dealt with first. *Death in Winter* concerns the fall out in the Romulan Empire from *Nemesis*, while *Resistance* and *Before Dishonor* address the continued threat from the Borg. "It is the 20th anniversary, and I thought the Borg had been defanged on *Voyager*, so I wanted to take them back to where they were when we first met them," she notes. "I told all the writers the story of me being a little kid, and the monster who lived under my bed. If I put my foot down, the monster would drag me under the bed and eat me. One night I promised it my baby brother and it ate him. I put my foot on the floor... and the monster ate me anyhow. That's what the Borg is: that elemental terror.

"You have to kick the table over and change all the rules to make the Borg interesting again. I always wanted to take them back. I thought when I first saw them that Maurice Hurley created the most fantastic thing. *TNG* never had a pure villain with no redemptive qualities, but they were a soulless monster. They were the things under the bed, and with Picard with a new ship and a new crew, and the new hope that the Federation was going to rebuild, I thought bringing them back was the right thing to do."

The Borg arc continues from their last chronological appearance on screen in *Star Trek: Voyager*'s *Endgame*. "They're a wounded animal: they've had their Transwarp Conduits destroyed so the Borg that are left in the Beta Quadrant are cut off, and can't hear the Collective. It's like a wolf chewing its leg off in the trap. Assimilated life may not seem great to Federation eyes but to them, it's a religion, it's a drive. Assimilation, absorption – they have always wanted to bring the harmony of the Collective to these people and they don't understand the Federation's resistance to it. They decide that there are certain persons standing in their way, and they need to stop them. The first person that they decide they're going after is Locutus.

"Meanwhile, the Borg that are left in the Alpha Quadrant are trying to create an integrated

STAR TREK THE NEXT GENERATION BEFORE DISHONOR — PETER DAVID

STAR TREK THE NEXT GENERATION Q&A — KEITH R.A. DECANDIDO

STAR TREK THE NEXT GENERATION RESISTANCE — J.M. DILLARD

Collective by creating a Queen on their own, which is something the Federation never knew they could do. That is what *Resistance* is about: Picard hears the song of the Borg, and realizes that they're not gone. The idea is to give the Borg back that elemental edge of pure terror. They are the best villain, for want of a better word, that *TNG* created. You know you can't reason with them. The idea is to build Picard's crew, and also lay open the plan that the Borg have to finally conquer these humans so they can bring the harmony of the Collective to all of them.

"*Resistance* and *Before Dishonor* are both Borg-oriented. In *Q and A*, Picard does get to explore, but we discover in *Before Dishonor*, you should never turn your back on the Borg."

As well as bringing back old adversaries, the novels also continue the holistic view of the *Star Trek* universe, incorporating characters from all the different elements of the franchise, both visual and literary. "The idea is to use other characters that make sense," Clark says. "In the excerpt in this issue, you see Janeway, who is obviously the foremost Borg expert apart from Picard that the Federation has. And of course the Federation has a Borg drone. *Before Dishonor* has some interesting guest stars: Ambassador Spock, Seven of Nine... although if you look at the cover, it's not Seven of Nine, it's Annika Hansen. (It's a seventh season beauty shot of Jeri Ryan not in her make-up.)

...THE BORG THAT ARE LEFT IN THE BETA QUADRANT ARE CUT OFF, AND CAN'T HEAR THE COLLECTIVE... THEY'VE DECIDED THAT THERE ARE CERTAIN PERSONS STANDING IN THEIR WAY, AND THEY STEP OUT TO STOP THEM. THE FIRST PERSON THAT THEY DECIDE THEY'RE GOING AFTER IS LOCUTUS.

But, despite the appearance of several old friends, Clark is determined that not everything on board the *Enterprise* is going to be sweetness and light. "The idea of bringing new people in is great – they're not all saying that whatever the Captain says is fine," she says wryly. "You need new officers who have never served under Picard before. He's not a legend: he's a man. He's flawed, he makes bad decisions, even after years of captaincy. He

assumes he knows what he's doing: he's been doing it a long time but nobody can know everything, especially when the rules change in the middle of it. In one of these stories, he makes a bad decision on how to deal with the Borg and it goes horribly wrong. What are the ramifications of that?

"In each of the subsequent books I'm asking the writers to plant that seed of doubt and despair in Picard's head: 'Will I never be free of the Borg? Will they never stop coming after us? Have I actually helped them?' There's a throwaway scene in *Q and A* where he talks about seeing the faces of the people that the Borg first took from him. He wonders for a moment if there is something about him that was responsible for the Borg coming and if that was why they made him Locutus. Is he now the reason why they keep coming after humans? He realizes he has to come up with a way to stop them. Janeway thinks she's found a way to stop them, but the Borg keep flipping the rules!"

For those concerned that the story will be left hanging for a long time, Clark explains that, with the exception of the *Star Trek: Enterprise* novel *Kobyashi Maru*, Pocket Books' output for 2008 will focus on the 24th Century. "We're at the end of 2380 at the end of *Before Dishonor*, and then we have another storyline that will go into the next year, which will come out in 2008. We have made a conscious decision in 2008 to stay away from the 23rd Century, and let the vision of the 23rd Century be J.J.'s."

Warped Reflections

They hail from different backgrounds, different eras –
different *universes* – but do Captains Jean-Luc Picard and
(Mirror) Gabriel Lorca share more in common than we
might otherwise suppose? *Star Trek Magazine* investigates.

Words: Jay Stobie

On the surface, Captain Jean-Luc Picard and the Mirror Universe's Captain Gabriel Lorca appear as polar opposites to one another. Picard, an impassioned explorer, embodies the Federation's ideals of goodwill and diversity. Mirror Lorca, a ruthless manipulator, sought domination over his fellow Terrans and the destruction of his foes. But despite their differences, the two share a surprisingly extensive roster of commonalities, ranging from minor quirks and personality traits to significant life experiences.

The First Duty

Picard and Mirror Lorca (simply referred to as Lorca in this article from this point on) both display an unwavering dedication to duty that quite possibly borders on an unhealthy obsession. Upon finding himself in an alternate universe, Lorca meticulously plots his return home for over a year, skillfully deceiving countless people on his journey. Lorca plays his role as his Prime counterpart until the last possible moment, when he finally frees his compatriots in the *Star Trek: Discovery* episode "What's Past Is Prologue." Of course, Lorca's perseverance lacks the altruistic and honorable qualities that distinguish Picard's tenure in the captain's chair.

Picard's acting abilities receive accolades from his crew, but he never utilizes his Shakespearean talents for anything as nefarious as Lorca's charade.

Nevertheless, Picard's adherence to his work proves infamous, so much so that the *Enterprise*-D crew practically force their leader to take a vacation in the aptly named *Star Trek: The Next Generation* episode "Captain's Holiday." When Picard finds himself living out the life of an alien named Kamin in "The Inner Light," five years seem to elapse before the La Barre native finally gives up on his hope of returning to his *Galaxy*-class vessel. The captain's fierce determination to man his post in these circumstances eerily echoes Lorca's

> Picard and Lorca both display an unwavering dedication to duty that quite possibly borders on an unhealthy obsession.

desire to lead the Terran Empire.

These merits do not go unnoticed, as both men receive praise from their superiors during the early portions of their careers. Emperor Philippa Georgiou entrusts Lorca with vital Imperial missions and the safety of her adopted daughter. Prior to the Battle of Wolf 359, Admiral Hanson similarly declares, "I never met anyone with more drive, determination, or more courage than Jean-Luc Picard."

That said, neither captain's walk

01

02

through life remains spotless. Both men lose their prior commands in combat and suffer the consequences. Lorca's survival of the *U.S.S. Buran*'s destruction brings scrutiny upon him, whereas Picard endures a court martial before being cleared of all charges.

Starship Mine

These downfalls do not prevent either officer from securing incredibly prestigious postings. Picard's next turn in the big chair arrives in the form of the Federation's state-of-the-art flagship, the *U.S.S. Enterprise*-D. Starfleet tasks Lorca with leading the crew of the *U.S.S. Discovery*, a top-secret vessel whose development of an experimental spore drive technology possesses the potential to turn the tide in the Klingon War of the 2250s. Of course, Lorca's assignment owes a great deal to the record of Prime Lorca.

Upon receiving their new positions, each captain exercises their prerogative to recruit certain crew members who personally impress them. Geordi La Forge and Tasha Yar awe Picard with their devotion to the uniform when their paths first cross, and the Frenchman famously selects William T. Riker as his Number One upon learning the commander confronted his former captain over away team procedures. Ash Tyler dazzles Lorca with grit during their

ordeal on a Klingon prison ship and receives a senior role on *Discovery*, while Lorca's pursuit of Michael Burnham centers more on his feelings for her Terran counterpart.

Correspondingly, each captain opts to show leniency for hard luck cases when filling out their crew manifests. At the time of Lorca's courtship, the professional trajectories for Burnham and Tyler trend downward. Burnham's imprisonment for mutiny at the Battle of the Binaries tarnishes her record, while Tyler's status as an emotionally compromised prisoner of war leads Admiral Katrina Cornwell to question Lorca's decision to rehabilitate the security officer.

Captain Picard's genuine compassion for those needing a second

chance contrasts with Lorca's ulterior motive of wanting skilled officers to help him return home, as shown in the stints of Ensigns Ro Laren and Sito Jaxa. Ro previously served time in a Federation prison for disobeying the orders of the *U.S.S. Wellington*'s captain, while Sito participated in an unapproved maneuver with her Starfleet Academy flight squadron that resulted in the death of a fellow cadet. Believing in the potential of the Bajoran ensigns, Picard bonds with Ro during a mission near Cardassian territory and personally requests Sito's appointment to the *Enterprise*-D.

Histories of Violence

Perhaps the most stark comparison between Picard and Lorca stems from the very serious issue of post-traumatic

Ships That Align

Prior to their assignments aboard the *U.S.S. Enterprise*-D and *U.S.S. Discovery*, both captains commanded starships outfitted with four warp nacelles. Picard's *Constellation*-class *U.S.S. Stargazer* and Lorca's *Cardenas*-class *U.S.S. Buran* fell in combat against the Ferengi and the Klingons respectively. While the *Stargazer* crew successfully evacuated after the Battle of Maxia, the *Buran*'s entire complement perished when Gabriel initiated the self-destruct sequence, leaving himself as the vessel's sole survivor. The *Stargazer* position marked Picard's first captaincy, whereas Lorca never mentioned holding the center seat on any ships other than the *Buran*.

04

Star Trek Nemesis adds context to how Picard might have fared living a lifestyle comparable to Lorca's formative years.

stress disorder. The scars Admiral Cornwell finds on Lorca's back, combined with the brutal nature of his universe and the phaser stashed under his pillow, indicate that Lorca endured a tumultuous past of disturbing savagery. Even before Burnham concocts a numbing agent to dull her captain's nervous system in preparation for his time in the agonizer booths aboard the *I.S.S. Charon* in "Vaulting Ambition," Lorca's ability to persevere during his encounters with the *I.S.S. Shenzhou*'s torture device suggest he has suffered such sessions on numerous occasions.

Lorca's surprisingly violent reaction to Cornwell's touch as he sleeps (in "Lethe") demonstrates the severe mental and emotional stress commonly faced by PTSD patients. The symptoms manifest in such a pronounced way that they even crack Lorca's carefully crafted performance as *Discovery*'s commanding officer and provoke Cornwell's decision to recommend his removal for treatment by physicians. Lorca's pain runs so deep that the admiral remarks, "I can't leave Starfleet's most powerful

weapon in the hands of a broken man."

Picard, whose upbringing occurred on a utopian Earth devoid of poverty and war, underwent a far different childhood than Lorca. However, the Borg Collective introduce Picard to his own universe of horror when they assimilate the captain in "The Best of Both Worlds." Stripped of both his humanity and the vital information about Starfleet's defenses held in his head, Picard remains trapped in his own body to witness his Borg alter ego, Locutus, lead a massacre at the Battle of Wolf 359, where over 11,000 people and almost 40 starships fall to a single Borg cube.

Despite his inability to control his actions, memories of the torturous violation haunt him for years afterward. Just as Cornwell lacks faith in a troubled Lorca, Vice Admiral Hayes and Starfleet Command express uncertainty over Picard's history with the Borg and sideline the *Enterprise*-E from joining a Federation fleet tasked with intercepting another Borg cube in the Typhon Sector

01 Impressed by his grit, Lorca assigns Tyler a senior position on *Discovery*.

02 Lorca, as seen in "Si Vis Pacem, Para Bellum."

03 Shinzon, clone of Picard.

04 Picard is forced to take a vacation (of sorts), in "Captain's Holiday."

prior to the Battle of Sector 001 in *Star Trek: First Contact*. Other Starfleet officers, including Benjamin Sisko and Rear Admiral Norah Satie, also express discomfort over Picard's actions as Locutus of Borg.

Parallel Lives
Intriguingly, *Star Trek Nemesis* adds context to how Picard might have fared living a lifestyle comparable to Lorca's formative years. Shinzon, cloned from Picard's DNA as part of an abandoned Romulan plot to infiltrate the Federation, grows up in the cruel conditions of the dilithium mines on Remus. Rising to become the Praetor of the Romulan Star Empire, Shinzon lures Picard to Romulus and explains the trials he experienced, from starvation to a broken nose and jaw.

Picard admits to Doctor Crusher that Shinzon shares the selfish and ambitious tendencies of his own youth, but Shinzon's assassination of the Romulan Senate and plans to eradicate Earth distance his character from Picard's. While the focus here is on the correlation between Picard and Lorca, it is worth noting that both Shinzon and Lorca seek power, initiate a coup, and perceive their "own" race as superior. Shinzon explains his perception of the rift dividing his lifestyle and Picard's

when he claims, "Had you lived my life, you'd be doing *exactly* as I am. So look in the mirror, see yourself. Consider that, Captain. I can think of no greater torment you."

Although Shinzon braved harsh punishment on a more frequent basis, Picard's tenure as Locutus does not constitute his only encounter with torture. Following his capture during a secret mission on the Cardassian world of Celtris III, Picard deals with a rigorous interrogation filled with deprivation and mental manipulation at the hands of Gul Madred, in "Chain of Command." The *Enterprise*-D's captain displays incredible resilience, unwilling to acquiesce to Madred's demand for Picard to state that five spotlights emanate from behind the Cardassian when only four exist.

Picard exhibits a similar level of determination in "The Best of Both Worlds, Part II," when he doggedly resists the Borg collective and manages to tell Data that the most expedient way to defeat the Borg cube involves transmitting a command for the drones to sleep. Lorca reveals his own irrepressible nature when he voluntarily submits to the pain of an agonizer booth on the *Shenzhou* for days as part of his master plan to become the emperor of the Terran fleet.

The trials faced by Picard and Lorca fuel each man's obsession to enact their own form of justice on their torturers. Lorca's desires to lead the Terran Empire and take revenge on Emperor Georgiou remain sharp even as he finds himself in another universe. The brutality of

Lorca's crusade reveals itself as he joyously executes Captain Maddox and Mirror Paul Stamets aboard the *I.S.S. Charon*.

The Borg Collective serves as the target for Picard's ire in *First Contact*, as the usually measured man angrily yells, "And *I* will make them *pay* for what they've done!" Fortunately for Picard, Lily Sloane breaks through his blind rage by accusing him of deriving enjoyment from killing Borg drones and comparing the captain's quest to that of the ill-fated Ahab from the novel *Moby-Dick*. As a result, the return of Jean-Luc's thoughtful sensibility allows him to defeat the Borg Queen – whereas

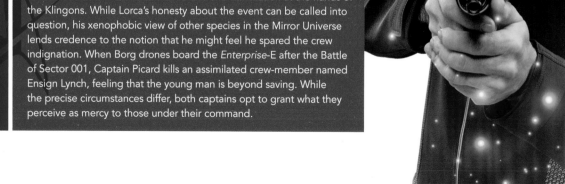

Sacrifice Of Ensigns

Gabriel Lorca claims that he purposely sacrificed the *U.S.S. Buran*'s crew to save them from the trauma of torture and humiliation at the hands of the Klingons. While Lorca's honesty about the event can be called into question, his xenophobic view of other species in the Mirror Universe lends credence to the notion that he might feel he spared the crew indignation. When Borg drones board the *Enterprise*-E after the Battle of Sector 001, Captain Picard kills an assimilated crew-member named Ensign Lynch, feeling that the young man is beyond saving. While the precise circumstances differ, both captains opt to grant what they perceive as mercy to those under their command.